Religion, the Independent Sector, and American Culture

ÆR

American Academy of Religion
Studies in Religion

Editor
Lawrence S. Cunningham

Number 63
RELIGION, THE INDEPENDENT SECTOR,
AND AMERICAN CULTURE

edited by
Conrad Cherry
Rowland A. Sherrill

RELIGION, THE INDEPENDENT SECTOR, AND AMERICAN CULTURE

edited by
Conrad Cherry
Rowland A. Sherrill

Scholars Press
Atlanta, Georgia

RELIGION, THE INDEPENDENT SECTOR, AND AMERICAN CULTURE

edited by
Conrad Cherry
Rowland A. Sherrill

© 1992
The American Academy of Religion

Library of Congress Cataloging in Publication Data

Religion, the independent sector, and American culture / edited by
    Conrad Cherry, Rowland A. Sherrill.
    p. cm. — (American Academy of Religion studies in religion ;
    no. 63)
    Includes bibliographical references.
    ISBN 1-55540-584-3 (alk. paper). — ISBN 1-55540-585-1 (pbk. :
    alk. paper)
    1. United States—Religion—1960- 2. Voluntarism—Religious
aspects. 3. Voluntarism—United States. 4. Church charities—
United States. I. Cherry, Conrad, 1937- . II. Sherrill,
Rowland A. III. Series: AAR studies in religion ; no. 63.
BR515.R45 1991
306.6'773—dc20   91-28447
                                                  CIP

Printed in the United States of America
on acid-free paper

For
Ellie and Joy

CONTENTS

INTRODUCTION

Conrad Cherry and Rowland A. Sherrill

The analysis of American culture according to its various sectors, and of religion as a conspicuous instance of the "third" or "independent" sector in America, is of recent vintage. In his contribution to this collection of essays, Max Stackhouse traces the origins of contemporary sector analysis to the widespread adoption of the work of Antonio Gramsci in the 1960s. Wherever one might locate its roots, interest in the independent sector and in religion's role as a participant in that sector has grown dramatically within the last two decades. In the 1970s, American intellectuals committed to social change through citizens' movements and non-governmental organizations touted the independent sector as the hope for a just and responsible social order.[1] During the 1980s, a strong political/economic accent was introduced into talk of the independent sector with Ronald Reagan's emphasis on voluntary, as opposed to government, solutions to social problems, an emphasis continued by George Bush's "thousand points of light" philosophy of self-help. Over this two-decade period, approximately 20 research centers for the study of the independent sector were established on American college and university campuses, and a coordinating and research organization, the Independent Sector, was founded with the support of over 600 foundations, corporate programs, and voluntary organizations.[2] Robert Payton, Director of the Center on Philanthropy at Indiana University, has proposed the creation of "philanthropics" as an academic field for examining the independent sector cross-culturally, and he has suggested that the study of religion should occupy the heart of this new interdisciplinary field since, to his way of thinking, the philanthropic act presupposes the religious posture of the transcendence of selfishness, acquisitiveness, and greed.[3]

But what is the "independent sector?" The literature on the subject

1. See Theodore Levitt, *The Third Sector: New Tactics for a Responsible Society* (New York: AMACOM, 1973) and Peter Berger and Richard Neuhaus, *To Empower People: The Role of Mediating Structures in Public Policy* (Washington: American Enterprise Institute, 1977).

2. Richard Magat, *Prospective Views of Research on Philanthropy and the Voluntary Sector* (New York: The Foundation Center, 1990), viii; Virginia A. Hodgkinson, "Research on the Independent Sector: A Progress Report," in Robert L. Payton, *Philanthropy: Voluntary Action for the Public Good* (New York: Macmillan Publishing Co., 1988), 228.

3. Payton, *Philanthropy*, 45.

reveals no clear, uniform definition. The definition *via negativa* that is sometimes invoked—the independent sector is neither government nor commerce—scarcely unravels the mysteries of the category, and few students of the sector are willing to rest content with the negative way. Payton admits that the category is protean and that his own working definition of it as "philanthropy" or "voluntary action for the public good" does not represent a consensus among its students, but he claims that beneath the shifting forms of definition lies an irreducible core: the sector's voluntary dimension.[4] And, indeed, much of the literature on the subject proposes that the distinguishing characteristic of the independent, third, or non-profit sector is voluntaryism—that drive of humans to join together and work together for common goals not dictated by the demands of the state or the marketplace.

Voluntaryism has long been viewed as something distinctively, if not uniquely, American, and institutional religion in a nation without a religious establishment has long been understood as a voluntary organization. Contemporary sector analysts often suggest that, in comparison with other nations and cultures in the West, the United States today relies heavily upon social voluntaryism to meet the cultural and social needs of its citizens.[5] But more than a century and a half prior to this contemporary claim, the French observer of American life Alexis de Tocqueville remarked that in his time "Americans of all ages, all conditions, and all dispositions constantly form associations."[6] Tocqueville was persuaded that the democratic environment, lacking the human alliances created by firm class lines, stimulated Americans to form alliances voluntarily in associations. And a full generation prior to the emergence of the sector analysts, a collection of American scholars insisted that the environment of democratic voluntaryism has accounted for the distinctive shape of much American religion. Sidney Mead proposed a thesis now widely accepted that the "denomination," a voluntary association formed by like-minded people consenting to a common objective and fully tolerated by the culture, rather than a state-supported "church" or a marginalized "sect," characterizes most religious groups in this country.[7] James Luther Adams devoted a long and influential academic career to reflection upon the religious and ethical implications of voluntary associations as agents of democratic values.[8] And Timothy L. Smith advanced the authoritative argument that most social reform in ante-bellum America was carried out by

4. Ibid., 61.

5. See Kenneth W. Thompson, ed., *Philanthropy: Private Means, Public Ends* (Lanham, MD: University Press of America, 1987), 131–32.

6. Alexis de Tocqueville, *Democracy in America*, ed. Phillips Bradley, II (New York: Vintage Books, 1945), 114.

7. Sidney E. Mead, *The Lively Experiment: The Shaping of Christianity in America* (New York: Harper & Row, 1963), 103–33.

8. James Luther Adams, *Voluntary Associations: Socio-Cultural Analyses and Theological Interpretation*, ed. J. Ronald Engel (Chicago: Exploration Press, 1986).

voluntary associations generated by Protestant revivalist religion.[9] If voluntaryism is taken as the irreducible core of the independent sector, there is a grand scholarly tradition for making that sector an appropriate means for understanding crucial traits of American culture and of religion's role in that culture.

That tradition, however, by no means assures the accurate placing of religion in the culture. Even when specified by the heritage of voluntaryism, the analysis of religion and culture in terms of "sectors" is inherently problematic. Are the divisions between the sectors high and insurmountable walls, or fluid and permeable lines? If religion exercises influences upon government and business, or government and business upon religion, at what point do the sectors lose their integrity? Are there only three major sectors—government, business, and non-profit—within which Americans organize their lives in a complex and multifaceted social order? What about the family? the professions? educational institutions? And what, anyway, is so disinctively voluntaristic about the independent sector in a culture in which political parties depend upon volunteers and business may be conducted by neighborhood cooperatives?

These and a surfeit of other questions receive no ready answers with the invocation of the categories of sector analysis or with the assignment of religion to the independent sector. In fact, a great advantage of sector analysis is its heuristic character, in that it scares to the surface compelling issues respecting the role of religion in American culture when some of its underlying assumptions are challenged. That end is accomplished by the essays in this book. Originally presented as papers at a series of symposia funded by the Lilly Endowment and held at Indiana University-Purdue University at Indianapolis on the topic "Religion, the Independent Sector, and American Culture," the essays take nothing for granted about religion's alleged "independence" or the nation's arrangement according to "sectors." Each essay offers reflections on religion's influence upon American culture, and the culture's influence upon religion, by attending to issues raised when religion is conceived as an occupant of the independent sector.

The essays deal chiefly with three themes:

1. *The manner in which the growing complexity and bureaucratization of American society have transformed the social sectors and their relationship.*

Max Stackhouse argues that traditionally every society has consisted of the axial sectors of family, economics, politics, culture, and religion. These interpenetrating systems have been crucial to the formation of persons and communities. With the rise of modern technical, bureaucratic civilization, however, these axial sectors have been altered by the power exerted by new, massive, complex institutions—what Stackhouse calls the "new corpora-

---

9. Timothy L. Smith, *Revivalism and Social Reform: American Protestantism on the Eve of the Civil War* (New York: Harper & Row, 1957).

tions." One of the consequences of the appearance of new corporate institutions like the multi-national business, the modern university, and the contemporary health-care system is that the religious and moral ground on which a society fashioned by these institutions might stand is rendered unclear. Stackhouse concludes with a call to religious and ethical thinkers to face the challenge of clarifying that ground which, in more traditional societies, provided at least a modicum of spiritual and symbolic cohesion for the social order. Though more circumscribed in the scope of their concerns, the essays by Mary Oates, Dorothy Bass, and William Dinges take up much the same issue raised by Stackhouse. Each is a case study of the manner in which the arrival of a "rationalized" post-industrial society has entailed the merging of the aims of the various sectors and, most especially, the powerful incursions of government and business into the domain of religion.

Mary Oates' concentration on the character of Catholic charities over the course of a century and a half, from the early national period up to 1940, depicts one religiously-based endeavor in the independent sector called continuously to sustain its efforts but to adapt its strategies to altered social and economic circumstances. Oates demonstrates how Catholic charities in America evolved from relatively simple measures for providing relief to poor immigrants, to their organization into benevolent societies, to their consolidation into large institutions complete with diverse professional staffs, to their eventual collaboration with government assistance programs. Catholic charities, inspired by an uncomplicated philanthropic motive to provide direct relief to the poor, were transformed by economic conditions in the country and by the changing economic status of Catholics into institutions of a complexity and a diversity equal to those of government and business. And although they continued to maintain many of their basic benevolent concerns, the charities struck alliances with the sectors of government and business. Oates' story of the increase in Catholic charities' size, scope, and influence also points to the possibility that the only groups in the independent sector likely to remain clearly differentiated from other sectors are those that work in small, local, face-to-face relationships. Given the complexities of the public realm, however, these other groups are unlikely to create systemic changes in the social order.

Dorothy Bass traces marked transformations of the role of Protestantism in American higher education. As major players on the 19th-century college scene, mainline Protestants have witnessed in the 20th century a diminution of their function in higher education. The appearance of the modern research university with its enormous support from the foundation, government, and corporate worlds, its devotion to specialization and the secular professions, its attraction of the large majority of American students, and its shaping of the educational philosophies of colleges that had previously taken their bearings from religion has driven mainline Protestantism to the margins of the culture of higher education. The influence of the sectors of government, commerce, and philanthropy has reduced the presence of religion at large institutions of higher education to religious studies and campus ministry. No longer moored to liberal Protestantism, religious studies has become an academic specialty among a welter of specialties in the modern university. And the campus ministry has become a program without a home, fully honored neither by the churches nor by the universities. Bass' essay thus raises an important but difficult question respecting the independent sector: What is the future of religious groups whose efforts in a given area have failed or have been stymied, absorbed, or marginalized by other forces in the culture?

In his case study of a soup kitchen in Montgomery County, Maryland, William Dinges chronicles the transformation of a neighborhood institution. Founded by a Baptist congregation, the Shepherd's Table quickly became cut off from its religious roots. The staff of the Shepherd's Table turned professional, the organization became bureaucratic, and significant financial support for the insitution began to flow from government and business. Religion, which had originally inspired the entire undertaking, becomes for the volunteers who now work at the soup kitchen diffuse, privatized, non-institutional, and largely unrelated the social-ethical components of Christian piety. Dinges' essay conducts us into a microcosm of the radical modification of religion and its voluntaristic ventures by the forces of the modern world which do not respect the boundaries separating social sectors. The essay also raises the possibility that the sharp edges of discrete religious communities (found in their doctrine, exegesis, and ethics) may inevitably be blunted when they throw themselves into cooperative efforts that require civic concert, public credibility, and broad social support.

If the rigid separation of spheres of life into sectors obscures the alterations of religion by other forces in modern American culture and ignores the tendency of religious groups to join in concert with those forces, the opposite analytical perspective—one that refuses to recognize the distinctive contributions of religion to that culture—is equally myopic.
The essays in this volume thus speak to a second theme:
2. *The ways in which religion has participated in the formation of public policy.*

For all of the frequent blurring of the lines dividing religion from the other sectors of society, religion has continued to express itself forcefully on issues touching the public lives of the American people. That feature of American religion is described in all of the essays in this book, but it is developed at length by Bryan Hehir and James Smurl.

Hehir takes the Catholic Bishops' declarations on nuclear arms as an instance of religion's role as an independent participant in matters of public policy. Although separated from the state, religious organizations in the

United States have by no means been separated constitutionally from society. Like other voluntary organizations, religious groups are free to contribute to the shaping of the national public life and to assist in the formation of a coherent moral framework within a pluralistic social order. That freedom has permitted, indeed stimulated, the Catholic Church to enter public policy debates on its own theological terms and to speak to both the religious and the civic communities on issues such as nuclear armament. Hehir shows how the shifting emphases, broadening categories, moral independence, and increasingly wide reception of the Bishops' statements on nuclear arms betoken the manner in which religion can join persuasively in a debate not controlled by the governmental sector. By concentrating on the influence of the Bishops' letters, Hehir's essay also raises the issues of what determines the "success" of religion in the shaping of public policy, and by so doing evokes the prospects of other kinds of voluntary groups. There are religious groups within the independent sector, especially those emerging quickly on single-issue matters, that might initially lack the foundations of intellectual leadership, institutional vehicles of dissemination, and an extensive community. What are their opportunities for success in the formation of public policy? The implication of most of these essays is that their opportunities are few.

Although more concerned than Hehir with the plurality of voices that speak to public moral issues, James Smurl proposes that the work of hospital ethics committees offers an instance of how the voluntary sector may free itself from the demands of other sectors, an instance as telling as the Bishops' declarations on nuclear arms. In a hospital environment that mirrors the American values and postures of economic profit, professional technologies, and government regulations, ethics committees have found ways to defend the values of choice, charity, and community on behalf of patients and their friends and families. Religion joins in the deliberations of these committees less as a voice of expertise and more—along with representatives of the medical, nursing, and legal fields—as one human voice among others directed to the very public and the very personal quandaries of health, death, and survival. Smurl is realistic about the difficulty of "sticking to the subject" and avoiding the standards of "power and profit" on the part of ethics committees, but he finds in them an occasion of the relative independence of the independent sector. He suggests that while American religion has frequently succumbed to becoming nothing more than an indistinguishable configuration of the cultural values of power, profit, and efficiency, at its best it can create a broader sense of the public and a voice for people. Smurl's essay also intimates that separate religious convictions, languages, and offices may have to broaden themselves to become credible and effective in a pluralistic public sphere. That suggestion leads to still another theme that arises from the sector analysis of religion:

3. *The identity of religion as a distinctive voluntary activity.*

This theme, like the second, is in the foreground of each essay, but it receives its most extensive treatment by John Witte and Brooks Holifield.

In his historical analysis, Witte describes two legal legacies informing the tax exemption of religion: a common law tradition that favors a religious establishment as a function of the state; and an equity tradition that grants exemptions to all churches because they dispense charitable benefits to society. Elements of both of these traditions continued to be invoked in judicial deliberations even with the disestablishment of religion and worked to create a deep rift in American attitudes, leading some to endorse religious exemption rights universally and others to plead for their abandonment altogether. The confusion of traditions has been exacerbated by the failure of courts and commissioners to offer a clear definition of "religion" or of "religious uses of property." Witte believes that the lack of clear definitions, the origins of "religious usage" in religious establishment, and the recent proliferation of groups calling themselves "religious" endanger the identity, indeed the very integrity, of religion as an occupant of the independent sector. He proposes, therefore, that the properties of religious groups "be exempted from taxation not because of the internal, cultic, sacerdotal uses but because of the external, cultural, social uses to which they are devoted." He also submits that this proposal be acted upon by the churches themselves so that they may safeguard their distinctive identities in a society driven by motives of wealth and promote more visibly their commitment to the commonweal. Witte's analysis and suggestion press the issue of the identity of religious groups in their relation to other sectors of the society. Centered on questions of possession, capital, and gain—each significant in the American pantheon of values—government concern about the tax exemption of church property has usually expressed itself in a vocabulary appropriate to other social sectors than the religious and in terms often oblivious to the public good.

Brooks Holifield, in his historical perspective on the "cure of souls" in America, is not at all concerned with the legal ramifications of religion's independence, but he is no less interested than Witte in the maintenance of religion's identity in relation to other spheres of social existence. In the Emmanuel Movement and its successor, the Pastoral Care Movement, Holifield discerns how religion has offered the American people alternative sources of care that both business and government were unwilling to provide. But in aligning themselves with modern medicine, those religious health-care movements adopted self-defining models that sometimes made them indistinguishable from other sectors of society. Drawing upon the deep American traditions of the cure of souls, harmonial religion, and public service, the movements inserted into the environment of professionalized medicine and bureaucratized hospitals concern for whole persons and their

larger cultural circumstances. Eager to mesh with the scientific and professional worlds of medicine and hospitals, however, practitioners of pastoral
care emphasized the methods of psychotherapy and counseling borrowed
from psychiatry. Holifield's essay clearly illustrates the ways in which a
religious institution in the public sphere can be shaped, even absorbed, by
other institutions, thus exemplifying the problem religious groups encounter
in maintaining their integirty in the midst of shifting cultural circumstances.
But the essay also suggests that the maintenance of religious integrity by
hardening the lines between religion and other social agencies would make
religious groups extraneous to the very human needs they seek to address. In
any case, Holifield sees in recent developments evidence that religion's
helping traditions have been breaking through the psychotherapeutic mold
to claim a multitude of self-definitions strictly imposed by neither modern
medicine nor modern hospitals.

   In the conclusion to his essay, Holifield maintains that for all of the
problems of identity presented to religion in its bid for significant connections with modern American culture, without the voluntary endeavors of
religious institutions "the American health system would be decidedly
poorer" since those institutions often have assumed the burdens of health
care neglected by other service agencies. The same claim could be made
about religion's voluntary efforts in education, relief to the poor, public
policy debates, and ethical discussions concerning many dimensions of the
social order. The essays in this volume illustrate how religious voluntaryism
has been shaped by other social sectors in post-industrial America, sometimes to the point of the loss of its social influence and the obliteration of its
distinctive identity. The essays also demonstrate, however, the continuing
role of religious voluntaryism as a vital force within the culture, one proven
capable of assuming new forms and developing new strategies appropriate to
a constantly changing social structure.
   Both the vitality of religious voluntarism and the pressures exerted upon
it by other sectors call attention to the potency of pluralism in American life.
Assessments of American religion as an occupant of the independent sector
must recognize, as all of our essayists do, that religious groups must find
their places in a social space defined by radical cultural diversity. Even when
pursuing goals and following motives defined by their own distinctive traditions, religious and other voluntary groups, when they make a bid for
attention in the public domain, compete with other parties for their share of
public space and thereby willy-nilly seek their own forms of gain and empowerment. Furthermore, in their public roles religious groups have found it
difficult to maintain their distinctive religious identities not only because of
the influence of external cultural forces. That difficulty has sprung, as well,
from religious groups' deliberate adoption of forms and strategies suitable to
cultural and social influence. Religious groups have ever been tempted to

tone down their traditional accents in order to gain social influence and attain a creditable cultural vocabulary. Given the diverse forces of American life, it is remarkable that so many groups have succeeded in making their influence felt, have made their voices heard, and have retained connections with their religious legacies. If they did not always attain their ends in ways they originally imagined, religious voluntary associations *have* made a difference in the shaping of American culture.

RELIGION, SOCIETY AND THE INDEPENDENT SECTOR: KEY ELEMENTS OF A GENERAL THEORY

Max L. Stackhouse

The idea of analyzing society according to its "sectors" is not new, although the contemporary use of "sectoral analysis" seems to derive from the appropriations of the thought of the Marxist-revisionist, Antonio Gramsci. Several of his works, written in an Italian Fascist jail between 1928 and 1937, were published in the late 1950's and adopted with enthusiasm by younger intellectuals wanting to change the world in the 1960s.[1]

Gramsci placed special focus on the place of the intellectual in transforming modern civilization toward the new order. He emphasized the interdependence of cultural factors with the economic, political, and social sectors of society. He rejected the hegemony of one sector over others and accented the interdependence of economic, political and cultural factors in social conflict and development. He also tried to overcome certain anti-intellectual and anti-religious implications of the Marxist dictum that it was not consciousness that determined existence, but existence that determined consciousness. Gramsci stressed the creative role of those who, like the Protestant Reformers or the philosophs of the French Revolution, were clearly thinkers, but were "organically" related to decisive groups of society.

Gramsci's thought was attractive to a number of groups struggling for social change, including socialist Christians who thought, against Marx, that religion was not simply an epiphenomenon that would fade away as the revolution progressed;[2] political activists who found the linkage of theory and

---

1. A. Gramsci's *Opera* were published in Turin in six volumes between 1947–54, although many of them were written in jail under the Fascists, in the 1930's and 40's. Translations of his *The Modern Prince* was published in London, and of his *The Open Marxism* in New York in 1957. The term "sectors" does not appear in the dictionaries and encyclopedias of the social sciences as an analytical category before that time.

2. Many who recount the intellectual pilgrimage of an enormous number of Religious Socialists and advocates of Liberation Theology through the 1960's to the 1990's have taken their clues from Gramsci. For example Rene Coste writes in his *Marxist Analysis and Christian Faith* (Maryknoll, N.Y.: Orbis, 1985): "Of all the historical leaders of the Marxist movement, however, it is the writings of Gramsci that I find the most stimulating (p.9)" and: "The principal

"community organization" empowering;[3] and reformist professionals work-ing in "establishment" institutions who found great promise in the "move-ments" of the 1960's and 1970's.[4]

But a basic idea that Gramsci articulated—namely, that society was a system of sectors which are partly autonomous, analytically distinct, but mutually influential—was not entirely new. This idea had appeared in other key theories of society with distinctly pluralistic, non-Marxist roots, and this offshoot has increasingly been re-grafted on to them. Deeper roots can be seen in Abram Kuyper's analysis of the "spheres" of society,[5] in Walter Rauschenbusch's program for Christianizing "areas" of society reform,[6] and in Max Weber's sociological and Ernst Troeltsch's social ethical treatments of the "departments of life."[7] In all these analyses, the idea is influenced by the

---

development of the Marxist analysis of culture has come from the introduction of the concept of . . . *ideological apparatus* by Gramsci. . . . It extends to all the systems (or "sectors")—religious, the different churches; educational, both public and private schools; political; juridical; trade union; familial; and so forth—that function in the service of the dominant ideology (p. 18)."

3. I draw this observation from my own participation in social change groups in this country where sectoral analysis became standard during the 1970's, but also, more interestingly, from a human rights commission sent to the Philippines by the American Committee for Human Rights to investigate the violation of the rights of religious workers under Marcos, a few months before the victory of Aquino. Fr. Robert Drinan and I sat through session after session with church-related advocates of change as they not only explained the ways they were harassed, threatened, and arbitrarily arrested if not beaten; but also as they explained the current situation in the Philippines in terms that derived directly from Gramsci, with sector by sector analysis. During coffee breaks, I found out that only some of the leaders knew his name; even fewer had read him; but everyone used his language with nuance. His mode of sectoral analysis had become standard there also. Similarly, Harvey Cox reports on the basis of his experience in Latin America, that "Gramsci has become the theorist of choice." My hypothesis is that it is from these sources that the terminology of sectoral analysis entered our common vocabulary as categories of Fabian socialist analysis entered our vocabulary through the Social Gospel at the turn of the century.

4. See, for example, Theodore Levitt, *The Third Sector: New Tactics for a Responsive Society* (New York: AMACOM, 1973), which is interesting especially because he wrote this as a professor at Harvard Business School, and it was published by an arm of the American Management Association. More recently, Michael O'Neill has taken up and extended this analysis in *The Third America* (San Francisco: Jossey-Bass, 1989).

5. His famous 1898 *Lectures on Calvinism*, delivered at Princeton and outlining his account of the nature and character of a profound pluralistic and theistic understanding of society were republished by Eerdmans Publishing Co. in 1976. He was both prime minister of Holland who helped establish democratic pluralism in Holland, and a founder of the University of Amsterdam on explicitly Reformed theological principles.

6. See his, *Christianity and the Social Crisis* (New York: Macmillan, 1907), and his *Christianizing the Social Order* (New York: Macmillan, 1912). I analyzed his theories of sectors in society in relationship to his vision of the Kingdom of God in "Eschatology and Ethical Method," Ph.D. Dissertation, Harvard University, 1965.

7. In his introduction to *The Protestant Ethic and the Spirit of Capitalism*, attached to his revised 1904 essay in 1920 (Tr. by T. Parsons) (New York: Scribners, 1958), Weber begins by surveying the "various departments of life and . . . areas of culture (p. 19)," echoing his

recognition of the socio-historical importance of the religious sector distinct from the cultural one—a matter of considerable consequence for those interested in the "independent sector."

In all these forms, "sectoral analysis" intends to supersede, in part by inclusion, its two most significant forerunners in terms of a general social theory. One is the classical view, rooted in those forms of political theory which understand the task of social analysis in terms of guiding the regime so that the *olis* may be ordered according to the "natural hierarchy" of life. This is the view advocated today by the contemporary advocates of a return to the political theories of Plato and Aristotle, as well as the defenders of the Indian caste system.[8] The other is the post-modernist, romantic theory of "class analysis," which understands the social task as emancipation from every residue of alleged natural hierarchy or from any idea of constant and necessary social structures and the simultaneous actualization of autonomous individuality and spontaneous communalism. Sectoral analysis suggests that these two alternatives can neither adequately map such decisive matters as the relations of religion to politics or of culture to economics, nor give normative guidance to modern civilizations. As we will see, this is especially the case if we understand the relationship of more "traditional" sectors to distinctly modern ones as the "multiversity," the "multi-national corporation," and the explosion of professional organization. Ultimately, we will also see, theological issues are directly pertinent to the analysis of social and civilizational development.

If we today attempt to extend sectoral analysis to grasp and guide life, we shall have to focus on the "independent sector," and to recognize that, neither the classical "natural hierarchy" view nor the anti-institutional, romantic view, nor even the revisionist socialism of Gramsci has anticipated the possibility of modern pluralistic democracies being renewed morally and spiritually by religion centered in the independent sector. To attempt such an analysis invites us to suggest that the multifaceted character of such analysis may reveal to us more about the way the common life works and ought to work than do the alternatives.

To extend sectoral analysis will require, first, some identification of the primary systems of society, which we will call the axial sectors; second, the delineation of the differentiated development of these systems which introduced new sectorial complexities and professional institutions in modern

---

colleague Ernst Troeltsch's used of the phrase "departments of life" in *The Social Teachings of the Christian Churches* (New York: Harper, 1960), (tr. from the German edition of 1911 by O. Wyon in 1930).

8. This view has been most vigorously advocated in the modern world by Leo Strauss and his students, who strongly resist anything like sectoral analysis in favor of classical political philosophy. See his *Natural Right and History* (Chicago: U. of Chicago Press, 1953), and Allan Bloom, *The Closing of the American Mind* (New York: Simon and Schuster, 1987). Cf. Louis Dumont, *Homo Hierarchicus* (Chicago: U. of Chicago Press, 1970).

civilization; and third, a sketch of some key religious influences which shape the values and the polity of all these systems. Finally, we shall turn to prospects for the future.

The Axial Sectors of Society

Every human community, to be viable, must have at least five ordered and ordering systems: a family system, an economic system, a political system, a cultural system, and a religious system—one capable of providing (as some claim ideologies and philosophies do also) a vision of metaphysical meaning for the whole and moral guidance for the several parts of the whole. When these systems coherently interact, a society can be said to exist, and each related system constitutes a sector, or subsystem, of the whole.

The five basic sectors often overlap; they reinforce one another; they inevitably interpenetrate one another. In a myriad of ways, they mutually influence one another although they develop at different rates, and intentional changes in one may only marginally alter another—or do so in unintended ways. In every village and among every tribe, in every city and throughout every empire in the history of humanity, times, spaces, material and human resources are set aside for these systems whatever differences there may be in these societies. The smallest town or the greatest metropolis has homes, workplaces, political authorities, cultural events, and centers for religious observance. And that is because sex, wealth, power, communication, and piety are, everywhere and always, possible, necessary, and simultaneously in need of both respect and constraint in human communities.

Each of these sectors organizes an indispensable aspect of human existence by forming institutions which meet a basic human need critical to personality and to community. Our personal identities are indelibly stamped, for example, by the family from which we come, by the ways we get our daily bread, by the kind of polity in which we live, by the way our language names the world, sings its songs and bewails its woes, and by the more or less ordered interpretations of ultimate reality which lends meaning to the whole when things go well and gives purpose to the parts when all else fails.

Each sector has its own characteristic institutions, and these institutions—partly malleable, partly determinate—pattern our lives. They are fateful not only for persons but also for peoples. Institutions may sometimes oppress, but chaos destroys any who dispense with them. It is never a choice of whether we can have or not have institutions in these various sectors. Without them we die. The only question is what shape they will take. The whole community suffers if one or another of these institutions fails. If they fall apart, or if a sector declines, the society's demise can only be arrested by the mobilization of the other sectors to reconstruct a viable institutional structure for the deficient sector. We can call these indispensable, organized aspects of life the "axial sectors" of society, for on them the destiny of civility turns.

Orders of Creation?

The classic theological traditions of the West knew that something like this was the case. Theologians recognized that the institutions of each of these sectors served to channel one or another of those great potentialities of life which can also become great sources of human temptation to sin and idolatry. Sex, wealth, power, communication, and piety can, rightly ordered, ennoble life; distorted, they destroy it. Theologians were concerned especially because they believed that the most fundamental question of all of these sectors had to go with the kind of piety which served to integrate and give guidance to the whole. *How religion is related to the other axial sectors was seen as fateful for both the salvation of souls and the destiny of civilization.*

We can glimpse the story of Western theology in this area by noting that Martin Luther was already drawing on several centuries of the Catholic recasting of influences from Greek and Roman political philosophy when he spoke of those foundational "orders of creation" established by God—*ecclesia, imperium,* and *dominum*—by which life was to be organized.[9] He simply presumed as obvious and scriptural the "estates" identified as decisive in late medieval law and theology and experienced daily in life. These structures, strengthened over four centuries in the new cities, prompted the notion that humans were supposed to live in what the French called a *"societe des ordres"* and the Germans *"Standesstaat."* Society is not essentially understood as a creature of regime, nor in terms of any natural hierarchy of master and peasant, nor as a solidarity formed by a contractual act of human will, although these are also acknowledged. Society is understood to be a *communitas communitorum.*[10]

Calvinist thought, with its more intense social interest, has been more influential in shaping the pluralism of modernity, on the basis of a theory of the covenants of civility—in spite of its sometime tendencies to theocracy. Calvin held that common institutional patterns such as those here called "axial" are earthly "arenas" in which people could work out their Godly callings and manifest covenantal responsibility in the world. These institu-

9. See, for example, John Witte, Jr. "The Reformation of Marriage Law in Martin Luther's Germany," *Journal of Law and Religion,* Vol. IV, No. 2 (1986), pp. 293ff.

10. Harold Berman has traced many of these developments in his monumental *Law and Revolution* (Cambridge, MA: Harvard U. Press, 1983). His evidence, in substantial measure, confirms hypotheses set forth by M. Weber in his "The City," *Economy and Society,* (tr. and ed. G. Roth and C. Whittich) (New York: Bedminster Press, 1968).

tions were not quite "orders of creation" (since they arose only after the Fall).
Yet, neither are they simply manifestations of the order of sin to be overcome
either by taking vows to lift one above the world, as some Catholic monastics
thought, or by trying to live a faith that stood against all authorities in the
world, as some sectarians taught. Rather, they were providentially-given
occasions to form covenantal alliances under God in the midst of sin, to
exercise ascetic discipline in this life, to constrain the grossest manifestations
of evil in a fallen world, and perhaps by rightly ordered living to give humble
witness to the glory of God.[11]

The heirs of this tradition held, as Althusius argued, that sustaining the
common life depended on forming "symbiotic associations" of piety and
justice which, when well formed, could avoid anarchy and tyranny in a
genuine commonwealth.[12] Other heirs in the Puritan tradition held that the
family and the state and the economy could be reformed much as the church
had been on the basis of this understanding.[13] Still, these arenas of human
activity were not inevitably redemptive; rather, they were partially pliable
manifestations of common grace wherein sanctification might be approxi-
mated.

More recent theological reflections about these arenas of existence have
taken a number of directions, including extensive treatments of the "orders"
in terms of their "functions of preservation and service" in the reflections of
the Swiss theologian Emil Brunner;[14] and extended treatments of "emergency orders" or "mandates of God" in the thought of Lutheran thinkers
Helmut Thielicke and Dietrich Bonhoeffer when they faced the Fascists.[15]
American thinkers such as James Luther Adams argue that theological and
ecclesiological forces created the basic covenantal patterns of the "indepen-

---

11. I have tried to show how this was mediated to contemporary American life through the
Puritan heritage as it joined with the traditions of liberal philosophy in my *Creeds, Society and
Human Rights*. (Grand Rapids, MI: Eerdmans Publishers, 1984), Ch. 3 & 4.

12. See the translation of Johannes Althusius, *Politics* by F. S. Carney, (Boston: Beacon
Press, 1966). See also Carney's article, "Associational Thought in Early Calvinism," and those of
George H. Williams, "The Religious Background of the Idea of a Loyal Opposition," and Karl
Hertz, "The Nature of Voluntary Associations" in *Voluntary Associations: A Study of Groups in
Free Societies*, ed. D. B. Robertson, (Richmond, VA: John Knox Press, 1966).

13. See, for examples, A. S. P. Woodhouse, ed., *Puritanism and Liberty* London: J. M.
Dent, 1938; James J. Johnson, *A Society Ordered by God* (Nashville, TN: Abingdon Press,
1970).

14. See his Gifford Lectures of 1948, published as *Christianity and Civilization*, 2 Vol.
(New York: Scribners, 1949).

15. Helmut Thieliche includes, transforms, and systematizes the work of D. Bonhoeffer on
these points in his *Theological Ethics*, 3 Vol. (Philadelphia: Fortress Press, 1966), where his
purpose is "to give a Christian interpretation of human and historical reality in general. . . .
This aim impels (him) to inquire concerning the shape of the social, political and economic
structures in which we must live and act . . . (and concerning) the relation of these structures to
God. . . . Are there "orders of creation" . . . and does our obedience . . . depend on our
acquiescence in the claim of these orders?" (p.xiii).

dent sector" by establishing a new kind of "social space" in society.[16] Such views are today advanced by voices as diverse as William Everett, Dennis McCann, Daniel Elazar, Michael Walzer, plus both Sarah Evans with Harry Boyte and Peter Berger with Richard Neuhaus.[17]

The Modern Social Sciences

Of course, many who worry about society are suspicious of normative approaches to it, theological or ethical, and some forms of the analysis of the decisive sectors of society were specifically developed to overcome what they perceived to be dogmatic bias in the study of human phenomena.[18] Indeed, it may even be the case that the social sciences miss what they seek because the bonds which finally hold human life together are "supranatural" and not merely natural, and theology is as much required to understand society as the social sciences are to understand religion.

The social sciences are, in short, inclined to reductionism. But let us note a most interesting thing: *we can identify the competing reductions of the modern social sciences by identifying which sector of society is taken to be explanatory of other sectors, and thought to be decisive also in the formation of religious and moral norms.* Thus we gain a clue as to what, according to the particular social science under consideration, is the root issue of the "independent sector." Whatever intramural disputes there may be within psychology, economics, politics, cultural studies, or anthropology and so-ciology, each of these great subdivisions of modern social science engages in a kind of intentional, methodological reductionism to try to show how much

16. James L. Adams is the premier American interpreter of the importance of the "inde-pendent sector" in modern societies, and the ways religious ideas have influenced their development. See his *On Being Human Religiously*, ed. M. L. Stackhouse (Boston: Beacon Press, 1976); *Voluntary Associations*, ed. J. R. Engel (Chicago: Exploration Press, 1986); and *The Prophethood of All Believers*, ed. G. K. Beach (Boston: Beacon Press, 1986).

17. William J. Everett, *God's Federal Republic* (New York: Paulist Press, 1988), from a Baptist point of view; Dennis P. McCann, *New Experiment in Democracy* (Kansas City, KA: Sheed and Ward, 1987), from a Catholic point of view; Daniel Elazar, *American Federalism* (3rd rev. ed.); (New York: Harper and Row, 1984), from a Jewish point of view; Michael Walzer, *Sphere of Justice* (New York: Basic Books, 1983), from a philosophical point of view; as well as by those advocating social change in a "radical" direction, such as Sara M. Evans & H. C. Boyte, *Free Spaces: The Sources of Democratic Change in America* (New York: Harper and Row, 1986), or in a "neo-conservative" direction such as Peter Berger and Richard Neuhaus, *To Empower People: The Role of Mediating Structures in Public Policy* (Washington: American Enterprise Institute, 1977). See also Robert Wuthnow, *et al.*, eds., *Faith and Philanthropy in America* (San Francisco: Jossey-Bass, 1990), espec. Ch. 1 & 2; and my "The Sociology of Religion and the Theology of Society," *Social Compass*, Vol. 37, No. 3 (Sept. 1990), pp. 315–330.

18. One thinks of Marx in Germany and Comte in France in this connection, of course; but the American Traditions have been somewhat more subtle. See Arthur Vidich and Stanford Lyman, *American Sociology: Wordly Rejections of Religion and Their Directions* (New Haven, CT: Yale U. Press, 1985), especially Ch. 2 & 3.

of the whole of the common life can be accounted for by revealing that the particular dynamics, structures and processes behind one or another of these axial institutions "decisively determines" all the other structures of society and hence the course of human affairs. Each draws its governing "myths, models, and paradigms" from a particular sector:

Psychology. Since (at least) L. H. Morgan's studies of kinship systems and ways these shape economic, political and aesthetic dimensions of "primitive cultures" in the 1870's through Freud's analysis of the psychodynamics of kinship relationships that dominate existence, to the new French studies on family, sexuality and social relations,[19] psychological (including many psychoanalytic and social-psychological) branches of the social sciences have opted for the paradigms of family life. The relations of males and females and of parents and children in various stages of the life cycle are seen as those determinative for religion and society.

Economics. From Adam Smith through Karl Marx and John Maynard Keynes to today's honored pundits, economists have proposed the view that material motivations, the means of production, and the structures and dynamics of exchange are the primary motors of society and determine the general patterns of family life, politics, culture and religion.[20]

Political Science. Since Machiavelli, Hobbes, Rousseau, and Lenin broke with the efforts of classical thought to identify how regimes ought to be organized, so that virtue and the laws of God were promoted, "Political Science" in its many forms has attempted to identify everything that happens in economics, family life, culture and religion by the use of "power analysis."[21]

Cultural Studies. From the Grimm brothers through Heidegger to the hermeneuticists of every text and context, cultural critics honor the creativity of the story-tellers, playfully decode the myths of the world, and deconstruct the meanings of every other sector of society because they are convinced, with Nietzsche, that these represent only the arbitrary constructs of artful genius.[22]

Why They Are Right, and Wrong

Each of these perspectives has seen something that is undeniably valid. Human activities everywhere fall into ordered patterns because a certain *lex*

19. See, especially, Philippe Aries, *Centuries of Childhood* (New York: Random House, 1962); and Emmanuel Todd, *The Explanation of Ideology: Family Structures and Social Systems* (Oxford: Basil Blackwell, 1985).

20. One of the best summaries can be found in Robert Heilbroner, *The Worldly Philosophers*, fifth ed, (New York: Simon and Schuster, 1980).

21. Sheldon Wolin, *Politics and Vision* (Boston: Little, Brown, 1960), remains unsurpassed in my judgment.

22. The best overview of the literature in cultural and cultural-linguistic interpretations of society is, in my view, Robert Schreiter, *Constructing Local Theologies* (Maryknoll, NY: Orbis Books, 1985).

societas is everywhere in effect. Modern social science has partly re-discovered, and refined, the "orders of creation." Because humans are male and female, and certain percentages of them get together with some regularity, every society has to have a patterned way to deal with the interactions of the sexes and the generations. Family and its psycho-sexual dynamics influence everything else.

Simultaneously, every group has to derive energy (and water and shelter) from the environment and distribute it in ways that sustain life. Thus every society develops economic techniques that intervene in the biophysical order. How it does this limits or expands the possibilities in every other axial institution of life.

Similarly, every society has problems of internal conflict and external threat. Thus, every society has some kind of structure of governance in which some dominate others. How a regime gets structured influences a good number of other things—such as family life, economic life, cultural life, and religious life.

And every society has to have common, characteristic ways of communicating while doing all of the above things. It needs organized ways to convey information, thought and emotion—through language, song, dance, images, or gesture. The ordering of these constitutes the cultural institutions of life, and how a society's artists construe things shapes sexual, economic, political, and religious relationships.

Each analysis is mistaken, however, when it tries to make a particular axial sector explain all the others. This is implicitly acknowledged by the constant creation of hybrid social sciences (cultural anthropology, studies in political culture, analyses of sexual politics, revivals of political economics) and as many interpretations of the nature and function of religion as there are social sciences (psychology of religion, sociology of religion, political ideology, etc.).

However, the developments over the last century in sociology and anthropology have recognized that societies are a complex of interacting systems as can be seen in the work of Malinowski, Eliade, and Geertz as well as that of Weber, Durkheim, Parsons, Berger, and Bellah. Further, these scholars also have a distinctive place for religion, although they recognize that much that passes for religion can be shown to be a projection of psycho-sexual desires or relations, a manifestation of economic wish or resentment, a transcendentalized political ideology, or a collective cultural folkway or memory. They have not yet, however, offered a compelling account as to how civilizations are renewed by religious revitalization in the face of (supposed) increased secularization.

Not infrequently, historians are especially suspicious of the social sciences, for they note that the particular forms these axial sectors of life take and the way these various "departments of life" interact are not constant over time and place. Those who think it is possible to get a clean purchase on the *lex societas* by using one fulcrum are suspect. The sectors of society can be variously related and do develop at different paces in different directions as widely varying institutions are formed within them and as external pressures prompt change. The variables of historical existence are more complex than most social sciences acknowledge. Time undoes narrow schemes. Still, historians know that the common life is not simply "one damn thing after another," as Henry Ford once said. Societies may well have a certain tendency to re-assert their deepest ethical presuppositions and to reintegrate the "blooming, buzzing confusion" of multiple variables according to a normative vision of how life ought to be lived—by, above all, religious renewal.

In other words, what governs the general direction and relative importance of these axial institutions, what holds them into some modicum of cohesion, what serves as the inner guidance system of the whole is religion—especially as it becomes internalized by the people and woven into the fabric of practical life to create an ethos.[23] That is, a religious vision becomes social ethics—carried by the voluntary institutions of society, which find their locus in the independent sector. Such ethics sustain their credibility only if they help sustain the axial institutions or help create new sectors that accord with the ethics implied by the original vision.

It may well be that to depend on voluntarily sustained social ethics is to depend on a frail reed, for oddly this most important area exercises its influence through the weak effects of beliefs, convictions, voluntary contributions of time and treasure, and intermittent promptings to honor truth, justice, holiness, sacrifice and service above all else. Even when such promptings are strong, social ethics not infrequently botch the job of guiding people's lives and civilizations—sometimes because they are based on beliefs that are in fact untrue or unjust, sometimes because they do not know how to do well what is well worth doing. Besides, the social sciences have taught us, through Durkheim, that religion sometimes becomes little more than society worshiping itself, and ethics becomes little more than the self-conciousness of the professional group—in either case a fragile and artificial collective consciousness grown out of some particular social experience, interest, or need.[24]

Nevertheless, any attempt to deal with any sector in society requires attention to the way the independent sector and its voluntary institutions interact with the other parts of society. And decisive in this is religion, for it may point to the only foundation that is not reductionistic.

---

23. This, I think, is the main point of Max Weber's *Gesammelte Aufsaetze zur Religionssoziologie*, which were unfinished at his death in 1920. These volumes remains among the most suggestive, if controversial, "classic" social scientific works that have implications for our questions.

24. See, especially, Emile Durkheim, *The Division of Labor in Society* (Tr., 1933) (Glenco, IL: The Free Press, 1960). CF. His study of the consequences of the failure of these, *Suicide* (Glencoe, IL: The Free Press, 1966).

Society and Civilization

Two factors make it very difficult to speak with precision on these matters, and we must note both of them. The first factor is this: only some religions can guide and sustain the fabric of a social system over time. Only some religious ethics can supply an interpretation of the meaning of life capable of guiding life in all its departments in a way that is, at once, true, just and practical, although it is very bad form to suggest today that all religions are not of equal worth. When a religion does not provide such guidance, we can expect a great number of religious conflicts, questings, conversions, enthusiasms, and fanaticisms—not to mention spiritual quackery and ethical fraud. When that occurs, a society is in for turbulence, for the sense of normative order by which human groups established patterned institutions to form a more or less viable society has become unglued, and the foundations for reconstruction are not available.

Axial institutions can coast for a time, perhaps for decades, for the hymns of the elders sung from the mountaintops of faith echo as morality in the valleys of the heirs. The blessings as well as the sins of the parents are visited unto the children unto the third or fourth generation. But without a valid guidance system—that is, a basically true religion that renders a basically just ethic, voluntarily held by the people—a subversion and exploitation of the ordinary institutions of life will eventually lead to the decay, corruption, or implosion of the axial sectors of society. Then heavy is their fall, and great the human suffering.

The second factor is the one which deserves examination at some length. Modern life is not only shaped by society-sustaining interactions between the axial sectors, but also by *civilizational* developments which increasingly make every society subject to new transformations. Modern civilizations construct new sectors that alter the axial ones. Many of the social sciences were born as the West underwent a transition from primary communities to complex society. We are moving from a complex society to a cosmopolitan civilization.

People do not always consciously choose these changes; indeed, some religious and ethical systems actively resist them. But the new sectors, usually claiming the sanction of alternative religious and ethical systems, cannot easily be opposed. Enough people find new patterns sufficiently helpful or attractive that they begin to prefer them. The cumulative impact of millions of minor decisions engenders a civilizational shift. The poor, the illiterate and the weak may be especially victimized by these changes, for fragile grips on society's institutions are endangered further. Yet the forces often seem so inexorable that the affluent and privileged also experience a powerlessness. It is not always clear who or what is in control of contemporary civilization, and the sense of impotence provokes innumerable alienations, conspiracy theories, and competing ideologies.

The great strength of modern social theory is the attempt to demystify these transformations. Psychology, political science, economics, cultural sociological and anthropological analysis and the various hybrids have indicated that we are leaving behind a world filled with discrete societies—some of which, like India, China, and Europe, had a remarkably common and resilient culture over long periods of time and wide reaches of space. Sectoral analysis helps us to see that what distinguishes modern civilization from earlier communities and societies is that key functions of the axial sectors are separated out from them and placed in distinct, new centers of organizational life. The common life is rearranged, on new terms. Invented institutions become indispensable. The axial sectors are modulated and made instrumental to new ends.

Under the impact of this transformation, every society, all of the great classic cultures, and a plethora of communities are challenged. They must adapt to modern, global civilization or die. People who resist the changes, or who cannot adapt quickly enough, experience the breakdown of the family as they were nurtured in it, the obsolescence of economic skills as they learned them, the absence of nobility in matters political as they honored it, the decay of the arts as they knew them, and hostile doubt about the meaningfulness of a religious vision as they believed it. Only those who experience religious conversion and/or are drawn into new voluntary associations to shape the transition can become involved in the shaping of the future.

Sophisticated civilizations, of course, have faced such troubles in the past, and some have overcome the difficulties enough to reach amazing levels of complexity. Few of the chief characteristics of modern civilization and none of its distinguishing institutions are *entirely* peculiar to modernity, but a shower differs from a torrent. We can see this if we look at the professions, which have produced the most visible new sectors of modern civilization. Contemporary education, law, medicine, engineering, journalism and business, all have many antecedents and predecessors. Yet only today does professionalization, technologization, communications, and commercialization begin to dominate the whole inhabited earth and produce new sectors of civilization. What once was episodic is now continuous; what was once confined to the cities now spreads to the countryside; what once was "North" is now also "South;" what once was bourgeois is today proletarian; what once was peculiar to the particular memory of the West is now transposed to the global future—in part because some people believed that some things were ultimately true and just, and thus *should be* carried to the ends of the earth.[25]

25. One can find both theological and social scientific treatments of a generation ago that anticipate this "universalization." See A. Van Leeuwen, *Christianity in World History* (New York: Scribners, 1964); and E. Tiryakian, ed., *Sociological Theory: Values and Socio-Cultural Change* (Glenco, IL: The Free Press, 1963). More recently, one might note the growth of the International Society for the Comparative Study of Civilizations which attempts to extend and refine the insights of Toynbee and Mumford on such questions.

Describing the process of transition is, from a personal viewpoint, easy; the cumulative structural effect, when millions of people experience it, is a civilizational shift of monumental proportions. We can take education as a primary illustration.

Every society teaches the children. In the simplest communities, children learn all sorts of quite subtle things from their parents. Their efforts are reinforced as elders inculcate values in dozens of ways; as grandparents, neighborhood and congregation, community festivals, and national rituals socialize and acculturate; as peers whisper, yell, tease, and insinuate a thousand lessons. Often, also, gifted persons are set aside to initiate the young into the arts of loving, learning, and believing, the crafts of production, the majesty of authority, and the lore of culture, especially through the inculcation of the mysteries of sacred myth and holy membership. Sometimes the young are taken, for a time, outside the community and taught through extraordinary modes of rite, instruction, and testing to encounter life, society, and its institutions in new ways.

Some religious leaders who believed that the true home of the mind was outside the world developed new places of learning. Schools took the young away from parents and traditional economy, local authority, mother tongue and pagan cults. Using the wisdom of ancient academies for youth of noble birth, they induced an intellectual alienation from, and thus a critical attitude toward, everyday experience. Monasteries of cathedrals became the centers of teaching and learning.

In the course of the development of schooling, three axial sectors were quite interested in controlling the substance of the lessons—the three "estates" or "orders of creation." In some places pedagogues were brought into the leading households for instruction. Every self-respecting villa, hacienda, mansion or manor had its resident guru to form the next generation of leadership. The young were "led out" to the wider world intellectually by an outsider, a servant, who tutored under the supervision of parental authority. Some argue today that parents are those chiefly responsible for education. In other places, rulers accented the importance of education and developed palace schools for royal purposes. And in still others, apprentice schools for training in the crafts or trade were established for economic purposes. The relationship between government, business, and education developed in distinctive ways, challenging the authority of parents.

And, of course, religious institutions which, at times, were not only interested in the cultivation of faith but in having a monopoly on culture also established institutions of learning—ironically legitimizing the relative freedom of schools from familial, commercial, and political control. Wherever, for example, the great missionary religions of the world spread, they formed schools to which young scholars went, abstracting them from the other axial contexts of their lives.

Educators who sometimes enlisted political authorities against the interventions of parents sometimes also enlisted the parents and the court against the church. When the masters of the University of Paris found a way to be economically independent of church, business interests, and political authority, a relatively autonomous new sector of society was born. Filled with conviction that both God and human welfare demanded the seeking of truth without interference, educators formed a variety of independent associations which, as they grew, extended their influence. Their heirs now establish the centers and institutes that populate the modern research multiversity.[26]

What is remarkable about modern civilization in this respect is that the young, from pre-school to graduate school, are now taken out of their homes into a permanent establishment, intentionally differentiated from every other organized sector of society, for the essential purpose of learning skills and developing critical thinking, according to abstract universalistic standards, about everything one might learn from ordinary experience. The youth, our nearest future, are put in the hands of teachers, professors, publishers of educational materials, and the academies which train them. They are to test the young and certify them as ready to be part of the civilization on the basis of encounter with, if not mastery of, thought which transcends their lives. Explicitly religious or ethical content is now hardly noticeable, or it is viewed as intrusive.

The education sector, with its various schools, academies, colleges, institutes and universities is a product of and an agent of the transition from complex society to cosmopolitan civilization. Many may argue today that education has lost its rudder, that it today rests on ultimate values that it cannot defend or induce. Many may join in the founding of independent schools in protest against public policies, and critiques of higher education may become best sellers; but pleas to "deschool society" will fall on deaf ears. The place of the massive educational sector is of enormous significance for any analysis of modern civilization and its future.

What is here exemplified by reference to education, however, is not unique. Functions previously reserved to the family, culture, and religion, for example, are removed from them and allocated to a new sector. Comparable examples could be drawn from law, medicine, or technology. These sectors of life separate us from our ancestors, sometimes alter and frequently alienate us from the axial sectors of life. They pose new challenges to the independent sector—and thus to the religious and ethical values by which it lives and which it must mediate to civilization if it is not to lose its basis for existence.

For all the transformations the modern professional sectors have brought to civilization, and for all that modern life depends on them, it is quite possible that no axial institution has become more differentiated, more

---

26. See H. I. Marrou, *A History of Education in Antiquity* (New York: Sheed and Ward, 1956); and William Boyd, *The History of Western Education*, eighth ed. (New York: Barnes and Noble, 1965).

complex or more global in implication than the economic sector. The political economy of modern civilization is characterized by differentiation of the economic sector into a technological sector on the one hand, and a business sector, dominated by corporations, interacting in a world market on the other. The corporations are (along with the professions and education) increasingly distinct from household, regime and culture.[27]

The New Corporation

The new corporation is a massive new kind of institution of considerable social complexity. It is not, in any clean sense, individualistic or collectivistic, public or private, or identical with either the axial or professional sectors of modern life. Yet it is highly interdependent with all of them. Indeed, it is in key ways as dependent on them as they are dependent on corporations. Universities, law firms, hospitals, publishers and nearly all the other useful institutions of modern life were organized as corporations—that is, as intentionally and voluntarily organized human communities that, while nongovernmental, have a distinct polity that links together, in new ways, as legal, intellectual and technological human activities in order to accomplish some particular task through a complex division of labor.

We Americans are self-conflicted about corporations. We live by them; they are nowhere more widely developed than among us; but our religious, moral, and intellectual leaders are alienated socially and morally from them.[28] We defend the family farm, but we buy our food (even health food) from agribusiness. We condemn a corporation's displacement of workers when it changes location or modes of production, but we also condemn American management for not moving to new locales and new modes of production while the Asian rim countries were establishing subsidiaries all over the world and developing robotics. We satirize the conformist, button-down mind of corporate thinking but are very pleased when our children get good jobs with a quality corporation and wear a buttoned-down shirt to work. The multinational corporations are portrayed as the beasts from the deep in modern demonology, but those who are most vigorous in trying to exorcise these demons find that their retirement funds are invested in blue-chip multinationals and that democratizing countries and those where various

27. See my *Public Theology and Political Economy* (Grand Rapids, MI: Eerdmans Publishers, 1987), especially Ch. 7 & 8. See also my "Godly Cooking: Ethical Reflections on Technology and Theology," *First Things* (forthcoming, May, 1991).

28. Compare, for example, Peter Drucker, *Concept of the Corporation*, second revised edition (New York: Mentor, 1983) to Richard Barber, *The American Corporation: Its Power, Its Money, Its Politics* (New York: Dutton & Co., 1970); to O. Williams and J. Houch, eds., *The Judeo-Christian Vision and the Modern Corporation* (Notre Dame, IN: U. of Notre Dame Press, 1982); and to M. Novak and J. W. Cooper, *The Corporation: A Theological Inquiry* (Washington: American Enterprise Institution, 1981), and Peter Berger, *The Capitalist Revolution* (New York: Basic Books, 1986).

socialisms have collapsed want as many of these corporations as they can get. We applaud national candidates who call for taxing the corporations, but we elect local officials who give tax-breaks to get corporations to move to town. The love/hate relation with what has become one of the most indispensable institutions of modern civilization is remarkable.

Asceticism Lives

It should not be surprising that we turn to religious categories to overcome the deficiencies of our present understanding and to find a guide for the future, but it will be to some. In spite of many models of social change that have held that progress would leave religion behind, the American experience generally and contemporary experience more widely suggests that we might well attend to new developments in just this area of religious ethical thought. And we should here note that the Roman Catholics, the Lutherans, the Presbyterians, the Methodists, and the United Church of Christ have all in recent years become suddenly active in developing pastoral letters, statements, and position papers on precisely the question of modern economic institutions. Indeed, we should also note the vigorous reassertion of the independent sector by conservative religious groups. They are not only forming new churches and new denominations, building alternative schools, proposing changes in the law, encouraging a new generation of Christian professionals; they are also developing networks of Christian businesses and charities organized by corporations.

There may be something of resentment in this. The towers of finance now dwarf the steeples of churches. And we may suspect some religious leaders are a little too eager to tell the less successful, for a donation, that if they think pious thoughts they too can join the rich and the famous. But at a deeper level, those who do not live in the corporate world suspect that what goes on in this new sector of civilization has no ultimate moral and spiritual integrity, even if its largess is welcomed. It seems to be premised on greed, on the playing of corporate and sexual politics, on the desire for material goods, on the making or getting of "more" by those who so obviously already have "enough." The corporations with their drive toward evermore efficient production and higher profits, making decisions based on tough-minded calculations that determine the bottom line, seem devoid of "human" factors. Indeed, some who are in the corporate life say that this is what makes it go.

In fact, dehumanizing factors are not unique to the corporation. Those who have lived in the villages, on the farms, or in small towns have faulty memories if they remember only folksy humor, close-knit affections, traditional festivals, and strong piety; and do not remember also the back-breaking drudgery, the petty-mindedness, the rapacious materialism, the exploitation and spiritual pretense barely held in check by faith and the associations of the independent sector.[29] It is simply not clear that greed, lust for power, or the love of material rewards are entirely absent from education, law, medicine, journalism, the military or the axial sectors of society. They may be part of the human condition, as theologians have claimed.

Yet, one thing that is different is that the modern economic sector does not have an explicit, overt, clear sense of why it does what it does and why it is valid—morally and spiritually valid—to do the things it does. The gospel of success and religious sanctifications of capitalism ring false. Business knows that what it does has its rewards, and nobody wants to support a system that doesn't work. But it is not clear that doing well is intrinsically related to doing good. There is the suspicion that the increase of one implies the decrease of the other; yet that does not seem exactly right either. This absence of an explicit moral and spiritual framework for self-assessment, self-guidance, and self-correction means also that, while people in business may be no less moral than people anywhere else, and while corporate life could not run for five minutes were it not for a remarkable degree of trust and trustworthiness, powerful elements in our spiritual heritage disapprove a life focused centrally on the accumulation of those things "where moth and rust consumes and thieves break in and steal."

We know that the axial institutions are necessary for human survival. Further, we can recognize the importance of the quest for truth in education (and the quest for justice in law, the quest for health in medicine, etc.); and we know that these have always been rooted in the deepest levels of faith as conveyed by our religious tradition. We know that a certain sense of the sacred remains in the classroom, the operating room, and the courtroom as well as in the house of worship. We even know that the fecundity of God's creation is a source of abundance and a reason for thanksgiving. But on what fundamental religious, moral or spiritual basis does the modern corporation stand? What is its governing principle? Gain? What is the chief end of the economic sector? Wealth? What is sacred to business? Profit? What do we get from the modern economic system? Rich? For what?

This is, I think, the most important single question facing Religion, Modern Society and the Independent Sector today. The spirit of asceticism lives; it has wrought what we have; it suspects what we have wrought. Are we not advised to "go, sell all we have, give to the poor, and follow" an entirely different model of life? Is there a religious ethic to guide our economic future? Can the voluntary institutions help define, evoke and implement a business ethic?

---

29. Edward C. Banfield, *The Moral Basis of a Backward Society*. (Chicago: The Free Press, 1958), has been much neglected, but it documents what is experienced in "communal societies" all over the world, as every young person who has escaped to the city already knows.

Future Accents

It has, quite recently, become fashionable to study the independent sector with special attention to ethics. If that fashion continues into the future, we would be well advised to identify those learnings from this sectoral analysis of our social situation that might preoccupy us for the next several tomorrows. Seven points are worthy of special mention:

First, such issues as are here posed can only be addressed with attention to the role of religion in modern civilizational life. This is partly because of the peculiarities of the American heritage, but it is also, and more profoundly, because we shall have to deal with a two-sided approach to the decisive questions. On the one side, we shall have to deal with the new sectors of modern civilization—especially with how the modern professions interact with the corporations and their relationship to voluntary organizations in the independent sector. And on the other side, we shall have to deal overtly with that which claims to point to what is, ultimately, reliable and sovereign in life—transcendent to the interests of society.

I think that, in the long run, a "public theology" is required because it provides a social ethic based on warranted argument and is capable of eliciting sustained commitment. Philosophy has arguments but does not evoke a committed constituency outside the classroom. Morality needs a foundation on which to rest, and religion can be, without the critical guidance of theology, quite esoteric, idiosyncratic and fanatical. However, it is beyond the scope of this paper to set forth a full explication of the idea of "public theology."

Second, we should expect that study in and study of the independent sector will continue to grow only so long as we continue to hold the view that social problems cannot or ought not be solved by government policy alone, and as long as we preserve the legal framework that allows the formation of communities of commitment for public good. This involves also the formation of character and the clarification of values built into pluralistic and inclusive structures that provide a sense of the meaning of life. Any who take up the study of this sector shall have to be willing to wrestle with the moral and spiritual issues, for it is only in terms of these that we can see the importance of having a flourishing independent sector.

Third, we can expect the continued, intense, even frantic organization of voluntary associations within the independent sector around the world whenever one or another of the axial institutions is felt to be threatened— Eastern Europe and the Mid-East are the most dramatic contemporary examples. Elsewhere "modernization," by the introduction of differentiated educational, legal, technological and business sectors, brings with it the acids which break down old bonds. The opportunities for comparative studies is wide open, and we may well feel that the prospects for the formation of independent sectors, pried open in the West by our religious history, may repeatedly be slammed shut in places where religious traditions identify the sacred with a particular form of familial life such as the tribe or the clan, or with a particular political, national, cultural, or economic system. We will then experience the intensity of fundamentalisms pitted against modernity, against the formation of open independent sectors, and against the religious traditions from which pluralistic civilizational patterns derive.

Fourth, where the social space for people to organize does come into being, we will find not only new religious formations but new accents on the defense of axial sectors that are under threat. In the United States, I expect one set of key debates to be posed around family life, for that is where many feel the loss of coherence under the impact of the modern professions and business.

We know that divorce rates, abandoned mothers, teenaged pregnancy, abortion, the changing roles of women, the breakdown of family in minority groups, the crisis of mobility in dual-career families, latch-key children, the struggles in many families with drug, alcohol or sexual abuse, patterns of "co-workaholism," and the debates over how society should respond to gay/lesbian advocacy, homosexual partnerships, and sexually transmitted diseases—all these already portend the battle over the family. Some key issues within this battle are economic and political; more are cultural, social, psychological, educational, medical, and integrally related to the economic sector in its contemporary form. In any case, religious, ethical, and ultimately theological questions are at stake, and no public or philanthropic organizations can duck them.

At a quite different level, it is likely that ideation-oriented voluntary associations will continue to grow. The fifth point is that the more cosmopolitan the civilization, the more abstract the conceptualities must be to organize its complexity, and the more refined the governing symbolic systems must be to maintain openness to both critical feedback and ultimate values, and the more widespread key values and understandings must be held among the people. Among the critical issues at this level will be those that face the sharp debates in the professions.

Absolutely central is the question of whether there is anything such as "Truth" to be properly pursued by the educational sector of modern civilization, and anything such as "Justice" to be pursued by the legal sector. Every profession has its parallel issues. Contemporary "anti-foundationalists" in education and "crits" in jurisprudence suggest that no reliable knowledge of objective standards is possible.

The sixth area is the one to which I alluded earlier: modern business and its values. Unlike the above axial and professional areas, business leadership—including many technological areas as well as management, personnel relations, marketing, advertising, etc.—has not had a tradition of professional standards, explicit norms, or even a theory of human relations that can guide the modern corporation. To be sure, many procedures for authority and negotiations are worked out, and many standards of stewardship, many meanings of what it means to be a trustee of social wealth, and many controls over overt deception have passed into liability law. But the inner sense of what it might mean to be a business professional does not seem to be developed in a way that is comparable to education, law or medicine.

Various efforts are, of course, under foot to clarify the practices that allow the executive to be truly effective, to identify the guidelines whereby business can engage in the pursuit of excellence, to state the conditions under which the corporations serve the common good, to identify the predominant rites and rituals of corporate culture, and to analyze the ways in which new models of business polity can enhance the social economy. All of these might well work, but the deeper and more difficult problem facing the corporate sector of modern civilization is that while it is, in so many ways, quite successful, it is held suspect by many who do not live for business or think that anyone should live simply for its stated ends.

It is doubtful that business can develop the guidelines for its own professionalization. It will have to rely, as did other professions earlier, on the independent sector to identify, develop, propose, and have accepted by modern business, clear and life-guiding principles of *what business is as a profession and what the corporation is as a moral member of a new sector of a cosmopolitan civilization.* If that is not possible, all the other sectors of society and many of business' own employees will simply try to seize its riches by all available means, for they will perceive that it gets its gain by draining the life out of families, the earth, and the poor, while turning the professions—education, law, medicine, journalism—into subsidiary businesses and destroying their reason for being. This will require the formation of professional business associations with a specific theological and ethical rootage, and a much larger vision for all those "prayer breakfasts" and "Christian Businessmen's Lunches" that already exist.

Finally, there is no evidence of a society or a civilization or a sector renewing itself unless it has the capacity, as Collingwood once reminded us, to overcome its own tendency to contract a "metaphysical disease." That tendency cannot be finally controlled by the social sciences, by increasing professionalism, and certainly not by parental, economic, cultural or political authority. Nor by the modern corporation. It can only be done by human spirits bonded together to seek and make actual what, ultimately, is worthy of commitment. That is where the independent sector must find its grounding and its future.

ECONOMIC CHANGE AND THE CHARACTER OF AMERICAN CATHOLIC PHILANTHROPY 1790–1940

Mary J. Oates

> Economic forces were turned loose a century and a quarter ago when the industrial revolution came. . . . The economic development carried all before it, and our social problem is the result.
> *William J. Kerby*, 1900[1]

The links between economics and the Independent Sector are both broad and deep and exist in times of prosperity and depression. Economic distress evokes calls from those most materially affected on the benevolence of those relatively secure from its attendant hardships. Periods of economic prosperity motivate social, educational, religious and cultural philanthropies to challenge citizens to support voluntary activities which will enhance the quality of the nation's collective life.

An analysis of the philanthropy of American Catholics demonstrates how economic forces shaped, internally and externally, the essential character of religious voluntarism. Changing economic conditions evoked new strategies to meet new needs and generated radical reassessment of traditional priorities and principles of giving. At the same time, an investigation of religious voluntarism, as interpreted and implemented by the Catholic community, illustrates the significant role of the private sector in the development of the Independent Sector. As the Catholic church grew in membership and acceptance by mainstream society, the altruistic values which prompted its tangible expressions of collective concern increasingly influenced the social context and basic identity of the Independent Sector.

The American Catholic community was, for much of its history, viewed as a socially marginal group. First, its religion was unpopular and, for extended periods, feared and detested by a majority of mainstream Americans. Second, over the course of the nineteenth century its membership became increasingly identified as "foreign" and impoverished. Its outsider status fostered the development of separate institutions in every sphere of

---

1. William J. Kerby, "The Priesthood and the Social Movement," *Catholic University Bulletin* 6 (January, 1900): 23.

church activity, a propensity which intensified as its numbers rose rapidly after 1840.

This paper explores some of the ways in which Catholic philanthropy responded to the challenges posed by major economic developments in American history, and it considers significant modifications in the focus and style of giving which these events provoked. Given that the proportion of its members who were impoverished immigrants expanded dramatically during the nineteenth century, it is to be expected that economic dislocations and fluctuations would play a critical role in shaping and transforming Catholic benevolence. The dedication of a high proportion of its charitable resources, both financial and human, to relief of destitution prevailed until the first decades of the twentieth century, a period marked by a decline in immigration and an expansion in the Catholic middle-class. Secular changes in the organization and location of industrial activity critically affected the philosophy as well as the strategies of Catholic philanthropy.

Catholic Charity and Economic Development Before 1840

When in 1789 John Carroll of Baltimore was named the first American bishop, his co-religionists did not exceed 30,000 nationally. A majority were poor farmers in the mid-Atlantic states, a small number were business owners, and a few French settlers were located to the west. The new nation as yet had no Catholic charities, although Ursuline nuns had been caring for orphans in Louisiana Territory since 1734. However, in 1791 the First Synod of Baltimore issued an urgent mandate for Catholics to ameliorate by generous gifts the ecnomic situation of the poor.[2]

The first charitable service undertaken by the Catholic community was the education of girls, a novel focus readily explained by the fact that the schools were established and managed by women. Visitation sisters in Georgetown opened a boarding school in 1805, using tuitions derived from it to finance a day school for poor girls and to maintain a number of boarding orphans. Three years later, with the aid of Bishop Carroll and lay patrons, Mother Elizabeth Seton and her Sisters of Charity established a similar school in Baltimore. Since the relatively poor Catholic population was unable to provide significant funding or endowments for charities, tuitions furnished revenues to cover living expenses of the sisters and to assist the poor. In order to reach poor children, it was necessary that sisters instruct more affluent girls, many of whom were Protestant.

Early converts to Catholicism like Seton, for the most part better educated and wealthier than their fellow Catholics, contributed disproportionately to the organization, management, and financing of these charities.

---

2. Joseph P. Chinnici, "Spiritual Capitalism and the Culture of American Catholicism," *U.S. Catholic Historian* 5, no. 2 (1986): 134.

Neither they nor Bishop Carroll foresaw any dramatic changes in the number, location, and economic status of the nation's Catholics. Writing to Mother Seton in 1810, Carroll observed that "a century at least will pass before the exigencies and habits of this country will require and hardly admit of the charitable exercises towards the sick, sufficient to employ any number of Sisters out of our large cities."[3] But within a generation, economic forces had begun to transform in radical ways the composition and the benevolent vision of the American church.

American society remained rural until mid-nineteenth century. Boston, with its good harbor, developing commercial sector, and approximately 6000 inhabitants, ranked in 1700 as the nation's most populous city, a distinction it retained until overtaken by Philadelphia and New York in the 1760s. Early growth of these cities arose from commercial rather than manufacturing expansion, and the supply of native labor was generally adequate for agricultural and local business needs. Transportation before 1820 was rudimentary and businesses and farms continued to serve local or regional markets. Domestic shipping was prohibitive in time as well as cost. In 1800 shipping goods to England cost less than transporting them thirty miles overland, while a shipment via horse-drawn wagon from Massachusetts to South Carolina took two and one-half months. In 1816, grain from midwestern farms had to follow a 3000-mile river and sea route to reach eastern markets.[4]

Marked economic and demographic change which commenced in the 1820s altered this picture considerably, and by 1860 the nation's land acreage and population had increased 300% and 100% respectively of 1790 totals. Since territorial acquisitions promised rich markets which could be exploited if transportation methods were modernized, pressures from eastern manufacturers and merchants generated intense construction activity, beginning in New York in 1817 with the Erie Canal, which opened New York ports to western markets. By 1830, 1300 miles of canals were in place in New England and midwestern states, a figure which rose by 1860 to more than 4300 miles. Railroad construction commenced in the 1830s and intensified after 1845 with the passage of land grant legislation. Since such large scale construction required huge numbers of workers and since the United States remained a labor-scarce country, canal and railroad companies actively recruited day laborers from Europe, especially from Ireland and Germany. The prolonged crop failure in Ireland in the mid-1840s spurred emigration of unskilled workers on an unprecedented scale. Land values rose and cities and towns along westward transportation routes prospered.

It was not long before Catholic communities in new towns as well as in

3. Sister Mary Agnes McCann, *The History of Mother Seton's Daughters*, Volume 1 (New York: Longmans, Green and Co., 1917): 59.
4. Alfred D. Chandler and Richard S. Tedlow, *The Coming of Managerial Capitalism*, (Homewood, IL: Irwin, 1985): 87.

older cities were appealing to sisterhoods for help in meeting economic needs of increasing numbers of immigrants, most of whom were impoverished and Catholic. While Mother Seton's Sisters of Charity managed most of the early charities, the extraordinary increase in the numbers of Catholics prompted the establishment of more sisterhoods devoted to benevolent works. The women's religious communities were absolutely essential to Catholic philanthropic ventures well into the twentieth century. They were relatively autonomous organizations which, while poor in material goods, were extremely rich in terms of labor service potential. Their formal religious approbation and the lifetime commitment of members brought stability to the charities they maintained. Of central importance, also, was the ability of sisterhoods to mobilize promptly as needs arose across the country. Their popularity as a life choice for single young women remained exceptionally strong until the mid-1960s.[5]

In contrast, many early lay philanthropies tended to be ephemeral and poorly managed. A chronicle of the development of a charity in Philadelphia reveals typical difficulties faced by good-hearted laity of this era. The yellow fever epidemic which struck the city in 1793 has been termed "the worst calamity of its kind in American history."[6] It recurred three times in the next five years, leaving many Catholic orphans with no recourse but the local poorhouse, public in name, but sectarian in philosophy. Their plight impelled several individuals to open an orphanage in 1797. But when the crisis of the 1790s passed, support for the project waned, resulting in neglected children and oppressive debts. Thus when yellow fever made its appearance again in 1814, Sisters of Charity were asked to assume responsibility for the institution.[7]

Charitable laity learned salutary lessons from such experiences. The New York Roman Catholic Benevolent Society (renamed the Roman Catholic Orphan Asylum in 1836) opened in 1817 only after its merchant founders had assurance from the Sisters of Charity that they would manage it. Intended "for the humane and laudable purpose of assisting and relieving the poor and protecting and educating orphan children,"[8] its financial support was the responsibility of a male Board of Managers, while sisters took full charge in its day-to-day operation, aided by a benevolent auxiliary of laywomen. This structure quickly became the model for most charitable institutions.

5. For a study of the lives and works of sisters in a major urban diocese after 1870 see Mary J. Oates, "'The Good Sisters': The Work and Position of *Catholic Churchwomen in Boston, 1870–1940,*" in Robert E. Sullivan and James M. O'Toole, Editors, *Catholic Boston: Studies in Religion and Community, 1870–1970* (Boston, 1985): 171–200.

6. Robert H. Bremner, *American Philanthropy* (Chicago: University of Chicago Press, 2nd edition, 1988): 35–38.

7. John O'Grady, *Catholic Charities in the United States,* (Washington, DC: National Conference of Catholic Charities, 1930): 21.

8. "The Catholic Charities of New York," *Catholic World* 43 (August, 1886): 681–682.

Religious Philanthropy and Antebellum Industrialization

With the industrial growth which accompanied westward expansion and improved transportation came the business cycle. The country experienced its first (and the century's worst) depression between 1839 and 1843. Financial institutions appropriate to expanding markets and growing investment in manufacturing had not yet developed, and while late eighteenth-century banks issued notes freely, only those of the First Bank of the United States were honored nationally. This large bank had been federally chartered in 1791 and was fairly effective in serving the financial needs of commerce, business and government, but for political reasons its charter was not renewed in 1811. Inflation spread as "wildcat banks" and their worthless notes multiplied, and calls for reform led to the establishment of the Second Bank of the United States in 1816. While this institution did much to stimulate economic expansion, formidable opposition prevented its rechartering in 1836. This setback and a Specie Circular of the same year, mandating payment for government lands in gold coin, induced a nation-wide banking panic in 1837 which was followed immediately by a national depression.

Among the most severely affected by the protracted depression were large numbers of immigrant Catholic day laborers and unskilled factory operatives. The high unemployment and falling real wages which persisted well into the 1840s worked enormous distress on families which were already barely surviving. The challenges to Catholic philanthropy presented by the 54,000 Irish immigrants of the 1820s paled in comparison with the scale of the problems ahead. In 1840, American Catholics numbered 663,000, but with the flood of immigrants (including 1.5 million from Ireland in the 1840s) total membership soared to 3 million by 1860, making Catholicism the largest as well as the poorest religious denomination in the country.[9]

During the 1840–1860 period, the labor force in manufacturing increased at a faster rate than in any other sector of the economy. Demand was so strong for unskilled labor for textile, iron, and metal mills that companies once again sent their brokers abroad. The need for labor intensified during the Civil War years as industries operated at capacity to produce war-related goods. As immigrants crowded into the mill towns, they made every effort to develop separate ethnic neighborhoods and were intensely committed to establishing parishes served by clergy of their own cultural background.

In the antebellum years, Irish and German benevolent institutions developed independently, usually within the parishes. Since parishioners were themselves working poor, they had to raise funds by cooperative efforts.

9. R. Emmett Curran, "Confronting 'The Social Question': American Catholic Thought and the Socio-Economic Order in the Nineteenth Century," *U.S. Catholic Historian* 5, no. 2 (1986): 169.

Usually a benevolent society was formed and a subscription list drawn up. After leasing a building, an appeal for furnishings would be issued and a sisterhood approached to provide managers for the institution. Operating expenses for the establishment were met through association dues and special collections. A popular strategy among Germans for support of orphans was the benevolent insurance association which promised care for a subscriber's children should he die. Sisters normally opened day schools in conjunction with early orphanages and tuition revenues derived therefrom supplemented other sources of funds.[10] A few important ethnic associations, notably the Irish Catholic Benevolent Union and the German Central Verein, crossed parish (but not ethnic) lines to establish large widows' and orphans' funds. Since both Irish and German priests were in short supply in this period, close collaboration of sisters and laity permitted a working-class population to address significant problems facing the needy among them.

Wealthy Catholics in industrial centers of the East and Midwest gave generously in the early nineteenth century, but their numbers were sparse. The first hospital-orphanage in the West opened in 1828 with the financial backing of St. Louis philanthropist John Mullanphy, an Irish immigrant who made his fortune trading land and cotton. Upper-class and working-class Catholics concurred that the need for housing and care of orphans should take priority over church and seminary construction, but funds accumulated slowly. It took from 1832 to 1841 for Boston Catholics to raise $9000 for St. Vincent's Orphan Asylum, the city's first Catholic charitable institution, and that sum included a $1000 gift from Mullanphy and generous assistance from Andrew Carney, an Irish immigrant, who became a director of the John Hancock Insurance Company and New England's richest Catholic.[11]

The transformation of the United States from an agricultural to an industrial economy was well underway by the close of the Civil War. By that date, also, the Catholic Church had become an urban church whose membership comprised a major proportion of the industrial labor force. Technological innovations and falling transport costs permitted business to increase productivity and take advantage of economies of scale in production, but it was the availability of plentiful cheap labor, more than any other factor, that made the postbellum expansion possible.

Industrial Growth, Urbanization, and Benevolence, 1860–1880

Because industrialization and the settlement of the country occurred at about the same time, urban development proceeded at an amazing pace. City populations grew far more rapidly than the national population, and immigrants figured very importantly in the differential. Boston's 1850 census

10. O'Grady, pp. 22–24; 79.
11. O'Grady, pp. 26–30.

revealed that the Irish-born already represented over 25% of city residents, and by 1860 immigrants accounted for 48% of the inhabitants of New York City, with the proportion even higher in Chicago and Pittsburgh (50%) and St. Louis (60%).[12] While there is little question that urbanization was a critical factor for industrial expansion, its rapidity brought acute problems for the urban poor. It is not surprising then that Catholic philanthropy began to modify its approach to respond more effectively to unprecedented and varied hardships.

The sheer numbers of urban poor had already begun to affect the structure of charities by the 1850s. The pre-war girls' school which accommodated a small number of orphans was giving way to the larger orphanage in which some education was provided. Scattered, independent parish orphanages were less successful as urbanization progressed. With needy Catholics increasingly clustered in the poorest of the large city parishes, the limited resources of these congregations were quickly exhausted. A situation in which the care of the destitute was being borne disproportionately and independently by the poorest of working Catholics called for adjustment in philanthropic style.

By 1860 the large diocesan institution was identified by charity leaders as the best way for a church with relatively limited financial means but abundant labor resources to reach the largest number of urban poor. Protestants and Catholics alike shared as their paramount concern the plight of destitute children, but differed in their views on how to deal with it. Thoughtful Catholics acknowledged that the Protestant approach, adoption or foster home placement, was in theory preferable to institutionalization. But since the supply of Catholic families able to adopt another child was utterly inadequate to meet the need, and since placement of Catholic children in Protestant homes was to be avoided at all costs, institution-building seemed to be the only practical solution.

Typical of the new diocesan charity was Boston's Home for Destitute Roman Catholic Children, which opened in 1864 with a Board of Directors which represented in its membership "the different parishes of Boston and vicinity."[13] The new style was reflected also in the organization in the same year of Chicago's St. Joseph's Orphan Asylum which was to be supported through assessments on every parish.[14] While the new arrangement de-

12. Robert F. Dalzell, Jr., *Enterprising Elite: The Boston Associates and the World They Made* (Cambridge: Harvard University, 1987): 140; Chandler and Tedlow, p. 486.

13. Rev. P. A. Baart, *Orphans and Orphan Asylums,* (Buffalo: Catholic Publication Co., 1885): 56.

14. Baart, p. 62. In his annual report of 1871, Rev. George Haskins, founder of Boston's House of the Angel Guardian, a diocesan institution for boys, noted that destitute orphans "are usually supported in part by the charitable societies of the parish whence they come." (A Friend of the House of the Angel Guardian, *The Life of Father Haskins* (Boston: Angel Guardian Press, 1899): 116.

veloped as economic exigencies dictated, the growing propensity of Catholics for larger institutions was, in part, also, an honest admission of the fact that the problem was getting worse. The Board of Directors of the New York Catholic Protectory argued in its 1863 appeal for funds that "the children of Irishmen make up by far the largest proportion of ruffians for whom we are called upon to provide."[15]

Another need which exacerbated with industrialization was that of the indigent sick. Antebellum Catholic hospitals were few and informal, intended chiefly for victims in the typhoid, cholera, and smallpox epidemics which appeared regularly. Only the truly impoverished would voluntarily enter a hospital which at this time "was defined primarily by need and dependency, not by the existence of specialized resources."[16] By 1860 eighteen cities had small hospitals staffed by nursing sisters who treated all regardless of denomination or type of illness. Among early religious philanthropies providing hospital care for the insane poor was Baltimore's Mount Hope Retreat, opened by Sisters of Charity in 1840.

These hospitals were pioneer institutions in one-third of the states, and numbered 154 by 1855, a figure exceeding the count of all hospitals, public and private, two decades earlier. Unlike orphan asylums, they were usually owned as well as managed by sisterhoods and financed by the contributed labor of the sisters and a small weekly charge from those who could afford to pay it. In addition to supporting the institution, the fee had a psychological benefit for the patient, since by paying it "a mechanic or domestic could avoid the stigma of receiving charity in an alien institution."[17] Probably because some payment was made for services, hospitals received few donations from clergy or laity and sisterhoods borrowed in their own name to

15. Cited by O'Grady, p. 78.

16. Charles E. Rosenberg, *The Care of Strangers: The Rise of America's Hospital System* (New York: Basic Books, 1987):5. Their unspecialized character is seen in the fact that in 1869 Boston's new Carney Hospital reserved 20% of its space "for old people who may not be sick but come here for a home." (Morris Vogel, *The Invention of the Modern Hospital: Boston, 1870–1930* (Chicago: University of Chicago Press, 1980): 73; Richard H. Clarke, "Catholic Protectories and Reformatories," *American Catholic Quarterly Review* 20 (July, 1895): 625. Elite Protestants had confidence in the care provided by the sisters in desperate cases. When in 1854, Buffalo Judge Nathan K. Hall "concluded that his ailing son could not be treated at home, [he] was quite willing to send him to Sisters of Charity Hospital for care." (David A. Gerber, "Ambivalent Anti-Catholicism: Buffalo's American Protestant Elite Faces the Challenge of the Catholic Church, 1850–1860," *Civil War History* 30 (June, 1984): 130.

17. Rosenberg, p. 111; John J. Flanagan, S.J., "The Catholic Contribution to Medical Care," in Marguerite T. Boylan, Editor, *The Catholic Church and Social Welfare: A Symposium* (New York: Greenwich Book Publishers, 1961): 149. In 1852 patients paid $3 per week for care in the Catholic hospital, a charge which was lower than that of other private institutions because the sisters did not receive regular salaries. Nor was this fee prohibitive for many poor patients. "Their ordinary board in town is $2.50, [so] they are put to a cost of only 50 cents per week additional, for which they receive medicines and medical attendance." (Rosenberg, p. 240, citing *Minutes,* Medical Board, Episcopal Hospital of Philadelphia, October 5, 1852 entry.)

cover their construction and operating costs. But since the fees for service were paid by the working poor, they continued to be minimal and by late nineteenth century the sisters were confronting serious financial difficulties in mounting equipment, medicine, and patient care expenses.

Women were among those who benefited disproportionately from rapid expansion of specialized services introduced in the 1840s. Thousands of young Irish women who each year emigrated alone to urban centers, without work or money, were aided by "houses of protection" which resembled in structure and goals those of similar Protestant establishments. In them, residents were taught basic domestic skills and were assisted in finding work as servants. In 1847, Sisters of Mercy in New York City reported that their "House of Protection for Virtuous Female Domestics" placed 1217 women and sheltered an average of 200 residents nightly in its first year of operation.[18] By the 1860s these benevolent institutions were found in every major city.

A related and innovative enterprise focusing on women was the house of reformation for those who had violated moral or legal codes of behavior. Protestant philanthropists preferred to concentrate their efforts on preserving young women from dangerous environments rather than on rehabilitating those who had already fallen into criminal activities. Thus those convicted of certain crimes as well as delinquent girls were referred for reformation to the Sisters of the Good Shepherd, a sisterhood founded solely for this purpose. The first such institution appeared in the 1840s, and within two decades Houses of the Good Shepherd were established in urban centers cross the country. A small per capita stipend was paid by city governments for the expenses of those referred by the courts, but operating funds were derived mainly from laundry and sewing work of the residents, who in the process were prepared to find employment upon their release.

The military experience of Catholics during the Civil War testified that despite differences in ethnic origin, they could unite in a common cause. Enthusiasm for consolidated action in philanthropic efforts ran high in the late 1860s, finding expression primarily in the popularity of the St. Vincent de Paul Society, a benevolent association of laymen. Originating in Paris in 1833, the society was introduced in America in 1845 at the parish level to enable the more prosperous in the congregation to help the poor through personal service as well as alms. By the 1870s, with membership climbing, the society had set more ambitious objectives. Chief among them were citywide programs for orphaned children who might otherwise turn to Protestant agencies like the Children's Aid Society. Since proselytizing by Protestant charities was a pervasive threat in the minds of Catholic philanthropists throughout the nineteenth century, the society's focus on child-caring proj-

18. S. M. D., "The Sisters of Mercy in New York," *Catholic World* 50 (December, 1889): 384.

ects is understandable and unexceptional. What is distinctive, however, is that the heavily Irish St. Vincent de Paul Society, unlike the thousands of ethnic benevolent associations, claimed as its vital unifying factor only its Catholic and national character.

The postwar push to open the West intensified as entrepreneurs moved to exploit potential markets and develop rich agricultural and mining resources. The astonishing expansion of railroads encouraged heavy capital investment in midwestern cities, and by 1875 nine-tenths of agricultural and industrial freight between east and west went via railroads. Technological advances in production processes continued and the advent of telegraph, cable, and steamship made communication with distant markets and financial centers much more efficient. The merging of railroad companies in the 1880s resulted in a few giant systems and precipitated a new phase in American economic development. Mergers became common in other major industries and the era of "big business" in the modern sense had begun.[19]

Leading Catholic clergy and journalists from the 1860s onward had expressed concern that the increasingly immigrant and working-class texture of the church which accompanied economic expansion was alienating it further from mainstream life and values and reinforcing its outsider status. They urged that Catholics improve their collective image by building larger charitable institutions to demonstrate more tangibly their commitment to social progress. At the same time, they displayed a yearning for acceptance by middle-class society in their ardent declarations that the free market was the best means to the good life for all Americans.

Charity workers joined in the anxious efforts to mold respectable citizens in whom the church could take pride. The New York Catholic Protectory described its aims in 1864: "Here can be found a variety of industrial pursuit—filling the mental and physical needs of the inmates, to prepare them to take their place in the world with self-reliance, and the capacity to add to the wealth and virtue of the community, instead of taking from the one, or being a disgrace to the other."[20] Three decades later, similar sentiments continued to be voiced about the Protectory. Its goal now was to develop "the Christian, the citizen, and an industrial producer in the general public economics of the nation."[21] Most bishops remained staunch supporters of laissez-faire economics, convinced that business expansion and an unregulated market would inevitably bring better employment opportunities, higher real wages, and a decent living standard for their working-class flock.

But the promise that a better life would emerge from the rapid and

19. Chandler and Tedlow, p. 398.

20. *A Short Sketch of the New York Catholic Protectory from its Origin to the Present,* (West Chester, NY: New York Catholic Protectory, 1885): 15.

21. Clarke (1895): 616.

unregulated postwar industrialization was not to be realized by many workers and their families. In fact, the distribution of income nationally became
more rather than less concentrated with succeeding decades. With unabated
immigration, wages and living standards continued to be low and slum
tenements became more crowded than ever before. Crime, disease, and
industrial accidents resulted in death or disability of parents, leaving children and dependent elderly to fend for themselves. "With its rapid expansion, its exploitative methods, its desperate competition, and its preemptory
rejection of failure, postbellum America was like a vast human caricature of
the Darwinian struggle for existence and survival of the fittest."[22]

Catholic Philanthropy, the "New Immigrants" and the Expansion of Big Business, 1880–1900

The large protectory with its industrial school attached was evolving by
the 1880s as the most visible Catholic philanthropic response to the height-
ening crisis of the American city. Just as industrial progress was achieved
through the large corporation, so too would the large scale and hence more
efficient charitable establishment produce more lasting results than the small
independent agency. In addition, it would testify dramatically to the willingness and ability of Catholics to care for their own children. Between 1875 and
1885, seven new protectories appeared in New York City alone. A conservative estimate of the number of orphans in Catholic asylums and protectories nationwide in 1886 was 20,000, with the large cities accounting for
about half of that figure. Within a decade, the national total had escalated by
54%.[23]

By 1900 these child-caring institutions were huge and comprehensive.
The New York Foundling Hospital reported in 1897 that it cared for 3274
infants and 536 homeless mothers, while the New York Catholic Protectory,
with 3296 boys and girls, held the distinction of being the nation's largest
child-caring institution. Operating expenses were met by Christmas and
Easter collections in all city parishes, supplemented by a city allotment of
$.30 per child per day.[24] The protectories were integrated establishments in

22. Richard Hofstadter, *Social Darwinism in American Thought* (Boston: Beacon Press,
1955): 44.

23. John Gilmary Shea, "What Can We Do For the Orphans?" *American Catholic Quarterly Review* 11 (January, 1886): 81–82; Clarke, (1895): p. 609.

24. Richard H. Clarke, "Catholic Life in New York City," *Catholic World* 67 (1898): 212. A
good summary of the establishment of the Foundling Hospital is given by George Paul Jacoby,
Catholic Child Care in Nineteenth Century New York (Washington, DC: Catholic University of
America Press, 1941): chapter 7, pp. 176–190. The idea of a comprehensive institution was not
new. Charity workers had long been concerned about children, especially boys, who were not
usually kept in the orphanages beyond the age of twelve. Between 1846 and 1854, religious
brotherhoods and clergy in Indiana, Maryland and Massachusetts introduced institutions which
incorporated trade programs and kept boys until they were sixteen. The innovative aspect of the

which children remained until they were trained in an industrial skill and were old enough to take their places in the world as self-supporting citizens.

Occasionally particular Catholic charities received general encouragement and financial support from mainstream society. A perennial favorite was the asylum for abandoned infants. The New York Foundling Hospital, at its establishment in 1869 was unique in the nation in its exclusive focus on infants. A rapid rise in infanticide and the fact that very few abandoned infants survived the care of inmates of the Blackwell's Island Almshouse made the hospital and others like it across the country extremely popular. Contributions from the public were handsome and other legislatures followed the example of New York City which in 1870 voted land and $100,000 toward a building for the Foundling Hospital.[25]

When "new immigrants" from central and eastern Europe began to arrive in the 1880s, the option open to earlier immigrant groups, and popular among Germans, to settle on free western lands had all but disappeared. In any case, most of the newcomers had emigrated in response to the promise of jobs at good wages in the expanding manufacturing sector. The American population had increased by 140% to 75.5 million between 1860 and 1900, providing a lucrative market for producers of consumer goods, services, housing and transportation, and immigrants readily found menial jobs in iron and steel mills, textile mills and garment sweatshops, mines and meat-packing plants.

The second great wave of immigrants brought critical challenges to Catholic philanthropy. The church added millions of new members, most of them poor and unable to speak English, just at the point when integration into mainstream society appeared reasonably near-at-hand. In the three decades after 1880, immigration accounted for a membership increase of 4.8 million persons from Canada, Italy, Hungary, Poland and Lithuania. Over half were from Italy and nearly all, like their predecessors, clustered in the nation's cities.[26]

Urbanization complemented the rise of industry, with big business breeding big cities. By the 1890s, New York, Boston, Chicago and Philadelphia had become "big cities" in every sense of the term, providing huge profits to landowners as well as business firms. These metropolises, incor-

---

protectory movement of the 1880s was the rapid growth in number and scale of the establishments.

25. J. R. G. Hassard, "Private Charities and Public Money," *Catholic World* 29 (1879): 263. Approval of this form of philanthropy was by no means unanimous. Baart reports that some complained that foundling homes "tended to the increase of immorality and unnatural feeling on the part of the poor and thoughtless mothers rather than to the good of society." (Baart, p. 157).

26. O'Grady, p. 276. Typical of newcomers were Polish immigrant workers in Chicago, two-thirds of whom were unskilled laborers in 1911. Until the 1930s, labor unions did not make much effort to organize this class of worker. (Edward R. Kantowicz, *Polish-American Politics in Chicago*, 1888–1940 (Chicago: University of Chicago Press, 1975): 28–29.

porating the core of the nation's manufacturing, banking, transportation and commerce, accounted for over 40% of its industrial output. But city services progressed after 1880 far more slowly than city populations. Chicago alone saw the number of its citizens rise by 100% during the 1880s to one million. External diseconomies were particularly acute in the area of sewerage, schools, police and fire protection, and housing. Crowded cities were soon distinguished by shocking poverty, pollution, slum housing, and crime. Undernourished immigrants, densely packed into tenements, were susceptible to communicable diseases like diphtheria and tuberculosis. Contaminated water supplies promoted the spread of cholera, yellow fever, typhoid, and dysentery, with the result that by 1890 the industrial labor force registered a death rate 50% above that of the rural population.

The newer ethnic communities immediately formed separate benevolent societies to care for the destitute among them. At the same time, diocesan protectories and orphanages were enlarged and new ones constructed to meet rising needs. But the economics of urban life by this time was once again dictating a fundamental change in the traditional Catholic pattern of philanthropy. The problem was clearly linked to industrial change, since, except in the event of epidemic or natural disaster, benevolent Catholics in rural communities had little difficulty in providing adequately for the needy. One observer reported in the mid-1880s that "the orphans of the diocese of Davenport [IA] are provided for immediately by their friends and the clergy of the diocese without the intermediate aid of asylum."[27]

Although church philanthropists found it immensely challenging to meet the needs of millions of new immigrants who arrived within a very short period of time, they were nonetheless in a better position to formulate long-term strategies than they had been when the "old immigration" began five decades earlier. In the antebellum period, needy Catholics had little recourse but to public or Protestant charities. By the end of the century, thanks to the development of a substantial middle-class within the laity, more resources were available for charitable undertakings. The number of wealthy and generous Catholics, while still not large, was growing. Most of them had earned rather than inherited their money and they tended to identify with the plight of the urban poor. Among them were Myles P. O'Connor, an Irish immigrant, who achieved notable success in the California mining industry in the 1850s; Thomas Fortune Ryan, a New York orphan, who advanced from message runner on Wall Street to one of the country's leading financiers; and millionaire Katharine Drexel who donated her entire inheritance to the benevolent activities of the sisterhood she founded in 1891 to work among Blacks and Indians.[28]

27. Baart, 172.
28. John Tracy Ellis, "Catholic Philanthropy: Building the New American Church," in Robert F. Trisco, Editor, *Catholics in America* 1776–1976 (Washington, DC: National Conference of Catholic Bishops, 1976): 168–169.

By the end of the nineteenth century, Catholic philanthropists were beginning to recognize possibilities for greater effectiveness through cooperation among themselves as well as with Protestant charities and government agencies. Just as the dominant organization of the firm changed from the small proprietorship to the corporation as economic growth advanced, so too must the traditional structure of Catholic charities be transformed to address modern needs. As one churchman put it: "This is an age of organization and concentration. . . . Recently a great impulse has been given to combinations in the same trade or profession because less expense is required with consequent lower prices and greater profits. . . . Federation promises to unite all organizations composed of Catholics, whether they possess the insurance, the beneficial, or the religious feature."[29]

As vertical and horizontal integration became common in major industries in the 1880s, monopolies and giant trusts flourished. Despite the passage of the Sherman Antitrust Act in 1890, "the years 1898–1902 saw the most intense merger activity in American history."[30] The spread of large impersonal corporations brought better wages, on average, but also more widespread insecurity, since hundreds of workers could be laid off simultaneously in a single location without notice or benefits in times of recession and depression. And periods of rapid industrial growth were followed by severe depressions in 1873, 1886, and 1892. The impact of downturns of the business cycle on the working poor who had crowded into cities during boom periods was immediate and shattering. While the numbers of poor were large in good times, they rose to overwhelming proportions during depression years. "The hardship and destitution caused by the depression of 1873–78 were like the effects of a nationwide natural disaster."[31]

Not surprisingly, these frequent and protracted periods of unemployment gave considerable impetus to the nascent labor movement. When in 1877 the Pennsylvania Railroad sought to recoup some of the profits it had lost in the 1873–77 depression by inaugurating a general wage cut, workers joined in a massive and violent strike. Boston recorded 550 strikes of factory workers in the "great uprising" of the 1880s. The Depression of 1893 was especially severe, leaving millions out of work and hungry. In the city of Chicago in that year 186,000 workers were unemployed, 40.3% of the labor force. As late as 1890, among all the ethnic groups, the Irish remained relatively most affected, recording a rate of impoverishment of 7.5 per 1000. "Still 99 percent of the Irish subsisted without public assistance during [the depression of 1893] a period of great hardship. They did so through use of

---

29. James A. McFaul, "The American Federation of Catholic Societies," *Donahoe's Magazine* 52 (July, 1904): 87.

30. Chandler and Tedlow, p. 554.

31. Bremner, p. 92.

their own mutual aid societies and ethnic charities, along with the traditional intrafamily support network."[32]

The hierarchy, fearing further violent confrontations between labor and management, at first urged workers, a large fraction of them Catholic, to turn to religious philanthropic institutions for assistance rather than to unions. But they were sufficiently dismayed by the effects of the recurring depressions to reject the laissez-faire attitude of their predecessors and to endorse government action in the areas of employment, regulation of business, and taxation of profits. "The government should disregard the law of supply and demand, and 'help the poorer classes in time of need.' "[33]

The papal encyclical *Rerum Novarum* (1891) put the church officially and solidly on record as supporting the right of workers to organize and endorsing government intervention in the marketplace to rectify injustices inflicted on workers by corporations and to mitigate the effects of the business cycle. Because Catholic philanthropy had for so long focused on relieving the needs of the urban poor, it is not surprising that the labor movement was the setting for its pioneer involvement in social reform.

The ruthless environment of late nineteenth century cities and the enormity of the social problems engendered by unregulated economic activity mobilized charity workers to join in calling for reforms in the Catholic approach to philanthropy. In particular, they began, tentatively at first, to question the effectiveness of institution-building which for so long had identified the Catholic way of giving. For example, when New York City pastor Rev. Edward McGlynn could not gain places for parish orphans in the diocesan asylum in 1885 because it was filled to capacity, he followed accepted practice and opened a parish orphanage and infants' home where 635 children were cared for by Sisters of Charity. However, despite all his efforts and the generous support of his parishioners, he reluctantly conceded that the traditional approach was no longer viable. Deteriorating social conditions required far more than almsgiving and relief, and an economic

---

32. Seamus P. Metress, "The History of Irish-American Care of the Aged," *Social Service Review* 59 (March, 1985): 26; Chandler and Tedlow, p. 354; Arthur Mann, *Yankee Reformers in the Urban Age: Social Reform in Boston, 1880–1900* (New York: Harper & Row, Publishers, 1954): 2; John Albert Mayer, "Private Charities in Chicago From 1871 to 1915," (Ph.D. diss., University of Minnesota, 1978): 135.

33. Aaron I. Abell, *American Catholicism and Social Action: A Search for Social Justice, 1865–1950* (Notre Dame, IN: University of Notre Dame Press, 1963): 47, quoting from "In Answer to a Calumny." *Mcgee's Illustrated Weekly* 4 (July, 13, 1878): 114. Jay Dolan provides several reasons for the hesitance of Catholic leaders to press for social reform in the 1890s. First, conservative attitudes were growing within the Catholic community; second, the effects of renewed anti-Catholic campaigns were demanding full attention of bishops; and third, Catholics had not yet developed an intellectual system through which a concerted response to social justice concerns could effectively be made. Jay P. Dolan, *The American Catholic Experience: A History from Colonial Times to the Present* (New York: Doubleday & Co., 1985): 335.

system which generated and tolerated such widespread destitution had to be fundamentally transformed. "You may go on forever with hospitals and orphan asylums and St. Vincent de Paul Societies. But with them you can't cure the trouble. They relieve, not eradicate."[34]

Two important meetings of charity leaders in this period triggered strong interest in cooperating with Protestant and public benevolent enterprises. The first was the 1889 Congress of Baltimore, called to commemorate the centennial of the American hierarchy, and the second was held in 1893 at the Columbian Exposition in Chicago. At the 1889 meeting, an episcopal committee commissioned a study by Peter L. Foy of "philanthropic movements generally." In his paper, Foy argued that the labor movement had definite charitable perspectives and stressed the mutuality of public and private enterprises.[35] And at the 1893 gathering, Thomas F. Ring, leader of the St. Vincent de Paul Society in Boston, urged Catholic philanthropists to abandon their separatist mentality and collaborate "frankly and cordially with all our fellow-citizens for the common good of the community."[36] In the same year, speaking at the World Parliament of Religions, Cardinal Gibbons of Baltimore also warmly endorsed shared undertakings, noting that while "we differ in faith, thank God there is one platform on which we stand united, and that is the platform of charity and benevolence."[37]

Under the leadership of Thomas Mulry, the St. Vincent de Paul Society, prompted by the destitution accompanying the 1893 depression, became the first Catholic philanthropy to collaborate with a Protestant charity, specifically with the Charity Organization Society. The two agencies sponsored joint relief efforts in the nation's major cities and in 1895 the St. Vincent de Paul Society declared at its convention that "it is advisable and necessary to co-operate freely and fully within the bounds prescribed by our general law, with all organized charities."[38] Not only did charitable services improve, but

34. Edward McGlynn, New York *Tribune*, November 26, 1886; "The Catholic Charities of New York," *Catholic World* 43 (August, 1886): 686–687. Before 1880, among the nation's many Catholic child-caring institutions, only the Home for Destitute Roman Catholic Children in Boston was willing to adopt the Protestant approach by finding homes for the children in Catholic families. (Francis E. Lane, *American Charities and the Child of the Immigrant: A Study of Typical Child Caring Institutions in New York and Massachusetts between the Years 1845 and 1880* (Washington, DC: Catholic University of America Press, 1932): 126.

35. Abell, pp. 106–109, citing data in *Souvenir Volume Illustrated. Three Great Events in the History of the Catholic Church in the United States* (Detroit: William H. Hughes, Publisher, 1889).

36. Thomas F. Ring, "Public and Private Charities: How Can They Be Made More Effective and Beneficial—A Catholic Layman's Experience," in *Progress of the Catholic Church in America and the Great Columbian Catholic Congress of 1893* (Chicago: J. S. Hyland and Co., 1897): 42–44.

37. F. Tennyson Neely, *History of the Parliament of Religions and Religious Congresses* (Chicago, 1893): 45–56, 185–91. Cited by Abell, p. 118.

38. "Summarized Report of the General Convention, 1885," *St. Vincent de Paul Quarterly*

Catholics became convinced of the need for greater cooperation among their own agencies, many of which did the same work but remained completely independent of one another. They realized that centralized diocesan charitable bureaus were critical for effective representation of the Catholic perspective in cooperative ventures with public and sectarian charities.

The Movement to Charity Organization, 1900–1940

Rev. Peter Ronan, an experienced charity leader and a board member of St. Mary's Infant Asylum in Boston, described the actual situation in 1897: "Managers of the Catholic charities are so engrossed in each one's special house that he comes to have a sort of 'religious jealousy' of all other houses and all keep apart."[39] Thus consolidation of charitable institutions was not to be easily achieved in a church marked by numerous ethnic groups, but the St. Vincent de Paul Society spearheaded the campaign by opening a cross-parish agency for child placement in Baltimore in 1901 and by uniting its own local units in 1914 under a superior council, headquartered in Washington, D.C. The pioneering cross-parish organization paved the way for the establishment of the National Conference of Catholic Charities in 1910. Attending its first meeting were representatives from the St. Vincent de Paul Society, some women's benevolent societies, and a few clergymen. Not yet convinced of the merits of such coordination for their numerous institutions, sisterhoods declined to send delegates to this inaugural meeting.

After 1920, with the professionalization of social work, a more affluent and educated laity, restrictive immigration legislation, and the formation in 1919 by seventy-seven bishops of the National Catholic Welfare Conference, the environment became more conducive to some consolidation of independent charities. Whereas before World War I only five dioceses had charitable bureaus in place, by 1931 thirty reported their formation. Sisterhoods were responding more positively to the idea of charity organization by the 1920s and established a Sisters' Conference in the National Conference of Catholic Charities. They also began to educate their members as professional social workers and to modernize their methods and institutions. Not all Catholics looked with equanimity on the changing face of philanthropy, and particular

---

1 (November, 1895): 24–27. A good account of pioneer cooperative efforts with Protestant charities is provided in Thomas F. Meehan, *Thomas Maurice Mulry* (New York: The Encyclopedia Press, 1917) and Thomas M. Mulry, "Catholic Cooperation in Charity," *The Charities Review* 8 (October, 1898): 383–386. That the goal of genuine cooperation among Catholic charities themselves as well as with extra-church agencies was not shared by all is reflected in William J. Kerby's urgent appeal in the mid-1920s for more determined efforts in this area. *The Social Mission of Charity: A Study of Points of View in Catholic Charities* (New York: Macmillan Co., 1924, chapter 11).

39. Susan S. Walton, "To Preserve the Faith: Catholic Charities in Boston, 1870–1930," in Sullivan and O'Toole, 79.

concern was expressed about the prominent role assumed in the 1920s by bishops and clergy in pressing for reforms. In the judgment of some, consolidation was "a great force in divorcing the laity from active participation in charities."[40]

The 1920s were years of unparalleled prosperity in the United States, with the rate of economic growth the highest of any decade in history. However, income distribution was becoming more unequal and tax policies were magnifying the disparity between the incomes of wealthy and working-class citizens. As a result, "the proportion of profits going to rural Americans, industrial workers and other potential consumers was too small to create a market for the goods produced by American business."[41] While economic expansion brought more jobs and higher wages as employers bid for scarce workers, it also encouraged heavier speculation in securities markets and unrestrained use of credit. Investment in the construction industry alone accounted for nearly two-thirds of gross investment in 1926, so when investment in this volatile industry fell sharply in 1929, a widespread business slump ensued. Banks, unable to withstand accompanying pressures, failed and the Great Depression began.

As in earlier depressions, the most devastating effects were felt by urban workers. Although the proportion of the labor force unemployed nationwide was 25% in 1932, industrial cities recorded far higher rates. Cleveland, Akron, and Toledo, for example, registered rates of unemployment in that year of 50%, 60%, and 80% respectively.[42] Neither state nor local public relief structures were able to cope with problems of this magnitude. Catholic charities were much better organized by this date to contribute effectively and efficiently to alleviating the hardships imposed by the latest economic crisis. They cooperated readily with private and government agencies and were unequivocal in their calls for social change. When the public turned to the federal government for assistance, Catholics, hierarchy and laity alike, were well represented among mainstream advocates of New Deal relief programs and social and economic reform legislation.

Conclusion

Largely because of religious tensions, Catholic philanthropy, throughout much of the 1790–1940 period has been carried out in separate societies, institutions, and agencies. While these frequently served citizens of all denominations, their origins, management, and funding sources emanated from within the Catholic community. Handicaps accompanying isola-

---

40. O'Grady, p. 446; Donald P. Gavin, *The National Conference of Catholic Charities, 1910–1960* (Milwaukee: Bruce Press, 1962): 183; Abell, 229.

41. Chandler and Tedlow, 585.

42. Chandler and Tedlow, 584–85.

tion and a separatist mentality were amplified by differences among Catholics themselves, which occasioned the development of separate ethnic charities.

Since during much of the nineteenth century the Catholic population, in the aggregate, was becoming less rather than more affluent, the church's philanthropic response was profoundly challenged by increasingly severe social dislocations that accompanied industrialization and the business cycle. In particular, since financial contributions from working-class members were individually small, strategies for collective action had to be developed to meet rising needs. More than most religious philanthropies, Catholic agencies depended heavily upon contributions of service from its members, particularly women in religious communities.

Since 1790, the vision of philanthropy among American Catholics has evolved in important ways. Early and sustained identification of Catholic benevolent activities with the needs of the poor meant that national economic progress or decline affected the pattern and direction of its philanthropies more immediately than if they had been directed mainly to cultural or political causes. Only with the emergence of a significant middle-class in the twentieth century was Catholic philanthropy willing to broaden its sphere to include, to a degree, cultural and political activities. And only then was it able to acquire sufficient resources to begin to endow some of its institutions and to establish foundations.

The Independent Sector has benefited from diverse traditions exemplified in religious philanthropy in important ways, as this analysis of Catholic giving over 150 years clearly demonstrates. During this period Catholics were preponderantly working-class immigrants, who only gradually were integrated into the mainstream. While their religious tradition called them to give to those in need, the ways they would give were not mandated. Thus their charitable responses to social upheavals accompanying rapid economic change were remarkably innnovative and wide-ranging. Economic crises summoned resourceful organization and outgoing exploration of the meaning of religious teachings in the light of present needs.

Catholic voluntarism was characterized particularly by its enduring belief that philanthropy encompasses more than monetary donations. By its propensity to organize charities at the local level, its insistence that the needs of the poor take priority over other worthy causes, and its contention that every individual, regardless of economic circumstances, has a role to play in benevolent activities, the nation's largest church engendered valuable and ongoing public debate on the true meaning of philanthropy and social responsibility. In this way it contributed significantly to shaping the spirit as well as the form of the Independent Sector.

THE INDEPENDENT SECTOR AND THE EDUCATIONAL STRATEGIES OF MAINSTREAM PROTESTANTISM, 1900–1980

Dorothy C. Bass

During the past century, higher education in the United States has undergone at least two major changes. In the first, the modern research university completed its emergence as the society's dominant and normative institution of knowledge, with major implications for all educational institutions. In the second, a large influx of government funds led to an enormous expansion of colleges and universities. Each of these changes contributed to altering the place of religion in American higher education. During each, philanthropic foundations played important roles in encouraging change or in helping those concerned about religion in higher education to adapt to change. Both government and organized philanthropy have exercised immense influence on religion's status in the Independent Sector.

The relationship of higher learning in the West to religious communities and traditions has a long and complex history. In the twentieth century, as in the more distant past, the most determinative issue in this relationship has most likely been one that is philosophical in nature. During the period under consideration here, this is the issue of whether and how the citizens of the modern university were to understand the general truthfulness and relevance of religious knowledge, in view of the university's prevailing epistemologies and fragmented disciplinary structures. This issue is beyond the scope of this paper. However, the universities' responses to this issue—implicit and explicit, including both benign neglect and positivistic cri-

Portions of this paper have appeared in my essays "Ministry on the Margin: Protestants and Education," in William R. Hutchison (ed.), *Between the Times: The Travail of the Protestant Establishment in America, 1900–1960* (New York: Cambridge University Press, 1989), and "Revolutions, Quiet and Otherwise: Protestants and Higher Education during the 1960s," in Parker J. Palmer, Barbara G. Wheeler, and James W. Fowler (eds.), *Caring for the Commonweal: Education for Religious Public and Life* (Macon, Ga.: Mercer University Press, 1990). I appreciate the comments of Merrimon Cuninggim, Robert Lynn, Robert Rankin, and Winton Solberg on a draft of this paper, though they are not responsible for its argument and conclusions.

tique—surely influenced the changes that do lie within the paper's scope: changes in the structure and ethos of higher education.

These changes affected "mainline" Protestantism, a stream of American religious life that has had a formative and well-known role in the development of American higher education, in ways that afford an intriguing double angle of vision into the complexities attending the place of religion in higher education during this period. When the influence of religious institutions within the general system of higher education diminished during the late nineteenth and twentieth centuries, this group was disproportionately affected. Yet the story of mainstream Protestantism's involvement in the changing relationship of religion and higher education is far from a simple tale of loss. For this religious family came by its very nature to relatively friendly terms with the modern university and produced numerous leaders—educators, ministers, philanthropists—who did not simply react to change, but who promoted it.

Church-Related Colleges and the "Comprehensive System" of Higher Education

The fact that mainstream Protestantism's role in higher education has changed dramatically during this century is readily estalbished by statistics. At the beginning of the twentieth century, almost half of all undergraduates attended church-related colleges, the majority of which were affiliated with mainstream denominations. In 1980, 78% of all students were enrolled in state-supported institutions. Only 38% of the others were in church-related schools, of which less than a third were related to mainstream denominations.[1]

The extraordinary growth of higher education under the auspices of other institutions (governments or other religious groups, particularly Roman Catholicism) accounts for most of this quantitative change. But the fact that other kinds of institutions thrived can account neither for decline in the absolute numbers of church-affiliated colleges nor for the recurrent crises of identity that have plagued them and their sponsors throughout the century. For these, more important than numbers was the cultural shift that gave the

---

1. William C. Ringenberg, *The Christian College: A History of Protestant Higher Education in America* (Grand Rapids: William B. Eerdmans, 1984), p. 132; Manning M. Patillo and Donald M. Mackenzie, *Church-Sponsored Higher Education in the United States: Report of the Danforth Commission* (Washington: American Council on Education, 1966), p. 21; *Digest of Education Statistics* (Washington: United States Department of Education, 1988), pp. 146–47. By "mainline" and "mainstream" I mean the seven denominations identified by William R. Hutchison as constituting the Protestant Establishment in *Between the Times: The Travail of the Protestant Establishment in America, 1900–1960* (New York: Cambridge University Press, 1989): Episcopal, Presbyterian, Congregational (now UCC), Methodist (now UMC), Baptist (now ABC), Disciples, and Lutheran (now ELCA).

authority to define higher education to modern research universities and their philanthropic backers.

Denominational colleges had flourished during the nineteenth century, when westward expansion, denominational assertiveness, and flexible academic standards provided opportunities and demand for founding numerous small institutions. What linked such colleges to their sponsoring churches were a common ethos and constituency, expressed in religious activities on campus and shared visions of the world beyond it. Official sponsorship, reflected in varying degrees of financial assistance and policy control, was often regional rather than national. The presence of sizable numbers of clergy on faculties further enhanced the connection. Located in "college towns" of manageable size and drawing students and faculty from a like-minded social group, these schools, which rarely had more than a few hundred students, offered a fixed curriculum and a strong communal life. The nineteenth century was the age of the college.

In the prevailing view of education historians, however, by the early twentieth century American universities had completed the impressive emergence begun after the Civil War. Emulating the research universities of Germany and explicitly differentiated by their leaders from "the old-time college," the great private and state universities of the age promoted a model of the academic enterprise that was specialized, secular, and attuned to national and international communities of scholarship. A new breed of professors appeared, members of the newly-founded disciplinary guilds that corresponded to the now segmented departments of the university and at least as committed to advancing knowledge as to teaching undergraduates. For students, the elective system, the introduction of professional studies and the practical sciences, and the larger size of the university added elements of freedom and vocational utility to the college years. Moreover, the university-builders of the late nineteenth century explicitly asserted that sustaining church ties was incompatible with their educational vision. President Charles W. Eliot of Harvard announced in 1891 that "it is impossible to found a university on the basis of a sect." President Andrew D. White of Cornell took sides against religious emphasis in *The History of the Warfare of Science with Theology* (1896), and the ceremony opening Johns Hopkins in 1876 included no prayers of invocation or benediction. In instance after instance, the new universities separated themselves from the religious values and practices that had previously informed American higher education.[2]

During the first quarter of the twentieth century, many of the distinctive standards of the modern research university came to exercise substantial

2. Hugh Hawkins, "The University-Builders Observe the Colleges," *History of Education Quarterly* 11(1971):354–58; Mark A. Noll, "Christian Colleges, Christian Worldviews, and an Invitation to Research," in William C. Ringenberg, *The Christian College*, pp. 26, 29.

influence not only within institutions like Harvard, Chicago, and Hopkins but also in colleges throughout the land. The interventions of two leading philanthropic foundations were crucial in promoting this expansion of the university's influence. Their activities, which exemplified the quest for national order and standards shared by reformers in various fields of American life at the time, were by no means single-handedly responsible for the educational changes that took place. Yet a consideration of the policies of these foundations will provide important evidence of the changing role of religion in higher education during this formative period.

The decades that witnessed the emergence of the modern university also saw the accumulation of the great industrial fortunes of such men as Andrew Carnegie and John D. Rockefeller. At the turn of the century, each of these two magnates had already made sizable philanthropic contributions and expressed the intention of making more. Like some of their peers, they had grown weary of fending off suppliants and were coming to rely on experts to guide and administer their giving. It was more convenient and more effective, they concluded, to conduct philanthropy "wholesale" than "retail."[3]

In 1905, both Carnegie and Rockefeller made multi-million-dollar gifts for the purpose of improving American higher education. The experts to whom they entrusted these gifts and the millions more that would follow believed that a "comprehensive system of higher education in the United States" was sorely needed. Frederick Taylor Gates, the philanthropic expert who persuaded Rockefeller to fund this system-building (which was after all not unlike the oil baron's own approach to the distribution of natural resources), recalled in his memoirs his impression of higher education around 1900: "I had a reasonably clear bird's eye view of the whole field, and while there was much to encourage there was much also to regret. The picture was one of chaos. Most of these institutions had been located in a soil which could not sustain them as colleges; in spots they were injuriously crowded together. They were scattered haphazard over the landscape like wind-carried seeds."[4] With the emergence of universities, new institutions had simply been added to the previous constellation, which was itself unregulated and widely variant. Thus demarcations between graduate and undergraduate education as well as between secondary and collegiate education were obscure. Many schools were built on shaky financial ground, and academic standards, for faculty as well as students, varied widely. These two great fortunes, the experts hoped, could provide the means of bringing order.

3. Merle Curti and Roderick Nash, *Philanthropy in the Shaping of American Higher Education* (New Brunswick, N.J.: Rutgers Univ. Press, 1965), pp. 212–17.

4. Frederick Taylor Gates, quoted in Raymond B. Fosdick, *Adventure in Giving: The Story of the General Education Board* (New York: Harper and Row, 1962), p. 128.

Historians of higher education treat these initiatives—particularly that by the Carnegie Foundation—as the culmination of efforts to standardize entrance requirements and accreditation that had been underway for more than a decade, and they judge that the strategists achieved their goals.[5]

Andrew Carnegie's 1905 gift of $10,000,000 to support professors' pensions initiated an important episode in this story. The donor himself placed no restrictions on the pension fund to be devised; he was simply appalled when he learned the facts about professorial pay and retirement. But the policymakers at the new Carnegie Foundation for the Advancement of Teaching quickly discerned that "there would be involved in the administration of this gift a scrutiny of education which would not only be desirable in the granting of pensions, but would go far to resolve the confusion that then existed in American higher education."[6] Under the leadership of Henry S. Pritchett, formerly president of MIT, the foundation explicitly announced its intention of limiting participation in the pension fund to selected colleges and universities that were willing to serve as models of the foundation's plan for standards in higher education.

Carnegie guidelines required colleges to be clearly differentiated from secondary schools, to have minimum endowments of $200,000, and to have at least eight full professors with earned doctorates, including all department heads. State institutions, which executives of earlier foundations had found to be uncooperative, were at first excluded, but in 1908 Andrew Carnegie gave an additional five million dollars to subsidize faculty pensions for those teaching at state-supported colleges and universities.[7]

Of particular importance for the place of religion in higher education was the Carnegie rule that excluded denominational colleges and universities from the plan. Placing institutions along a spectrum with five points from "absolute denominational control" through "no formal connection . . . but a strong sympathetic one," the foundation excluded colleges in the first

5. *The General Education Board: An Account of Its Activities, 1902–1914* (New York: General Education Board, 1915), develops this critique of the *status quo ante*, pp. 103–43. Education historians consider this depiction to be generally accurate; see Lawrence R. Veysey, *The Emergence of the American University* (Chicago: University of Chicago Press, 1965), and Frederick Rudolph, *The American College and University: A History* (New York: Alfred A. Knopf, 1962).

6. Henry S. Pritchett in the Carnegie Foundation's *Thirteenth Annual Report* (1935), quoted in Ernest Victor Hollis, *Philanthropic Foundations and Higher Education* (New York: Columbia University Press, 1938); Ellen Condliffe Lagemann, "The Politics of Knowledge: The Carnegie Corporation and the Formulation of Public Policy," *History of Education Quarterly* 27 (1978):210.

7. Hollis, *Philanthropic Foundations*, pp. 34–38; Curti and Nash, *Philanthropy and the Shaping of American Higher Education*, pp. 221–22. In 1918, with the early mission completed, the Carnegie pensions funds were reorganized as TIAA, and the requirements having to do with academic standards were dropped.

four categories and required colleges in the fifth to certify by trustee resolution that no distinctly denominational tenets influenced admission, instruction, or the choice of trustees, officers, or faculty.[8]

About fifteen denominational colleges and universities severed ties with their denominations in order to participate in the Carnegie pension fund, including Wesleyan, Drury, Drake, Coe, Dickinson, Goucher, Swarthmore, Bowdoin, Rochester, Occidental, Rutgers, and Brown.[9] Many, probably most, other denominational colleges would not have been accepted by Carnegie even if they had been willing to disaffiliate, since other measures of excellence were also applied. Some historically church-related colleges (particularly Congregational ones) were already sufficiently free from denominational control to qualify for the plan; Oberlin is a leading example.

These changes naturally evoked resentment of the Foundation in some quarters. A Methodist bishop published in 1909 *Dangerous Donations and Degrading Doles: A Vast Scheme for Capturing and Controlling the Colleges and Universities of the Country,* while a liberal Protestant weekly based in New York more temperately objected to the power of a private fortune to "effect profound changes in the constitution and management of our colleges, severing venerable denominational ties, tightening up requirements for admission, differentiating the college from the University, systematizing finances, raising salaries, and in more subtle ways modifying the life and work of thousands of educators."[10] In this latter quote, it is noteworthy that not all items in the litany of change were negative in content; this author seems to object mostly to the power of private funds to alter abruptly lives of long service. And, indeed, many liberal Protestants welcomed the advent of higher standards for the colleges. For instance, President Henry Churchill King of Oberlin College, a leading Congregationalist, served as an advisor to the Carnegie Foundation. True religion would be furthered by the application of the highest standards of scholarship, in his view. Not denominational ties but high ideals of inquiry within a general collegiate ethos of "moral and religious conviction and purpose" should typify the Protestant contribution to higher education.[11]

8. Paul M. Limbert, *Denominational Policies in Support and Supervision of Higher Education* (New York: Teachers College, Columbia University, 1929), p. 56.

9. I have found no exhaustive list but have combined data from Limbert, *Denominational Policies,* p. 57; Hollis, *Philanthropic Foundations,* p. 54; Rudolph, *American Colleges and Universities,* p. 433; Merrimon Cuninggim, *The College Seeks Religion* (New Haven: Yale University Press, 1947), p. 8; and W. Bruce Leslie, "Localism, Denominationalism, and Institutional Strategies in Urbanizing America: Three Pennsylvania Colleges, 1870–1915," *History of Education Quarterly* 17(1977):248.

10. Warren Akin Candler's *Dangerous Donations and Degrading Doles* is cited in Curti and Nash, *Philanthropy and the Shaping of American Higher Education,* p. 221. *The Independent* LXVI (June 17, 1909):153–54, is quoted in Hollis, *Philanthropic Foundations,* p. 52.

11. Henry Churchill King, "Religion in Our Colleges," address to the National Council of Congregational Churches, *Report of the Sixteenth Regular Meeting* (Boston: Office of the National Council, 1915), pp. 142–43.

By the early twentieth century, the faculties of the best denominational colleges included many modern scholars like King, who possessed an M.A. from Harvard and had studied with Adolf von Harnack at the University of Berlin, a prototype institution for the emerging system of higher education. Trained themselves in research universities and sharing in the valuation their era placed on standards, excellence, expertise, and order, this new breed of professor would presumably welcome Carnegie interventions in their own institutions. In some cases of disaffiliation, such as Swarthmore, strong forces within the college were already advocating changes such as those the Foundation required. On the other hand, changing educational ideals probably were not the only reasons for disaffiliation given the expense of higher education and the difficulty of finding funds for support in that age as in our own. At Brown, for instance, the trustees admitted that the financial attractiveness of pension fund participation was a reason for disaffiliation but denied that it was the chief one; instead, Carnegie money had given them a lever for liberalization that they already had been seeking.[12]

Denominational affiliation, or its abandonment, had a wide variety of meanings for different colleges, depending on peculiarities of denominational polity and institutional tradition. Particularly before the establishment of national denominational boards of education, which came in the early twentieth century as a response to the perception of crisis in church-related higher education, ties were usually local or regional, expressed through the constancy of a particular constituency and the predominance on boards and faculties of a particular sort of Protestant church membership. Disaffiliation did not necessarily break all these ties; surely disaffiliated schools with strong traditions, such as Oberlin and Swarthmore, continued to have a distinctive religious tone in the ensuing decades. Nor did continued affiliation necessarily guarantee that a school's religious commitment would be unmistakably manifest, as numerous studies seeking to discover the distinctive religious mission of church-related colleges would later report. Rather, the new climate of authority in higher education—a climate governed by the sun of national standards and the winds of university research—altered in important ways the ecology within which all colleges would henceforth have to live. A few who adapted remarkably well rose to national prominence; most others were probably strengthened in many aspects of instruction, but at the cost of having to adhere more closely to homogenous, non-sectarian norms.

The other great fortune shaping higher education in the first decades of the century belonged to a devout Baptist, John D. Rockefeller. Moreover, the chief architect and the steady administrator of this aspect of Rockefeller philanthropy (Frederick Taylor Gates and Wallace Buttrick, respectively) as well as the president of its flagship university (William Rainey Harper) were

---

12. Leslie, "Localism, Denominationalism, and Institutional Strategies," *loc.cit.*, pp. 248 ff.; Hollis, *Philanthropic Foundations*, p. 54.

one and all Baptist clergymen. Significantly, church-related colleges were not automatically disqualified from receiving assistance. Yet the effort to prune away the deadwood of American higher education—and the assumption that most of that deadwood was presently supported by misguided denominational rivals—was if anything more earnestly attempted by the Rockefeller grant programs.[13] If the triumph of the comprehensive, university-dominated system of higher education spelled a decline of Protestant influence in American higher education (as it clearly did), an explanation is necessary.

The General Education Board, the agency founded in 1902 through which Rockefeller education programs were administered until 1960, was originally and continuously most active in promoting education for both races in the South. Later it would also have considerable impact on medical education. In 1905, however, Frederick Taylor Gates persuaded John D. Rockefeller to make a large gift for the promotion of higher education nationally. Ten million dollars that year were followed by another ten million a year later and many more in coming years. These funds were consistently available to a wider range and number of colleges and universities than were Carnegie funds. In 1919, for instance, fifty million dollars were made available in matching grants to endow faculty salaries in 203 colleges and universities, among them six state institutions, forty secular private ones, and a diverse range of others including 36 Negro, 40 Methodist, 35 Baptist, 30 Presbyterian, and 15 Congregational colleges. Some of these, unable to raise matching funds, lost the grants.[14]

Gates, the strategist who conceived the comprehensive national system of higher education and devised the philanthropic means of promoting it, had already been involved in Rockefeller projects for more than a decade. In 1915, John D. Rockefeller would call him "the guiding genius in all our giving." A graduate of the modest Baptist college and seminary in Rochester (which would grow to much greater size and eminence during the era of philanthropy and standardization), Gates served as pastor in Minneapolis until his talents attracted the attention of the millionaire George Pillsbury, who sought his advice in making a bequest to a Baptist academy. By the time

13. Gates's 1908 recommendation against grants to any of the "no less than nine so-called Christian colleges" in the state of Nebraska is worth quoting. Their very existence, Gates argued was "destructive of higher education." Most of them, he believed, had been born "of real estate speculation and local town pride," with the speculators having "flattered the vanity and beguiled the simplicity of the children of light, who in yielding to these seductions little realized the burdens and responsibilities they were assuming." Quoted in Fosdick, *Adventure in Giving*, p. 131. Fosdick happily reported that Gates's appraisal of the prospects of these denominational colleges had been accurate, in that only one survived the next half-century.

14. Hollis, *Philanthropic Foundations*, pp. 36, 198, 271, 133; Fosdick, *Adventure in Giving*, pp. 127–31; Leslie, "Localism, Denominationalism and Institutional Strategies," *loc. cit.*, p. 246.

he first met Rockefeller in 1888, Gates was serving as the agent of the American Baptist Education Society, a newly-devised denominational agency that was pioneering educational fund-raising and reform. After turning down the presidency of the University of Rochester as too limiting a post, Gates worked with William Rainey Harper to persuade Rockefeller to support the development of an excellent Baptist college, and then university, upon the ruins of the old University of Chicago. Gates moved from this project into a New York office from which he would continue to direct Rockefeller philanthropic ventures, as well as some business dealings.[15]

Together, the activities of Gates, Harper, and Rockefeller forged an important bridge from the age of the college into the age of the university. The bridge was partly a structural one; Rockefeller made his early contributions to the University of Chicago through the American Baptist Education Society, and the 1890 charter required that the president and two-thirds of the trustees be Baptist.[16] More importantly, however, the bridge was built of ideas gaining currency among Protestant liberals at the turn of the century. On this foundation Harper, a biblical scholar who served as the University's first president until his early death from cancer in 1906, devised a philosophy of education that celebrated the modern university in nearly religious tones. The modern university and the learning and service it provided, Harper believed, would be the instrument of progress, equality, and goodness for society. Theologically, this acceptance of the scholarly scrutiny of all aspects of life and the extension of redemption from religious institutions into the whole secular order were wholly acceptable to this generation of liberals. Therefore, though nominally Baptist, Harper's university was able to avoid a sectarian stance, courting support from a wide public, displaying unusual religious and ethnic tolerance, and apparently aspiring to win the esteem of international scholars more than that of American Baptists.[17]

A similar religious position lay behind Gates's advocacy of university-style reform throughout American higher education. The pilgrimage that led him from the strict and gloomy Calvinism of his boyhood in an upstate New York manse to the pinnacle of Establishment philanthropy was accompanied by a process of theological liberalization that gradually reduced the doctrinal portions of his piety while enlarging the ethical ones. As a later Rockefeller

15. Frederick Taylor Gates, *Chapters in My Life* (New York: Macmillan, 1977), is the first publication of Gates's 1928 autobiography. It is published with two essays on his life and career by Robert Swain Morison, who quotes J. D. R.'s comment about Gates, p. 285. Gates's assistance to J. D. Rockefeller was mirrored a generation later by the assistance Raymond B. Fosdick provided to J. D. R., Jr. Although Fosdick was not a clergyman, his brother was the most eminent one of his time, and his twin sister was a missionary in Turkey.

16. Limbert, *Denominational Policies*, p. 224; Veysey, *The Emergence of the American University*, pp. 373–75.

17. William Rainey Harper, *The Trend in Higher Education* (Chicago: University of Chicago Press, 1905).

Foundation executive described him, Gates combined a nineteenth-century moral and religious character with a sensitivity to the scientific culture of the twentieth century.

> [H]e believed deeply and irrevocably in the perfectibility of man and especially in the advancement of knowledge as the best means for reaching perfection. The vigor and rigor of the old-time religion were in his bones. But the dogmas of original sin, arbitrary election, and salvation by faith had been metamorphosed. . . . Faith . . . changed its focus to include man as well as God. Faith that man can make himself better by his own efforts—that indeed he was already on his way—gave the best of Gates's generation a single-mindedness and a driving energy which have descended to few of their sceptical grandchildren.[18]

The portrait of Gates that emerges from his autobiography confirms this assessment—perhaps nowhere more clearly than in his breathless commentary on the Rockefeller Institute (for medical research):

> Do not smile if I say that I often think of the Institute as a sort of Theological Seminary. But if there be over us all the Sum of All, and that Sum Conscious—a Conscious, Intelligent Being—and that Being has any favorites on this little planet, I must believe that those favorites are made up of that ever enlarging group of men and women who are most intimately and in every truth studying Him and His ways with men. That is the work of the Institute. In these sacred rooms He is whispering His secrets. To these men He is opening up the mysterious depths of His Being.[19]

The changing sensibilities of Protestant educational leaders such as William Rainey Harper, Frederick Taylor Gates, and Henry Churchill King disclosed the significance of the emergence of the modern university for mainstream Protestantism as surely as statistics: whatever their pious intentions, the future path of American higher education lay in an essentially non-religious direction. In fact, the policies of the Carnegie Foundation and the General Education Board did not substantially reduce the number of colleges and universities affiliated with Protestant denominations, and the pension-chasing of some fifteen newly-disaffiliated schools is only evidence, not cause, of the change that was taking place. Rather, the importance of the foundation-supported triumph of a national comprehensive system of accreditation, entrance requirements, and faculty expertise is that it marked a major change in the climate of cultural authority prevailing among almost all

18. Robert Swain Morison, "Gates Lecture II," in Gates, *Chapters in My Life*, p. 283.
19. Gates, *Chapters in My Life*, pp. 187–88.

institutions of higher education. After the First World War, it became apparent that institutions able to draw on urban wealth and reflect the new national orientation became more successful, while colleges that continued to rely on traditional local and ecclesiastical sources of support and control gave up opportunities to grow and thrive. Although the leadership and constituencies of many colleges continued to reflect the membership of particular denominations, this fact increasingly denoted less particularity than previously. These forces pressed the secularization of some crucial aspects of a college's program even if not official disaffiliation.[20]

Black colleges were affected by the shift in educational authority in distinctive ways. In 1940, the pattern of black higher education was similar to what the predominant pattern had been in 1900: one-half of the undergraduates were in church-supported schools, of which about half were affiliated with mainstream Protestant denominations. Forty per cent of all black college presidents were clergymen; 75% of those in the denominational schools were. Through these colleges, the churches had an opportunity for broad impact in the larger black community, even if the students belonged to other denominations or none at all. Yet the relative strength during the pre-civil-rights era of these colleges' church relationships was counterbalanced by their marginalization from the newly dominant national comprehensive system. The great majority were not accredited at the highest level. And for this the General Education Board, which exercised the strongest philanthropic influence on Negro education in the South after 1902, must be held largely responsible. Well aware of the deficiencies of most black colleges and universities, the Board nonetheless pursued a policy of cooperation with white Southerners, thereby effectively defining "the retarded condition of private black colleges in years to come," as one historian of black higher education put it.[21] With a few exceptions, the Board supported vocational emphasis in Negro higher education and kept institutional control in white hands.

By the second quarter of the twentieth century, other changes also marked the declining influence of mainstream Protestantism in higher eudcation. Students began to protest chapel requirements at state-supported, independent, and church-related colleges alike, and the process of relaxing and abandoning such requirements began. There was a drastic decrease in clergy representation on boards of trustees, particularly in leading institutions such as Yale and Princeton where their presence had once been strong.

20. This is the argument of W. Bruce Leslie's study of Swarthmore, Bucknell, and Franklin and Marshall, "Localism, Denominationalism, and Institutional Strategies," *loc. cit.*

21. Richard I. McKinney, *Religion in Higher Education among Negroes* (New Haven: Yale University Press, 1945); Curti and Nash, *Philanthropy in the Shaping of American Higher Education*, pp. 168–77; J. M. Stephen Peeps, "Northern Philanthropy and the Emergence of Black Higher Education—Do-Gooders, Compromisers, or Co-Conspirators?" *Journal of Negro Education* 50 (1981): 265.

In addition, the practice of appointing clergy presidents practically disappeared in all but denominational institutions.[22]

Developing New Strategies of Protestant Influence

By 1920, church-related colleges had lost considerable status within the overall system of American education, and they were also beginning to lose preeminence as the locus of the churches' attention to students, professors, and research.[23] During the ensuing decades, concerned Protestant educatonal leaders devised three strategies for renewing the influence of religion in higher education, each of which has had lasting significance: campus ministry at secular institutions, promotion of the academic study of religion, and efforts to raise faculty consciousness about the religious and ethical dimensions of higher education. Some of these leaders were located in colleges and universities, others in denominations. As we shall see, philanthropic foundations would lend crucial support to their efforts at several points, though the quantitative expansion of higher education made it increasingly difficult for independent donations to make as great a difference as Carnegie and Rockefeller had made earlier in the century.

Campus ministry had begun to take shape around the turn of the century, when a few denominations placed on or near university campuses ministers whose primary duty was to serve Christian students there. The social analysis and basic strategy of this movement were expressed in the title of a 1938 book by Clarence P. Shedd, a professor at Yale Divinity School: *The Church Follows Its Students*. Since the demography and spheres of influence in higher education had radically changed, Shedd argued, students at tax-supported institutions now deserved a major share of the churches' attention. Shedd, the key figure in the development of the professional campus ministry, wrote with enthusiasm about the effectiveness of the two hundred university pastors currently active; and although their impact can hardly be assessed, it is clear that Shedd's argument had considerable impact on the perceptions of higher education held by religious leaders, whose imaginations had previously been dominated by church-related colleges.[24]

The growth of the modern academic study of religion at the college level made major strides in the 1920s. Whether to interpret this as a strategic

---

22. Evidence and references for these changes are detailed in Bass, "Ministry on the Margin," in Hutchison, *Between the Times*, pp. 49–57.

23. Cuninggim, *The College Seeks Religion*, pp. 13–14, identifies 1900 to 1918 as the period when "secularization" triumphed in higher education.

24. Clarence P. Shedd, *The Church Follows Its Students* (New Haven: Yale University Press, 1938), pp. 7–11, 219. On Shedd's considerable influence, see Cuninggim, *The College Seeks Religion*, p. 4, and Amos N. Wilder (ed.), *Liberal Learning and Religion* (New York: Harper and Brothers, 1951), p. 13.

effort of mainstream Protestants to attain greater influence within an increasingly secular system of higher education is problematic, of course, since not churches but individual scholars took the initiative in this arena. A key figure whose actions did seem to carry this strategic flavor was Charles Foster Kent, the long-time professor of Biblical literature at Yale who in 1922 founded the National Council on Religion in Higher Education. Kent's expressed hope was that religion could "once again" attain a significant place in college and university life, a place he believed must be won through the intellectual and educational respectability of religious studies. One description of Kent's and the Council's ideals discloses the closeness of this vision to some theological elements within mainstream Protestant liberal academic circles: the goal was "an intellectually respectable, modernist and liberal, scholarly and scientific approach to religion on campus, which would take all that science had to offer and come back for more, and which would move on a level beneath but respectful to all faiths."[25] During the second quarter of a century, a center of influence based at Yale and funded by the Edward W. Hazen Foundation did most of the important organizing and publishing related to the means of promoting the study of religion in higher education.[26] At mid-century, Hazen-supported studies showed that the academic study of religion had grown substantially since 1920, but that religion was usually either ignored or treated with scientific scorn in the textbooks most widely used in other departments.[27]

From the National Council on Religion in Higher Education there emerged a network of concerned educators who would dominate Protestant reflection on the religious and ethical dimensions of higher education into the 1960s. Originally based in a Council-sponsored, Hazen-funded Society of Fellows, this network developed a range of publications, conferences, and other programs designed to raise awareness of religious and moral issues among faculty, administrators, and graduate students, while also providing support to those persuaded of the importance of such issues. Membership in

25. Thornton W. Merriam, "Religion in Higher Education Through the Past Twenty-five Years," in Wilder, *Liberal Learning and Religion*, pp. 6–7.

26. *The Edward W. Hazen Foundation, 1925–1950* (New Haven: The Edward W. Hazen Foundation, 1950) lists the dozens of publications supported by this small foundation, which expended a total of $1,625,495 during these twenty-five years. Edward W. Hazen (1860–1929), of Haddam, Connecticut, made his fortune in advertising.

27. Cuninggim, *The College Seeks Religion*, pp. 300, 151; Merriam, "Religion in Higher Education," *loc. cit.*, p. 6; Virginia Corwin, "The Teaching of Religion," in Wilder, *Liberal Learning and Religion*, p. 169; and Howard B. Jefferson, "The Present Religious Situation in Higher Education," in Christian Gauss, *The Teaching of Religion in American Higher Education* (New York: The Ronald Press, 1951), p. 86. See also *College Reading and Religion: A survey of college reading materials sponsored by the Edward W. Haven Foundation and the Committee on Religion and Education of the American Council on Education* (New Haven: Yale University Press, 1948).

these programs was open to persons of all faiths, though informal mainstream Protestant dominance within them persisted into the 1960s.[28]

From mid-century until 1980, when it ended most of its activity in higher education, the Danforth Foundation was a lively source of stimulation and support for those concerned with these issues. Under the staff leadership of Kenneth I. Brown (1951–61), a former president of Hiram and Denison colleges, and especially of Merrimon Cuninggim (1961–77), a Yale-educated Methodist who had been centrally involved in the Hazen network, Danforth supported and sometimes reshaped all three of the strategies. The context within which this took place, however, was changing rapidly, particularly after 1960.[29]

A Ministry on the Margin: Religion in the University After 1960

In the view of sociologist Robert Wuthnow, the "enormous expansion of higher education" during the 1960s constituted a major cultural change for the United States, and especially for American religion. The total numbers of students enrolled in given years reflect that enormous expansion: 2.6 million in 1950, 3.6 million in 1960, 8.6 million in 1970, 12.1 million in 1980. The increased size of the college-aged cohort contributed to the expansion, to be sure, but the proportion of this cohort that enrolled was also rising dramatically, from 22% to 32% during the '60s. Moreover, the infusion of government funds into universities was based not only on the need to educate youth but also on the society's hunger for science and technology.[30]

Higher education's growth in size, which took place almost entirely in the government-sponsored sector, was accompanied by heightened awareness of its role in a complex modern society. "We are just now perceiving that the university's invisible product, knowledge, may be the most powerful single element in our culture," affirmed California Chancellor Clark Kerr in his noted 1963 address on *The Uses of the University*. In phrases that recall the tone of the Kennedy administration's best and brightest strategists, Kerr declared that the university was being called upon to "produce knowledge" for a wider range of purposes than ever before—"for civic purposes and regional purposes, for national purposes, and even for no purpose at all beyond the realization that most knowledge eventually comes

---

28. Hugh Hartshorne, Helen R. Stearns, and Willard B. Uphaus, *Standards and Trends in Religious Education* (New Haven: Yale University Press, 1933), p. 193; Merriam, "Religion in Higher Education," *loc. cit.*, pp. 3–23.

29. Danforth Foundation, *Annual Reports* (St. Louis: Danforth Foundation, 1965–73). The 1965–66 report noted that the immense increase in federal support of higher education constituted a major turning point for higher education and for philanthropy in this arena.

30. Robert Wuthnow, *The Restructuring of American Religion* (Princeton: Princeton University Press, 1988), pp. 154ff.; *1988 Digest of Educational Statistics*, p. 146; Seymour E. Harris, *A Statistical Portrait of Higher Education* (New York: McGraw-Hill, 1972), p. 269.

to serve mankind"—and to transmit knowledge "to an unprecedented proportion of the population." In the process, the university was acquiring a
web of complicated relations with government, foundations, and industry
that would further transform it.[31]

Kerr's image of the large, impersonal, fragmented, cosmopolitan "multiversity" hardly described the majority of colleges and universities in the
United States. Yet the multiversities—schools like Berkeley, Wisconsin,
Columbia, Michigan—were the decade's pace-setters. In one sense, Protestant ministries in such settings were in place: interested observers had
already noticed that there were, for example, more Methodists in Iowa's state
universities than in its Methodist colleges, and denominational programs
existed at the University of Iowa and similar campuses all over the country.[32]
In another sense, however, the continuing secularization and fragmentation
of knowledge and the institutions where it was "produced" (as Kerr put it)
placed ever greater distance between the dominant forces in higher education and the inherited educational style of American Protestantism. Church-
related colleges received relatively little denominational attention during the
1960s, and reports early in the next decade discovered widespread lack of
clarity about their mission. Within higher education, religious institutions
and studies came to occupy an ever smaller portion of the whole. More
importantly, the ever-increasing dominance and confidence of the cultural
forces represented by the multiversity seemed further to weaken religion's
claim to be a center of value.[33]

As in the earlier period, mainstream Protestant leaders charac-
teristically did not react negatively or defensively against the increasing
cultural claims of the modern university. Theological movements away from
neo-orthodoxy toward a celebration of the secular set the stage for an
innovative, politically active campus ministry. Increasing commitments to
ecumenism and pluralism confirmed mainstream Protestant educational
strategists' nonsectarian, academic approaches to religion in the curriculum
and on campus. And the discomfort with ecclesiastical institutionalism that
prevailed in mainstream circles sometimes made disestablishment from the
educational center seem almost attractive. "A society which once hinged
around the church is now more and more pivoting around the university, and
the church is marginal to that university," declared Robert W. Lynn in a 1966
address. Far from considering such a shift disastrous, however, this Pres-

---

31. Clark Kerr, *The Uses of the University* (New York: Harper and Row, 1963, 1972), pp. vi–
vii, 122.

32. Robert Michaelsen, "Religious Education in Public Higher Education Institutions," in
Marvin J. Taylor (ed.), *Religious Education: A Comprehensive Survey* (New York: Abingdon
Press, 1960), p. 306.

33. Pattillo and MacKenzie, *Church Sponsored Higher Education in the United States;*
and C. Robert Pace, *Education and Evangelism* (New York: McGraw-Hill, 1975); Wuthnow,
Restructuring, pp. 158–60.

byterian educator welcomed the churches' release from the tasks of building and sustaining institutions. This change, he argued, constituted "a new call of the people of God to be a critic on the margin of American society."[34]

Campus ministers lived upon this margin—an extraordinarily difficult position, where they were simultaneously squeezed between two mighty cultural forces and kept at arm's distance from each. Commentary on their role during the 1960s displays some of the ambiguities that the ministers themselves experienced. Typical campus ministers were too churchy, the secular theologian Harvey Cox charged; they were too caught up in the busyness of developing denominational programs, coordinating ecumenical activities, and sustaining a religious realm that was divisive of the life of the university as a whole. Sociologists analyzed the situation differently, observing that campus ministers were often isolated from the churches.[35] Both points of view, however, identified the enduring quandary of campus ministry: how to forge a relationship between dissimilar institutions with different aims. Moreover, two factors made this quandary, always a pressing one, exceptionally strong after 1960. One was theological and structural discomfort with the institutional church. The other was the massive self-confidence of the modern university.

During the 1960s, the old campus ministry goal of following the students into a setting where a church home-away-from-home was needed lost its persuasiveness. Propelled by genuine attraction to the vibrant political and intellectual life of the university as well as by frustration at the difficulty of building a traditional program in its midst, many campus ministers were seeking "wider-ranging and less institutionally inhibited roles." In the view of campus ministers at the University of Wisconsin, a mid-decade sociological survey concluded, "the traditional notion of the student relgious group is as archaic as it is ineffectual."[36] It is not surprising, therefore, that considerable confusion about the role of campus ministers appeared. A 1963 survey showed that they were disproportionately young, of short tenure, and uncommitted to long-term service in the field. They believed that the churches wanted them to produce quantitative successes, but they were unsure of how and even why to do so. They received little acknowledgement from either church or university. And, paradoxically, it seemed that they were caught in a spiral that must only make their isolation more severe. The

34. Robert W. Lynn, "A Ministry on the Margin," in Kenneth Underwood, *The Church, the University, and Social Policy: The Danforth Study of Campus Ministries,* 2 vols. (Middletown, Ct.: Wesleyan University Press, 1969), II, 20.

35. Harvey Cox, *The Secular City* (New York: Macmillan, 1965), p. 197; Phillip E. Hammond, *The Campus Clergyman* (New York: Basic Books, 1966), pp. 98–106; Jeffrey K. Hadden, *The Gathering Storm in the Churches* (Garden City, N.Y.: Doubleday, 1969), pp. 194–97.

36. N. J. Demerath, III, and Kenneth J. Lutterman, "The Student Parishioner: Radical Rhetoric and Traditional Reality," in Underwood, *The Church, the University, and Social Policy,* II, 139.

more cosmopolitan (i.e. less religious) their university, the more innovative their style became; and the more innovative their style became, the less acknowledgement were they likely to receive from the church.[37]

Faced with this conundrum, most chose innovation. In part their reasons were theological, but the financial generosity of denominational sponsors in a prosperous age may also have emboldened them. (The earliest signs of diminishing mainstream Protestant resources for campus ministry appeared in 1966, with a much sharper decline coming in the next decade.) The campus culture of the 1960s lent further impetus to campus ministers' innovative style and shifting identity. In a 1973 evaluation report prepared for the Danforth Foundation, Robert McAfee Brown conceded that campus ministry was having an "identity crisis"—but perceptively added that a similar problem afflicted both the campus *per se* and the ministry as a whole.[38]

The Danforth Foundation began to provide financial assistance to campus ministry in 1956, with a program to support seminary internships in this field. A year later, a program of campus ministry grants was initiated, which would fund special projects and conferences into the 1970s. In addition, a range of programs provided campus ministers with opportunities for professional growth, particularly through an annual fellowship program to support sabbatical study. The largest single expenditure was for a six-year, half-million-dollar study of campus ministry headed by the Wesleyan University ethicist Kenneth Underwood, who died of cancer in 1968 when the project was in its final stages.

Danforth programs in campus ministry found their justification in providing essential services to the university and its inhabitants, not to the church. A 1966 foundation report identified Danforth's goal in a range of programs in higher education, of which this was one, as "better education for persons of promise who can make a difference in their time and place, education that is aware of its own built-in sense of values and is prepared to uphold them."[39] And in his report, Brown emphasized the particular role of campus ministry in focussing attention on "values," which he was persuaded other agencies within the university overlooked.

The Underwood study reflected a fascination with the power and possibilities of the modern multiversity not unlike that earlier displayed by Clark Kerr. To the churches (whose support for campus ministry was needed) Underwood interpreted the university as a religious new frontier. "The vast intellectual, political, and social changes sweeping the world confront the leadership of the churches in the theories and data of the strategic centers of

37. Hammond, *The Campus Clergyman*, pp. 13, 70–71, 80, 101, 115.

38. *Church Society for College Work Report* XXXII:1 (January 1974): 2.

39. The Danforth Foundation, *Annual Report* (St. Louis: Danforth Foundation, 1966), p. 17.

higher education," he wrote. Campus ministers were thus pioneers on the challenging trails the whole church would need to travel in the not too distant future. To the universities, Underwood offered the services of campus ministers as "catalysts" who would bring together currently fragmented elements of knowledge and power for the purpose of "prophetic inquiry." Campus ministers, he argued, should and could be the free agents who would facilitate "the centering of theology, ethics, the humanities, the creative arts, the social sciences, history, and the natural sciences on the task of envisioning the nature of a humane urban technical society and determining the means of realizing that vision through responsible action within complex institutions."[40]

Of course it is difficult to assess the impact of a philanthropic venture of this kind. In a basic assessment, it can be reported that the Underwood study was well received by reviewers and influential among campus ministers, although its intricate structure and complicated prose hindered its appropriation by church and university leaders and perhaps even by some Danforth board and staff members.[41] Whatever its impact, however, the report did provide an exceptionally thoughtful example of mainstream Protestant thinking about higher education—one that was characteristic in its strengths and in its weaknesses. Underwood's vision was to place Christian ministry at a crossroads near the center of the university, where ethics and knowledge and symbol could interact as the university took its proper responsibility for the social good. This is a grand vision that was true to the best traditions of a public, pluralistic Christianity able to stand unthreatened, in its own estimation at least, in the presence of modern science. Yet it was also sadly unrealistic. Why should the Clark Kerrs of the world accept the proffered catalytic services? Underwood had seriously underestimated the extent to which higher education, and especially religion's role in it, had been restructured. The real difficulties of resolving the identity crisis of a pluralistic and ethically-oriented campus ministry (which is what most mainstream ministers attempt) still have not been resolved. The exit of the Danforth Foundation from this field beginning in the early 1970s has only exacerbated campus ministry's problems of identity and morale.

The difficulties of campus ministry (together with the demise of the

40. Underwood, The Church, the University, and Social Policy, I, xvi, 3, 8; New Wine: A Report of the Commission on the Danforth Study of Campus Ministries (St. Louis: The Danforth Foundation, 1969), p. 37.

41. For example, positive reviews appeared in The Christian Century 87 (April 22, 1970): 506–10; America 122 (January 17, 1970): 50–51; Commonweal 91 (January 30, 1970):484–87; and Theology Today 26 (January 1970): 471–75. Parker Palmer's 1973 evaluation study of Danforth's Underwood Fellowship program hints that some Foundation board and staff members were uneasy with the Underwood study (unpublished report shared with the author by Parker Palmer and Robert Rankin).

student Christian movement in 1968)[42] weakened the mainstream Protestant presence in American higher education, particularly in the large secular universities that dominated the system. Religion more broadly construed, however, did not lose ground in the universities during the 1960s. Rather, as a subject for study in accordance with the academic norms of those universities, religion attained much greater attention than previously. Reversing the trajectory of official Protestant presence, the upward movement of the field of religious studies won from the modern pluralistic university at least a grudging respect for the importance of religion in human affairs.

Mainstream Protestants, whose liberal theological perspective was not at odds with the historical and scientific study of human religious activity, were generally supportive of the trend. However, in institutional terms the advance of the academic study of religion was neither their initiative nor their victory. The social and intellectual location of the study of religion, once the territory of theological faculties and church-related colleges, had been changing throughout the century, and especially so since World War II. As higher education grew in size, self-confidence, and secularity, scholars in the field of religion addressed—successfully, on the whole—concerns about their academic legitimacy. Pursuing the 1935 Princeton University plan of drawing a clear distinction between "the study of religion and the practice of it," the field entered a formative period that brought it by 1968, in the judgment of John F. Wilson, to substantial self-understanding and clarity. James M. Gustafson agreed: the field had made great strides in the academy, and differentiation among the several types of concern for religion—in arts and sciences, in preparation of professional church leadership, in religious care of students—had made the crucial difference.[43]

Working from a "posture of analytical rigor, of disinterested objectivity, and sometimes of disinterested irreverence," the field of religious studies was showing great scholarly productivity and attaining substantial institutional success. Might this success have been related to the corresponding decline in the churches' influence? The differentiation of religion's various tasks in higher education, with one clearly at the center and others on the margins, would suggest that this was the case. In addition, John Wilson believed, theology's intellectual hold on thinking about religion had weakened. This was due in part to the current confused state of theology, he

---

42. The University Christian Movement, an ecumenical organization that incorporated the heritage of the Student Volunteer Movement and the National Student Christian Federation, voted itself out of existence in 1968 in a moment of radical student anti-institutionalism. Danforth had given this organization modest financial support. Only today are new organizations forming to take its place. A discussion of this episode appears in my "Revolutions, Quiet and Otherwise: Religion and Higher Education in the 1960s," loc. cit.

43. Paul Ramsey and John F. Wilson (eds.), The Study of Religion in Colleges and Universities (Princeton, N.J.: Princeton University Press, 1970), pp. 14, 332.

reported; no theological option "so articulated and expounded as to transform (or be intended to transform) cultural attitudes and social institutions" was on the intellectual scene. Moreover, theological schools played an ever smaller role in the social structure of the field, taking a decreasing place in the preparation of religious studies faculty members after 1950.[44]

If this analysis is correct, growth in the academic study of religion was partly the result, by a curious twist, of the expansion of secualr ways of thinking in the American academy. It was surely related to another event in the secularization of American education: the Supreme Court's 1963 ruling against devotional Bible reading in the public schools, which explicitly allowed and even encouraged teaching *about* religion at all academic levels. Programs in religious studies, which had grown steadily but unimpressively early in the decade, multiplied rapidly after 1964, until by 1970 nearly all accredited four-year institutions offered courses in religion, and two-thirds of them had a program or department. It should be added, however, that the numerical growth of other fields during the same expansive period kept religious studies from increasing its proportionate share of total enrollment and degrees.[45]

The Danforth Foundation offered a series of grants to support the development of departments of religion during the 1960s. Its most sizable and far-reaching programs in higher education, however, came in support of the third strategy originally developed by the old Hazen-supported, Yale-based network. Indeed, among the earliest actions of Merrimon Cuninggim, who became the foundation's chief executive in 1961, were transferring the program of Kent Fellowships from Hazen to Danforth, strengthening both this program and the program of Danforth Graduate Fellowships begun in 1952, and forming a Society for Religion in Higher Education to provide for the continuing association of Kent and Danforth Fellows with one another and with the issues of value judged central to their vocations. Although the impact of these programs is difficult to assess, program alumni/ae seem to recall their participation with great warmth and appreciation.[46] Danforth support of these programs ended by 1980. I know of no current official program to nurture young academics in the personal, moral, and intellectual ways the Danforth networks did, though some alumnae/i of these and other Danforth programs continue independently to perpetuate and renew the network through the Society for Values in Higher Education. (The transfor-

44. The "posture" phrase is Gustafson's, in *ibid.*, p. 335; Wilson, in *ibid.*, pp. 15–19.

45. Claude Welch, *Graduate Education in Religion: A Critical Appraisal* (Missoula: University of Montana Press, 1971), pp. 167–75, 193. See also Wuthnow, *Restructuring of American Religion*, p. 160.

46. Danforth Fondation, *Annual Report, 1965–66;* telephone interview with Robert Rankin, April 27, 1989; participants' recollections from many friends, including Parker Palmer and Mark Schwehn.

mation of a society for "religion" into a society for "values" is noteworthy as one more small indication of the secularization of American higher education.)

Clearly the direct role of philanthropy in shaping the place of religion in higher education was much greater during the first quarter of the twentieth century than it could possibly be a half-century later. After 1960, the sheer size of the system made it much more difficult for any foundation to have formative influence, and those that did have large resources were more interested in science or other areas of higher education. In general, the activities of government and business outweighed all others.

The relocation of religion from a determinant of ethos at most turn-of-the-century institutions to a position within the departmental structures of contemporary universities marks a significant change. In part, at least, it confirms Charles Foster Kent's prediction that religion's future place in higher education must rest on an intellectually respectable academic approach. Yet the concomitant marginalization of other forms of campus religion would probably have surprised even that modernist. And in this juxtaposition, the double-edged quality of the liberal mainstream Protestant approach is exhibited: since their very theology encouraged them to embrace both many features of the modern university and the persons of other or no religious faith who increasingly populated it, once they lost interest in church-related colleges they left behind few distinctive, identifiable traces of their strong commitment to higher education.

In one sense, the final chapters of this unfinished account do not belong particularly to mainstream Protestantism at all. The academic study of religion seems to have attained a genuinely pluralistic constitution by the 1980s. And Danforth programs always sought to be open to all ethically sensitive and vocationally thoughtful persons, whatever their religious views, though the mainstream leadership of the foundation was never in doubt.

In another sense, it is possible that the effects of the changes recounted here have been particularly telling in mainstream Protestant circles. There, the membership losses experienced by several denominations appear to be related to the defection of their best-educated young people, who some scholars believe turned away from religion during their university studies.[47] In addition, confusion about the goals and methods of campus ministry—and declining financial support from denominations—continues, as it does not in more conservative groups. Although members of this religious family cannot and should not seek to regain the dominant role in higher education they once held, it would seem to be in their interest to reflect with renewed

47. Wuthnow, *Restructuring of American Religion*, pp. 160–62. Dean Hoge of Catholic University is working on a study of the religious lives of baby boomers that hypothesizes that higher education has had a major impact on their disaffiliation.

clarity and seriousness upon the nature of their ministries on the margins of American higher education. And it would behoove them to consider the effects of powerful philanthropic enterprises upon their activities in this, and perhaps in other, aspects of the independent sector of American culture.

RELIGIOUS VOLUNTEERISM AND CARE FOR THE HOMELESS: A CASE STUDY OF THE SHEPHERD'S TABLE

William D. Dinges

The Shepherd's Table (hereafter ST) is a community-based, state-chartered, non-profit soup kitchen now in its eighth year of operation and service to the needy and homeless of Montgomery County, Maryland. Unlike many inner-city store-front soup kitchens, ST is located on the edge of a residential area—although within the legally defined commercial district. The only visible indications that the converted house on Bonifant Street is not an ordinary home are an unobtrusive wooden sign in the front yard mounted on a shepherd's staff and a sign near the front door posting mealtime and line-up procedures.

The "clients" who come to ST are mostly men. Many of them are disheveled. Some are intoxicated. Others have run out of food stamps. Many bear signs of ill health, depression, fatigue, and other symptoms of physical and emotional neglect. They are the American "untouchables," the urban underclass, the disinherited in the midst of a suburban county with one of the highest median incomes in the nation.

Serving begins at 6:00 p.m. every evening and continues through the next hour and one half. In the context of this most fundamental act of human solidarity, two very different social groups intersect. Public service and individual need are united in a public drama of "doing good."

To its many clients, ST is a hot and nutritious "free meal," an entry point into county social services, a temporary reprieve from social isolation and hard luck. To an extensive network of community supporters, it is a place to "give back" to society and pay "civic rent." To the religious institutions in the area, ST is a cooperative interdenominational effort that unites believing communities in a common moral responsibility and public service. And, to a minority of sometimes vocal opponents, ST is a "misguided" case of good Samaritanism, a "magnet" for derelicts, and a threat to the local community's public and commercial image.

Method

For the past six years, I have worked as a volunteer at ST. The description and analysis that follow are derived from this work experience and from both formal and informal "active interviews"[1] with other volunteers and ST staff members. I have also attended monthly ST board of directors meetings as an observer for the past two years. Although I did not attempt an extensive quantitative study for the purposes of this paper, some survey questionnaire data have been utilized.[2]

The first section of this paper provides background information about the origins of the ST project and its organizational structure. The second discusses some of the demographic factors and perceptions of the volunteers who work at ST. The third section focuses on the relationship between religion and volunteerism in contemporary American society in the context of the ST project.

My focus, however, is not hunger or homelessness *per se*. Rather, I want to direct attention to how a project like that of ST sheds light on the role of religion as a culture-shaping force in a society dominated by individualism, corporate managerial capitalism, and political bureaucracy. Questions relevant to this issue include: Is ST a form of public religion, or a form of civic virtue essentially uninformed by religious symbols and ideals? How is the religious dimension of a project like ST affected when engaged with the government and for-profit sectors of American society? What does a study of an organization like ST reveal about the changing relationship between religion and social problems? What is the primary vocabulary used by volunteers to describe (construct) their helping patterns? What is the connection between "charitable work," religious views and motives, and denominational affiliation? What does an analysis of ST volunteers suggest about the "ontological individualism," the culture of narcissism and self-interest, and the privatizing of religious faith that are alleged to characterize so much of contemporary American life?

I. The Beginnings

ST is a voluntary response to a national economic and social crisis, the most visible symptom of which is the growing number of homeless citizens.[3]

1. As described by Bellah, et. al., in *Habits of the Heart* (New York: Harper and Row, 1985): 305.

2. I surveyed 81 volunteers using a five-page questionnaire. Sixty of these respondents were interviewed in person over a two week period during the evening meal work shifts at the ST house. Another 13 volunteers were interviewed by phone; 8 responded by mail. The sampling is a stratified random one.

3. For an excellent empirical work on homelessness and extreme poverty in the United States see Peter H. Rossi, *Down and Out in America: The Origins of Homelessness* (Chicago: University of Chicago Press, 1989).

Until the 1980's, homelessness was not a media-visible problem in Montgomery County.[4] Social services for the homeless were few in number and relatively unorganized. A volunteer ecumenical organization called Silver Spring HELP, Inc., formed in 1967 under the auspices of the County Council of Churches and composed primarily of retirees, provided a few palliative social services. Several HELP, Inc., affiliated churches ran "outreach" programs that provided food, clothing, and limited financial assistance to the indigent, largely on a short-term and *ad hoc* emergency basis.

In 1981, N.S., an energetic activist with a background in social work, became chairperson of HELP, Inc. This tenure as chair coincided with a new awareness of the problem of homelessness in the county. During this period churches affiliated with HELP that were located along Colesville Road, a main East/West artery running through lower Montgomery County, began receiving an increasing number of requests for food and financial assistance. In addition, local clergy became aware that growing numbers of men were sleeping in the woods along the beltway and major corridors in the area. In response to the situation, several churches began putting up people in local hotels, a practice that proved both haphazard and expensive.

In January, 1983, HELP representatives and a group of concerned citizens met to assess the situation. Under the guidance of B.M., a local Congregational minister, and N.S., an *ad hoc* Committee on Housing for the Homeless (CHH) was organized. CHH checked police records and surveyed other area religious organizations—concluding that a definite need existed in the county for a shelter for homeless men. The findings of this survey were then communicated to the member congregations. Goals were established to set up a soup kitchen, open a homeless shelter, work with the community in understanding and accepting the needs of the homeless and hungry, and promote county and state services in these areas.[5]

Under the auspices of CHH, four public workshops on homelessness were held from June through September of 1983. The feasibility of a new county shelter was discussed. "Experts" from the metro area shelters were brought in. County officials were contacted and possible shelter sites were explored.[6]

Through N.S.'s persistent and aggressive leadership, CHH continued soliciting church support and pressing local political and civic leaders to address the homelessness issue. CHH leadership made it clear to county officials who were reluctant to acknowledge the extent of the problem that neither CHH nor the homeless issue would "go away" or conveniently evaporate.

---

4. This account is derived from my discussions with the principal individuals involved and from relevant documentation provided by N.S. and ST staff.

5. CHH "Purpose Document," n.d.

6. In September 1983, the county opened a shelter for the homeless (contracted to the Salvation Army) in nearby Bethesda, Maryland. This facility, however, proved inadequate to the rapidly-increasing number of homeless and indigent people in the county.

An answer to part of the CHH agenda finally emerged in the fall of 1983 when representatives of the Silver Spring First Baptist Church came forward with an offer to support the opening of a soup kitchen on property owned by and adjacent to the church.

First Baptist Church

Like many of the churches inside the I-495 Beltway, First Baptist was once a thriving middle-class congregation composed of urban professionals, many of whom were government employees. The congregation began aging in the 1960's. Younger families migrated to upscale county suburbs. The ethnic composition of the church also began changing as the black, hispanic, and asian population in the area increased dramatically.[7] By the early-1980's, First Baptist was rapidly transforming into an urban church, but one without a clear sense of mission and direction in its changing social milieu.

In 1981, a new minister, S.H., was called to First Baptist from a congregation in Arkansas. One of his first initiatives was to encourage the congregation to forgo the previous pattern of undertaking another formalized "study" of church administrative goals and objectives. He asked, instead, that a year be spent in prayer and community discernment to determine possible new directions for church ministry. Cluster groups were formed within the church to facilitate this goal.

At the end of this year-long process of prayer and discernment, and in conjunction with discussions with church deacons and cluster group leaders, a planning group was organized. This group, under the direction of S.H. and G.L., a local attorney and leading church deacon, came forth with a proposal that First Baptist respond to a call for a ministry to "feed the hungry" and "clothe the naked." This decision, in turn, coincided with N.S.'s canvassing efforts of area churches to gather support for the CHH soup-kitchen/homeless shelter initiative. Contact was subsequently made with First Baptist representatives.

A series of meetings followed between church and CHH representatives, leadership of the local chamber of commerce, and C.S., Director of the Country Department of Family Resources. These meetings culminated in a specific proposal calling for the opening of a community supported soup kitchen on the grounds of the First Baptist Church.[8]

In proper Baptist congregational fashion, the proposal was brought

7. Between 1980 and 1988, the black population of Montgomery County increased 33 percent, the asian 90 percent, and the hispanic 55 percent. See, M-NBCPPC Census Update Survey in the *Silver Spring Record*, February 15, 1990: 16.

8. During the early stages of the planning, some members of CHH were pressing for a shelter rather than a soup kitchen. It became apparent, however, that opposition—especially from the Chamber of Commerce—to a facility of this nature in a commercial/residential area would be too difficult to overcome.

before the church membership at a regular business meeting in the fall of 1983, and discussed at subsequent meetings convened to address a multitude of concerns that had arisen. S.H. and G.L. worked diligently to lead the large number of hesitant members of the congregation toward endorsement of a new and untried way of carrying out mission to the community.

On November 2, 1983, the critical meeting to vote on the soup kitchen proposal took place at the Church. As proposed, the plan called for a facility that would provide an evening meal to the hungry and needy along with information and referral assistance. The ministry would be "provided unconditionally" and would be administered by a steering committee composed of members of the Church and HELP, Inc.—rather than by an already taxed First Baptist administrative staff. The goal of the project was to get "the vagrants off the street and ultimately into a more stable situation whenever possible—by satisfying physical needs." Assurances were given that the venture would not entail a large financial investment on the congregation's part and that security would be carefully monitored.

The plan called for an initial six month commitment on the part of the church. At the end of that time, a formal report would be given to determine whether the original goals and objectives were being met. Members of the congregation were assured that the church would have "ultimate authority" over the project; if it became unworkable or undesirable, a majority vote "could simply shut it down."[9]

The initiative to commit First Baptist to permitting the operation of a soup kitchen met with strong resistance within the congregation, including threats to pull back pledges. Fears were expressed that First Baptist was becoming too much of an "inner city" Church, that the presence of a soup kitchen would inhibit efforts to attract younger families and jeopardize a large Church-sponsored daycare program. Some members of the congregation asserted that "street people" would bring violence and danger to the area, that the Church would face liability problems and be overwhelmed by panhandlers and vagrants. Others argued that First Baptist's primary ministry was evangelization rather than "social gospel" initiatives that too often and too easily became a "substitute" for preaching the Gospel. Questions also arose as to whether or not the soup kitchen would be an explicitly enough "Baptist" or "Christian" endeavor. Some members objected that the undertaking would involve some form of government regulation, thereby "bending" the long-standing Baptist principle of separation of church and state.

These and other issues were discussed at length during the evening meeting.[10] As a crowd of angry neighbors gathered outside the church, S.H.

---

9. "Statements of Purpose and Priorities for Consideration."

10. S.H. and G.L. were particularly helpful in shedding light on the discussions over the soup kitchen issue that occurred within the congregation.

put his leadership on the line with an impassioned appeal to the congregation to support the project. G.L. also exhorted the reluctant members of the congregation to endorse the soup kitchen initiative. N.S., who had been waiting in a side-room in the church, was called in to face hostile questioning from those opposed to the project.

After several hours of intense debate, a secret vote was taken. By a two-thirds majority, the proposal passed. First Baptist would carry out a soup kitchen ministry "shaped by the Lordship of Jesus Christ—do unto others."[11]

Not In Our Neighborhood

As might be anticipated, the soup kitchen project generated bitter opposition from the local residents, neighborhood civic associations, and much of the Silver Spring business community. Irate letters were sent to area newspapers. Pickets arrived at Church. Threat of an injunction loomed. The project was assailed as a misguided exercise in "good Samaritanship," as a *fait accompli* imposed on the neighborhood without its consent. While few openly disputed the need to do something about the growing problem of needy people in the area, it was clear that no one wanted a soup kitchen in his or her back yard.[12]

Much of the opposition, both echoing and fanning concerns that had already surfaced within the First Baptist congregation, centered on fears that a soup kitchen would lower property values, increase crime, and draw a derelict and transient population of "panhandling alcoholics" into the area, especially men from the adjacent District of Columbia. Fears were also expressed that the soup kitchen initiative would enlarge and become a much bigger endeavor than had initially been promised by its proponents.[13]

Local business leaders decried the "negative image" that a soup kitchen would project and the manner in which a facility of this nature would prove detrimental to efforts to "upgrade" an aging downtown business district.[14] Street people would allegedly "intimidate" customers and litter property. Charges were also leveled that a disproportionate share of the county's social

11. "Statements of Purpose and Priorities for Consideration."

12. See, for example, Mark Moran's "Feeding the Poor In your Neighborhood?" *The Montgomery Sentinel*, November 9, 1986. Because the soup kitchen was to be housed in church property, First Baptist was not legally required to hold public hearings on the proposal.

13. Strong hostility was directed against N.S. who was accused of "pressuring" the First Baptist Church to open the soup kitchen and of using her influence with county officials (her husband was County Council President) to "do her charitable work in someone else's neighborhood" where "none of the rich and powerful live." See, Allied Civic Association Meeting Notice, June 23, 1984.

14. ST was about a half block away from the heart of a proposed "Super-Block" development project in downtown Silver Spring.

service facilities was already located in the Silver Spring area. Counter proposals called for the establishment of a canteen or a "meals-on-wheels" program where needed.

Members of the First Baptist/CHH steering committee made a concerted effort to respond to these and other public concerns over the soup kitchen initiative. They set up a Neighborhood Liaison Committee to act as a vehicle for complaints, to build trust with the community, and to provide a means for communicating with the neighbors. (The head of this committee, a member of the CHH, was highly adept at defusing opposition and selling the soup kitchen idea in a way that did not "shake people up.") As a First Baptist representative, G.L. also worked tirelessly to allay the hostility and meet concerns surfacing in the local business community and Chamber of Commerce.

Over the next few months, a series of public meetings were held. Repeated assurances were given that the soup kitchen would be "well supervised and promote orderly behavior," that clients who needed "professional help" would get it, and that proper security would be maintained.[15] It was agreed that no "open advertising" of the soup kitchen would occur.[16] Notices were also sent to local merchants and civic associations assuring them that every reasonable step would be taken "to insure a smooth operation."[17]

Ironically, public resistance to the soup kitchen proved to be far more beneficial than detrimental. Opposition drew widespread media visibility to the effort. Every demonstration against the proposal highlighted the heretofore unrecognized problems of poverty and homelessness in the county and brought a new avalanche of calls to First Baptist and HELP, Inc., supporting the effort and offering help. Public opposition that had placed the First Baptist church in siege-like posture also worked to pull together members of the congregation who had previously been divided over the issue.[18]

Throughout the controversy the position taken by county officialdom was mixed. At the time of the CHH initiative, Montgomery County had virtually no social service network for the homeless. Funds for such services

15. Letter to K.B., president of a local civil association from J.M., chairperson of CHH, November 7, 1983.

16. Letter to C.S. from R.R., n.d.

17. As noted before, some opposition centered around concern that the soup kitchen proposal would include an overnight shelter for which some of the members of CHH had been pushing. CHH wanted to use the upper floor of the house for this purpose. (Letter from N.S. to Karen Burns of SOECA, May 12, 1984.)

18. Most, but all local citizen groups were opposed to the initiative. The Silver Spring Center Citizens Advisory Board formally endorsed the soup kitchen as a good "humanitarian commitment" to the less fortunate. Letter to S.H. from SSCCAB president, January 11, 1984.

were "not available." A strong endorsement for the project, however, came from C.S., the head of the Department of Family Resources. C.S. recognized the scope of the problem and was, at the time, seeking to encourage and develop grass-roots efforts on behalf of homelessness independent of government AFDC, food stamp, and entitlement programs. While county officials pointed out that the soup kitchen initiative was a "private effort" over which they had no control other than zoning, health and fire inspection, and other regulatory functions,[19] when the project finally got underway, C.S.'s office funneled a $16,000 Federal Development Block Grant to bring the ST facility up to codes and to make it accessible to the handicapped.

To conclude: after months of protracted debate, public controversy, individual soul searching, and tireless resolve on the part of N.S., S.H., G.L., and others committed to new directions in ministry and to civic responsibility in addressing the growing problem of hunger and homelessness in Montgomery County, renovations on a house owned by and adjacent to the First Baptist Church began.

Work on the house continued at a harried pace through November and into the following month. Finally, on the night of December 16, 1983, the soup kitchen served its first meals—with a staff of eager volunteers markedly outnumbering the three individuals who came to eat. Within six years of operation, ST had served its 200,000th meal.

Organizational Structure

When the first meals were served, ST had no employees except for one individual hired to cook. Since that time, however, the scope of the staffing and the number of services provided has grown substantially. In true Weberian fashion, ST has followed a pattern of routinizing and bureaucratization: what began as a hands-on and relatively free-wheeling project eventually evolved into an increasingly complex organizational initiative. This development resulted from concerns with efficiency and good management, from the desire to provide a greater array of services to the homeless, and in response to the ever increasing number of needy people finding their way to the ST facility.

As a tax-exempt, non-profit organization, ST is guided by a Board of Directors headed by a president and composed of nearly 35 individuals. Salaried employees include a part-time project coordinator, a manager and assistant manager, a full-time resource counselor and assistant, and security guard. Committees and special assignment groups exist for Community and Public Relations, Advocacy, Fund-Raising, Volunteer Coordinator, Facilities, Personnel, and so forth.

In addition to providing the needy with nightly meals, ST auxiliary

---

19. Letter from C.S. to South East Civic Association, June 26, 1984.

services also include operation of a clothes closet, medical clinic,[20] and various counseling and referral services (e.g., federal benefits, housing, detoxification). ST also provides showers, haircuts, metro tokens for travel to overnight shelters, and mail and prescription services.

ST's annual operating budget at the end of its first year was approximately $45,000. That figure has now reached over $100,000. Between 100–150 clients are fed nightly. Food comes from numerous sources: from "sell by" products picked up from local grocery stores, from government food banks and USDA surplus commodities, from area food coops, and from private individuals and corporations.

The bulk of ST operating funds come from local church and synagogue collections and from private individual and corporate donations. Funds are solicited directly from congregations biannually. Money is also received from canister collections and from interest on ST deposits. Fund-raising projects, including benefits sponsored by area service organizations and the ST board of directors, have also been undertaken. Although a non-profit organization, ST does not seek support from the United Way. This is primarily to avoid the "philanthropic imperialism" and loss of organizational autonomy that often accompanies receipt of such funds.

II. Volunteers

In addition to paid staff members, over 400 volunteers work at ST. They do so in "teams" of 8–10 individuals per evening. Each team is headed by a coordinator who is responsible for seeing that the appropriate number of volunteers is present, arranging for substitutes when necessary, and assigning team members to various tasks.

Volunteers come from a number of different constituencies. The largest group come from a network of nearly 30 local churches and three synagogues. These religious institutions provide volunteer teams drawn from a pool of individuals within their membership. Each participating church is responsible for staffing the operation one night a month.

A second group constituting about 20 percent of the work force are court referrals. Most of these individuals have been convicted of minor traffic violations, DWI, or bouncing checks. They normally work off sentences of 1 to 30 hours with arrangements made through the project coordinator and court probation officials. In 1988, 106 court referrals served 4,376 hours at ST.[21]

A third group of volunteers consists of high school students (from both

---

20. This service is provided by Mobile Medical Care, Inc. Mobile Med. is a nonprofit organization operating in Montgomery Country to provide health care for the indigent. It is staffed by two doctors and nurses and serves ST clientel twice monthly.

21. *ST News Report,* July, 1989.

public and parochial schools) doing "community service" requirements for graduation and of adolescent members of churches and synagogues fulfilling confirmation or bar mitzvah obligations. Normally, two or three students work each evening, along with a denominational team and several court referrals.

In addition to the above volunteers, a few unaffiliated "walk-ins" give their time and labor at ST. And occasional clients will also help out during the day by preparing meals, cleaning, painting, or doing yard work in appreciation for services they have received.

Fears voiced during the initial controversy over the ST project that volunteers would not be forthcoming, or that they would "melt away" over time, have proven unwarranted. To the contrary, management problems have occasionally arisen because of trying to coordinate *too many*, rather than too few, volunteers.[22]

For the most part (and with some seasonal variation), ST denominational volunteers remain faithful to their commitments in spite of the inherent frustrations of working with improverished clientele ravaged by chronic mental illness, substance abuse, and an assortment of personal and social maladies. In fact, many volunteers find their work at ST "addictive." While a few confess leaving "heart-broken" or "depressed," or report that they feel "hopeless" in the wake of their meal-time encounter with society's "walking wounded," they nevertheless willingly return each month. The average length of volunteer service among questionnaire respondents was 3.5 years.

When people do stop volunteering, it is usually because of a geographic move or due to the competition of work and family-related demands or commitments. "Burn out" on the meal shifts is infrequent, in part, because team members typically work no more than three or four hours one night a month. However, "burn out" and difficulty finding volunteers is more pronounced in respect to administrative positions on the board of directors and committee work—with which greater investments of time and responsibility are often required.

With some exceptions, court appointees and community service students do not normally continue working at ST after completing their required time, although a few students have stayed on over the summer months. Among the different volunteer constituencies, court referrals usually harbor the more negative attitudes towards both their work assignment and the clients—although it is not the work, *per se*, that is typically begrudged, but its mandatory and court-imposed character. Students tend to find their work experience enriching. This is attested to in conversations with

---

22. These problems usually involve people who show up unannounced to help when there are already enough workers on the team. One evening, for instance, a group of 25 grade school students arrived to help. During the holidays, in particular, the number of volunteers swells substantially.

adult who supervise them and by occasional remarks by students indicating an intention "to do something like this again" after graduation.[23]

Volunteer Profile

Volunteerism is a dynamic process in which individuals are influenced by a multitude of attitudinal, demographic and other background factors.[24] Denominational volunteers at ST are not screened by the ST staff. However, their profile generally matches the socio-demographic variables that correlate with voluntary action participation.

Among questionnaire respondents, the average age is 49. The majority are white (91 percent), female (67 percent), and married (52 percent). Three-fourths have college degrees; 47 percent have combined incomes over $45,000. Politically, 22 percent identified themselves as "conservative," 32 percent as "middle of the road," 37 percent "liberal," and 7 percent "very liberal." Most (78 percent) have previously done some form of volunteer work. However, only a little more than one-third (37 percent) have been actively involved in public issues or some form of community concern in the last two years—suggesting the importance of differentiating between the commitment to volunteerism and the commitment to social activism.

Although only a minority of volunteers (27 percent) indicated that they have had any personal experience with homeless people prior to the involvement at ST, the majority find their work experience both positive and transformative. Respondents often spoke of having their "consciousness raised," their "eyes opened" and their attitudes "turned around" after spending time at ST. Others said that they had become "more sensitive" and "more understanding" and were "less fearful" of the poor and homeless.

23. I spoke with a local parochial high school teacher whose students are required to do 40 hours of community service and to keep a journal of their experiences. Many of these students volunteer at ST. According to the teacher, students often begin with a voyeuristic-like attitude: they want to "see what the homeless are like." He also noted that students who work in shelters and who have more personal contact with the homeless tend to develop a more empathic attitude than those who work at ST where the contact is less direct. One of the most persistent views of the ST student volunteers was the gratitude they expressed that "thank God I don't have to live like that."

24. See, for instance, C. Smith and A. Freedman, *Voluntary Associations: Perspectives on the Literature* (Cambridge, Mass.: Harvard U. Press, 1972); A. K. Tomeh, "Formal Voluntary Associations Participation, Correlates, and Inter-relationships," *Social Inquiry* 43 (1974): 89-122; John C. Anderson and Larry F. Moore, "The Motivation to Volunteer," *Journal of Voluntary Action Research* 7 (1978): 120-125; T. DD. Kemper, "Altruism and Voluntary Action," Pp. 306–338 in D. H. Smith and J. Macaulay, et. al., eds., *Participation in Social and Political Activities* (San Francisco, California: Jossey-Bass, 1980); P.L. Benson, "Interpersonal Correlates of Non-Spontaneous Helping Behavior," *Journal of Social Psychology* 110 (1980): 87–95; J. Allen Williams, Jr. and Suzanne T. Ortega, "The Multidimensionality of Joining," *Journal of Voluntary Action Research* 15 (October/December, 1986): 35–45.

Others reported seeing the homeless in less stereotypical terms, as "more real" and as "individuals." For some, volunteering at ST made it more difficult to "walk by" destitute people on the street. For others, service at ST has generated an evangelistic-like zeal—they now want "to tell other people about homelessness."

The factors that contribute to these changed attitudes and perceptions may seem somewhat puzzling given the transient character of many of the ST clientele and the fact that the majority of volunteers have very limited personal interaction with them. Eighty-five percent of the respondents reported that they had not come to know personally *any* of the clientele who came to ST—other than recognizing a familiar face. In my own work experience, I have observed relatively little personal (as opposed to instrumental) interaction between clients and volunteers. Volunteers who actually socialize with clients (other than counseling and staff people) are few in number. Nor are there many opportunities to do so given the current practice of serving meals in twenty minute shifts, and the administrative concern with keeping clients "moving" after they have eaten in order to avoid public nuisance problems in the neighborhood.

Many of the middle-class volunteers who come to ST are animated with a desire to serve and help. However, they also bring with them fears and anxieties about homeless, alcoholic, and mentally disturbed people with whom they do not normally interact. Over time, these fears and anxieties seem to abate. Familiarity has a positive effect—even under circumstances of limited interaction—on many volunteers who come to discover the basic humanity and diversity of the poor.

Other volunteers bring an already highly empathic attitude to ST. Their good will is associated with the perception that "there but for the grace of God . . . ," or with the conviction that the line between their lives and those of the homeless and destitute is "thin" or simply a matter of "luck" or "fate." In a few cases, I spoke with volunteers who, themselves, had been homeless or in great need at one time. Out of their own real or sensed jeopardy, they have responded to the jeopardy of others.

However, the fact that many ST volunteers develop positive feelings toward homeless people over time, or the fact that some are already empathic, does not mean that their interaction with ST clients is without difficulties or tension. An hour or two at the evening meal can provide first-hand evidence of the difficulties arising out of the vast chasm that separates two very different social classes and the cultural styles each has created in response to its life-world and the exigencies of survival.

When asked what they "least like" about their work at ST, volunteers often complain about the "disrespect" from clients and the ingratitude of those who "demand things," who do not say "please" or "thank you," or who fail to manifest other normative middle-class social amenities. Volunteers are put off by the "smell" and "looks" of clients, their use of "foul language," and their demanding and impolite behavior—which is readily interpreted as arrogance and ungratefulness. As one volunteer complained, "They want us to treat them like kings." A few volunteers will not work in the serving area because of fears of harassment or because of a previous hostile encounter with a rowdy or abusive client. Racial tensions also surface at times as when one white volunteer expressed resentment over being called a "honky" or when another complained that some (black) clients treated him "as though I'm invisible."

The control mechanism in the above situations is refusal of service. In the more extreme cases of rowdiness or drunkenness, the client is removed from the premises. This authority is the prerogative of virtually any volunteer worker and will be assisted by the manager.

Although by no means a majority perspective, volunteers will occasionally voice concerns about "undeserving" and "manipulative" clients who are merely taking advantage of a "free meal" and the goodwill of others. Local merchants and opponents of the ST with whom I have spoken often use this "horror story" mode of symbolic degradation as a way of discrediting the ST project and many of its clients.

Where there is disdain for the "undeserving poor" and those who are not "truly needy," it is usually based on physical appearance rather than any actual knowledge of the situation of particular individuals. This (typically American?) concern with the "undeserving" poor reinforces disillusionment when the same apparently "able bodied" individuals return to the soup kitchen night after night. One volunteer who told me that he had started out at ST with the intention of helping "people in need," later complained in a tone of exasperation: "I never thought I'd be serving the same people after four years."

Negative volunteer perceptions of clients are generally tempered by the conviction that the occasional behavioral problems at ST are due to the stresses of poverty and the pervasiveness of mental and emotional problems and substance abuse among the homeless. Most volunteers recognize that the overwhelming number of those who come to ST are in genuine (sometimes desperate) need, that many do not have (and may never have) jobs, social skills, and the psychological resilience and toughness to bring order and discipline to their lives, that many are on the edge of the poverty line, and that few are "free-loaders." One volunteer put it this way: "I give Shepherd's Table the 90–10 test on this issue—and it passes."

While negative perceptions of clients can be found among volunteers, deeper misgivings and ambiguities (not directed toward ST, *per se*) sometimes surface over whether or not a project of this nature makes any substantive difference in the long-term problem of alleviating poverty and homelessness. This concern arises in discussions over whether or not an "exceptionalist effort" (which is aimed at helping victims) like that of ST is simply creating a "dependency relationship," eroding incentives for self-help, and promoting and reinforcing a class system—rather than addressing underlying structural causes of poverty and homelessness.

One volunteer observed that ST merely "keeps the lid on things." Another saw the project as an "antidote" to more radical social change. Others have observed that ST is essentially a middle-class structure where clients have no real power or authority, no meaningful input, and no evaluative opportunities. While ST does things *for* people, it fails to do so in a way that leads to empowerment and feelings of competence. ST "feeds the hungry" but without adequately addressing the broader range of individual and structural problems related to "why" they are hungry in the first place.

The concern that ST is no more than a band-aid approach to a serious social problem afflicting the entire nation is a minority one, offset for some by the solace of the biblical dictum, "The poor you will always have with you." However, even when questions about the long-term or structural impact of the ST project do arise, people recognize that such concern does not negate the urgency of the task at hand—hungry people need food before they need social or political theorizing.

Organizationally, ST has moved toward more advocacy in addressing political and economic issues related to homelessness—beyond the simple provision of food. Over the years the board has expanded ST services to reconnect people with sources of federal, state, and county aid. Efforts have also been increased to prevent the development of "permanent dependency" and to keep the number of clients from escalating indefinitely. The board has organized public discussions on homelessness and played an active role in informing public officials of serious gaps in social welfare service and housing. The board has also joined with other coalition groups working to raise public awareness about poverty and hunger. Informal lobbying occurs between ST board and staff members and representatives of the county council, government officials, business leaders, and social service agencies. The board has also become increasingly concerned in the last two years with the issue of affordable housing.

However, while the experience of ST staff and volunteers in service delivery has been an important factor in stimulating advocacy for social change, it is not a matter of consensus, either on the board of directors or among the volunteers, as to how far ST ought to move in this direction.

When a controversy erupted several years ago in an adjacent municipality over the enforcement of a ten-year old housing code that would have led to a large number of evictions, several board members expressed concern about ST representatives becoming too involved in the "political turmoil" surrounding the issue. After considerable discussion, the board decided that its president would speak at a People's Public Hearing on the matter; however, his remarks would be confined to "ethical and moral issues" surrounding the human costs of the evictions. Those who wanted a more aggressive/advocacy posture observed that comments of this nature meant that ST representatives would primarily be "talking to themselves" rather than addressing the political realities of the situation.

Questions have also arisen at board meetings regarding the role the ST board should play with respect to political campaigns and support or opposition to candidates vis-a-vis their position on homeless issues.

Volunteers who oppose a greater advocacy role for ST usually do so on the grounds that such activity will create legal problems, threaten the organization's non-profit status, and/or jeopardize the effectiveness of its primary function as a soup kitchen. Others view a "too political" role as threatening the precarious peace with the local neighbors and the truce-like status of ST's current relationship with the Silver Spring business community. The fact that most middle-class volunteers who work at ST do not identify closely with the destitute they serve may also account for their lack of a more radical advocacy commitment to them.

III. Religion, Public Virtue, and Shepherd's Table

The role of religious groups in establishing the "voluntary principle" and in charitable and reform initiatives in the United States is a well-established fact. Religious groups have long organized to promote a wide variety of humanitarian causes and projects for moral and social reform. Evangelical Protestantism stood at the core of the temperance and anti-slavery movements and worked to ameliorate many of the worst excesses of early industrial capitalism. Voluntary societies united the "best hearts, the most willing hands, and the most vigorous and untiring enterprise" in common tasks in which divided denominations pooled their efforts to meet particular needs. Nor were the goals of these enterprises strictly evangelical; as Winthrop Hudson has noted, they were also attempts to remake society, to shift the individual from a preference of self-interest toward a common good and the shaping of public life ("disinterested benevolence").[25]

A project like ST is situated in this historical legacy of religion motivating public virtue and social reform. The questions remain, however, as to what, precisely, constitutes the "religious" dimension of such a project and how this dimension relates to the role of religion in curbing self-interest, addressing social problems, and shaping contemporary American public life.

A Question of Identity

On the one hand, the religious dimension of ST seems readily apparent. In its public literature, ST is presented as a "mission to community" involving a cooperative effort on the part of churches and synagogues, community

---

25. See Winthrop S. Hudson, *Religion in America* (Charles Scribner's: New York, 1973), esp. pg. 150–154.

service organizations, and those who share common concerns for the disadvantaged. Although ST's legal status is that of a non-profit corporation, it is also a "Biblical mission" of the First Baptist Church[26] and a "ministry" to many of its volunteers. ST has been publicly described as "the work of the Lord."[27] This religious dimension is also symbolically encompassed in the soup kitchen's title—"the Shepherd's Table." As narrated above, ST would not exist as it is now constituted had it not been for the leadership and support of religion-based organizations such as HELP, Inc. and the First Baptist Church. And, as noted, a core network of mainline religious denominations make the daily operation of ST possible. These denominations provide the vast majority of volunteers and are the primary source of sustained financial support; nearly 40 percent of ST's current operating budget comes from these sources.

However, in spite of the above religion based characteristics, ST is, in fact, a social service project in which religion as an organizational identity has virtually no public visibility. ST is a non-profit "corporation." It is governed by a "board." It serves "clients" and functions along rational bureaucratic lines. The facility itself displays no visible religious symbols or signs. There are no organized prayers at meals, no "moments of silence." There are no scripture study or bible class programs, no religious music, no organized "spiritual counseling." No religious literature is made available to clients and proselytizing by volunteers is strictly prohibited. Public relations efforts "studiously avoid" any religious emphasis other than mention of the fact that ST is a inter-denominational initiative.

In all of the above respects, the religious identity of ST is problematical. It is questionable, therefore, whether or not ST can be viewed as an expression of religious cultural hegemony or even a form of public religion. While ST fulfills a prophetic role by reshaping a vision of public order—showing care and concern in the face of "Reaganism" and a culture of civic abandonment—the project also illustrates how a religious-based initiative is transformed into a religiously vague or markedly secular enterprise in the public sphere or, ironically, when it involves a cooperative endeavor among religious groups. What seems to be at work at ST is a process in which institutionalized religion functions not primarily as a visible and distinctive culture-forming force but as a social mechanism for the practice of private virtue and ritualized self-enhancement.

The flattening of the religious dimension of the ST project stems from two primary factors. To begin with, although ST is an independent sector

26. When the proposal for the soup kitchen was presented to the congregation, members were assured that no individual would be "handcuffed from or prevented from performing any spiritual counseling or ministry that that individual deems appropriate." *Soup Kitchen Proposal Doc.*, November 2, 1983.

27. See remarks by the public relations chair. See, *Woodside Messenger*, August 30, 1985.

initiative, it is hardly "independent" at all. ST is embedded in a web of relations with the government and for-profit sectors: government funds made renovation of the Bonifant Street house possible[28]; government funds pay the salary of ST's resource counselor; the county and municipal court systems provide labor resources in the form of referral workers; business organizations deliver an assortment of material and financial resources that make operation of the soup kitchen possible.

These entanglements preclude any explicit religious presence in the public operation or visibility of ST. They inhibit both a "too political" advocacy role by the board of directors that might challenge the local status quo *and* they inhibit a too prophetic religious role that might otherwise be expected of a denominationally-based initiative of this nature.

Second, ST's cooperative interfaith character also contributes to the invisibility of its religious dimension. Because ST involves joint denominational efforts, the project cannot have a "sectarian" orientation—lest some individual or denominational group take offense. The religious presence at ST must be one of "civility."[29] "Civility" in this case, however, means that the problem of cooperative religious pluralism is addressed by dissolving any specific religious presence, symbolism, or identity.[30] Thus it is not without irony that the religious cooperation which is lauded as one of ST's strongest features also manages to cancel out anything that might be construed as giving the project an organizationally explicit religion-based social identity.

Volunteer Perceptions of Religious Identity

The question of the relationship between the secular and religious dimensions of the ST project is not problematic for most volunteers or for the members of the board of directors. The overwhelming majority of those involved at ST support the policy of not allowing a religious presence in the form of proselytizing or overt religious "ministry" (including 89 percent of the questionnaire respondents). Most believe that a visible religious presence would "complicate things," constitute an "unfair exchange," and have

28. Equipment for the kitchen was also received from Montgomery County school surplus supplies.

29. See, John M. Cuddihy, *No Offense: Civil Religion and Protestant Taste* (New York: Seabury Press, 1978), 7.

30. For instance, a minor controversy arose over the issue of whether or not lilies would be placed on the ST tables at Easter time. A pictorial representation of Christ was also removed from the ST dining area because of an objection from a board member.

It is also noteworthy that, although an interreligious initiative, the interaction between religious groups in the operation of ST is limited. Volunteer teams consist primarily of members of the same denomination. Only one denominational team works any given evening. Volunteers thus have limited opportunities for interaction with members of other faiths. This is less true, however, with regard to ST board and salaried staff who interact regularly with different denominational groups and individuals.

the practical consequence of "scaring people away"—both clients and volunteers. Even where the idea of a more explicit religious dimension is endorsed, most individuals are uncertain as to what form it would or could take.

When volunteers express ambiguity over the religious dimension of ST's identity, they typically resolve the tension by equating religion with moral action and deed: ST is "theology of the dishpan," of "doing good" and "feeding the hungry"—rather than the religion of creed, ritual, or institution. As one respondent put it, "we don't preach religion, we practice it." (Whether or not clients interpret the activity in this way is another matter.)

Those volunteers who want a more explicit religious presence (typically in the form of a prayer before meals or a "moment of silence") argue for the necessity of some public affirmation of the Judeo-Christian tradition of the sponsoring organizations. For these individuals, ST is not first and foremost a corporate entity or a civic organization but a "church ministry," a "Gospel effort," a "Biblical call" that ought to bring people together, ennoble the disenherited "with an encouraging word," and feed the spirit as well as the stomach.

The manner in which the secular, bureaucratic character of ST as a public initiative conflicts with the vision and values of those who view the project as a form of religious ministry is illustrated by the following incident.

In response to loitering, crowdedness, and control problems, the board adopted a policy last year requiring clients to eat in three twenty-minute "shifts." Every individual must leave at the end of a shift and return to the porch to line up should they wish to eat again. This plan was hailed as both necessary and beneficial to volunteers and clients alike. As a result, there has been less disorder, meals are served more efficiently, people sit down to a clean table, and the serving area is less congested.

Not everyone approved of the changes, however. Volunteers who viewed their commitment through the lens of religious ministry felt that the new policy worked to depersonalize the client/volunteer interaction in the name of organizational efficiency. "Herding people" in and out recapitulated the bureaucratic and sterile professionalism associated with the government and corporate sectors of society while diminishing the charism of "personalism" and the radical "Gospel idea" of love and openness that some volunteers saw as integral to their "witness" at ST. These volunteers asserted that those who have fallen through the cracks of the welfare state "need more than food," that shift-serving diminishes their opportunity for experiencing genuine community, hospitality, and compassion. Shift-serving had the moral consequence of reinforcing the sense of powerlessness among the homeless clients, thereby further threatening their dignity and respect.

Individual Religion

While related to its corporate and civic character and to the practical problems surrounding interreligious cooperation, the invisibility of religion at ST also relates to broader social and cultural trends, notably the highly privatized character of religion in contemporary American culture—by which faith experience is removed from a community and institutional basis and reduced to the purely subjective dimension of individual opinion and attitude. In this context, the influence of religion is confined almost exclusively to the private rather than the public sector.

Observers of the American religious landscape have been noting for some time now the pervasiveness of "privatized religion," the weakening of mainline denominational loyalties, the loss of a common moral vocabulary, and the emergence of Durkheim's "cult of the individual"—a cultural ethos in which individual psychological, emotional, and social needs take precedence over inherited ties to a normative community.[31] These dynamics, in turn, have been associated with broader trends toward secularization marked by the increasing differentiation of religion from the public realm.[32]

While ST is hardly the New Jerusalem, it is a source of moral and religious energy in the community at large. It is a place in which people literally "serve others." Nearly all of the respondents (94 percent) belong to a denomination. Sixty percent attend church or synagogue "once a week or more"; another 23 percent "once or twice a month." Fifty-eight percent reported that religion was "very important" in their lives.

However, in spite of this profile of moral energy and religious affiliation and commitment, the vocabulary used by most volunteers to articulate why they work at ST is not primarily a religious one. It is, instead, predominantly therapeutic. During the interview process, individuals were asked to respond to the open-ended question: "Why do you do volunteer work?" They were then asked to indicate (on a four point scale) the importance in their own lives of each of the following reasons for volunteering: civic responsibility, religious responsibility, returning a favor, fulfilling a commitment or obligation, family tradition, personal psychological satisfaction.

The most frequently given responses to the open-ended question related volunteering to self-fulfillment or personal psychological satisfaction ("it makes me feel good," "personal satisfaction," "I get satisfaction out of helping," "it's good for me," "it makes me feel better," "it's part of a process of learning about myself and life"). Volunteerism was also clearly linked to self-perception ("it's in my bloodstream," "I'm issue oriented," "I'm a rescuer").

31. See, Bellah, et al., *Habits of the Heart;* Thomas Luckmann, *The Invisible Religion* (London: Macmillan, 1967); Christopher Lasch, *The Culture of Narcissism* (New York: Norton, 1978).

32. See, for example, Dean R. Hoge and David Roozen, eds. *Understanding Church Growth and Decline, 1950–1978* (New York: Pilgrim Press, 1979); Wade C. Roof and William McKinney, *American Mainline Religion: Its Changing Shape and Future* (New Brunswick: Rutgers University Press, 1987); and, Robert Wuthnow, *The Restructuring of American Religion: Society and Faith Since World War II* (Princeton New Jersey: Princeton University Press, 1988).

These responses were followed in frequency by the perception of civic responsibility and/or social reciprocity ("you just can't just take from society," "you need to give something back to the community," "I feel like I'm fortunate and I want to give back," "helping others is a part of society," "it's the pay-back-society thing"); followed by remarks relating to necessity and objective need ("something needs to be done," "it has to be done," "somebody needs to do it," "There's a need, I feel a person should do it"). Next came comments that emphasized the nature of the work itself ("it's a worthy cause," "the sense of sharing talents and common goals," "I wanted 'hands-on' experience").

What is most noteworthy is that very few volunteers described the motivations behind their helping behavior at ST with reference to religious values or symbols. Those who did used expressions such as "this is a response to who I am as a spiritual person," "this is part of what is required as a person of faith," "because the Gospel says so," "a good Jew should do something like this." However, these responses were infrequent and rarely the primary vocabulary of those who were interviewed.

When then asked to indicate how important specifically listed reasons (civic responsibility, religious responsibility, returning a favor, fulfilling a commitment or obligation, family tradition, personal psychological satisfaction) were to them for volunteering, respondents rated "personal psychological satisfaction" as "very important" or "most important" 87 percent of the time. This response was followed in frequency (sixty-eight percent) by "religious responsibility"—ahead of all other categories other than "personal psychological satisfaction." (The third most frequently given response to the question as to what they "most liked" about their volunteer work at ST was that it made them "feel good.")

These responses raise a curious issue: although the vast majority of volunteers did not use a religious grammar in their open ended responses, when asked specifically, sixty-eight percent rated "religious responsibility" as "very important" or "most important" as their motive for volunteering. We are left with the question as to why people view religion as important in their lives, impute religious meaning to their helping behavior, initiate that behavior through religious institutions, but resist describing it in religious terms?

If we approach volunteer work in terms of cost/benefit ratio and assume that people do not give something without the expectation of receiving something in return, we see that "personal psychological satisfaction" is a major benefit (and, by implication incentive) among ST volunteers. However, it is clearly a distortion to suggest that the majority of those who work at ST do so *merely* because of their own utilitarian self-interest and needs for personal psychological satisfaction. (Nor should it be assumed that there is something inherently wrong with the feeling of psychological well-being that accompanies helping others, as if compassion needed to be grim and dour.)

ST volunteers are motived by the awareness of an objective sense of need and societal responsibility—a fact suggesting at least a mid-range level of moral sophistication above purely egotistical and self-center needs. Intrinsic and associational rewards are also clearly important in ST volunteerism. The most consistently reported intrinsic reward was the opportunity for serving a "useful purpose," "doing good" and "helping others," or "seeing another person smile." Volunteers also clearly derive enjoyment and reward from the camaraderie of working with their friends and like-minded individuals, many of whom are drawn from their own denominations.

The concern with helping others, the perception of objective need, and the experience of social solidarity notwithstanding, the nature of volunteerism at ST nevertheless points to the power and pervasiveness of the pursuit of self-fulfillment and self-enhancement in contemporary American culture—whereby the incentives for helping behavior are not first and foremost articulated in terms of what such behavior does for the recipients but in terms of what it does for the individual volunteer. Many of the volunteers with whom I spoke made it clear that their involvement at ST is an association pursued primarily on the basis of the benefits they derive from it rather than because of the effect of their labors on the lives of others. This therapeutic perspective found its most extreme expression in the volunteer who remarked, "Look, let's face it, I'm selfish. No matter how much good the program [ST] does for these people [the homeless], the experience here does immesurably more for me!" This statement intimates a concept of "good citizenship" that is essentially privatized, self-serving, and individualistic— not civic or religious in character.

It is also relevant that even when a respondent used religious language to describe his or her motives for volunteering, the vocabulary often implied a churchless or a "do it yourself" religiosity. When asked specifically to what extent their work at ST was "shaped by your particular denominational perspective," 41 percent of the respondents indicated "not at all," while only 9 percent indicated that it was "exclusively" so. Although the vast majority of volunteers described their coming to ST *through* their denominations, they also made it clear that it was not primarily *because of* their denominations. The practice of religion that many volunteers associate with the faith dimension of their work at ST came from something inward and personal rather than from ties with the traditions of a historical community or an objective institution. Nor did this faith dimension involve normative consent or value consensus or commitment to corporate or community religious goals—other than the assumption that actions speak louder than words and that moral behavior *ipso facto* constitutes religious behavior.

The above responses need to be analyzed along more denominational specific lines than I have attempted here. They may reflect, in part, the emphasis (or lack of) on "social ministry" within specific religious groups and/or where these particular groups fall on the liberal/conservative religious spectrum.[33] In the aggregate, however, they point to the pervasiveness of the cultural separation of faith from church and the loosening of denominational loyalties that have been identified by other scholars studying mainline American religion.[34] Such responses indicate how deeply the privatizing and individualizing influences of American culture have penetrated religious institutions and how individuals conceptualize and act upon their religious identities. What seems to matter in American religious life is less the shared experiences and affirmation of a community of like-minded believers and more a person's own journey and quest in search of an acceptable belief system or a generalize and diffuse "spiritual" fulfilllment. Subjective aspects of faith have expanded as ascriptive and command attachments have declined[35]. This finding is entirely congruent with the emergence of the so-called therapeutic personality, a personality that interprets reality in psychological and individualistic terms and that expresses a declining commitment to community and goals which lie outside of the imperial self. It is also one of the principal reasons why the invisibility of religion is not problematic for most ST volunteers. Religion is a preeminently "private affair," not a matter of public policy, concern, or identity.

Conclusion

The story of ST demonstrates that individuals can and do make a difference, that persistence and resolve and risk-taking can bring about social change and turn people toward the needs of others. ST also shows that there are people who want to cultivate in their lives a larger form of purpose and humanity and that they will do so when encouraged and given an appropriate opportunity. Analysis of a project like ST also sheds light on the broader question of the role of religion in the culture of modernity.

In a recent article on the significance of religion and spirituality for the identification and alleviation of social problems in advanced industrial societies, sociologist James Beckford noted—following Simmel—that, as religion and spirituality have become more disconnected from institutional frameworks and more autonomous, they have also become more vulnerable to cooptation or "hijacking" by various interest groups and/or social activists trying to combat social problems.

This observation is relevant in some degree to the ST project. Although largely a church-based initiative in its inception, those who worked to mobilize people on behalf of the project also included activists who recog-

33. Impressionistically, I found volunteers who appeared to be more orthodox/fundamentalist in their religious orientation to be more insistent on the religious character of their ST volunteerism. This would substantiate the point that fundamentalism is an attempt to nullify the consequences of modernism and make religion relevant to all aspects of an individual's life.

34. See, especially, Roof and McKinney, *American Mainline Religion*.

35. Ibid.

nized the strategic utility (i.e., the financial and labor base) of involving religious organizations on behalf of the homeless.

Beckford further notes that religious organizations can have a diffuse influence in modern industrial society if their ideas and values are mediated and refracted by intervening networks.

ST is one such mediating structure. As such, however, the history of ST reinforces Beckford's observation that the effectiveness of religion in modern industrial society is largely a function of the degree to which it conforms to the generally secular logic of the process of politics and public administration. As Beckford notes, in this type of situation "religious actors and agencies do not specify the terms on which discussion of social problems takes place in public—they merely tailor their contributions to fit the secular template."[36]

In response to both internal and external exigencies, ST has to a large degree "tailor[ed] [its] contributions to fit the secular template." Some of this tailoring has come about as a consequence of specific policy decisions while other aspects have been of a more willy-nilly nature.

An initiative like that of ST clearly exemplifies the long-standing tradition in American society for religiously motivated and church-based civil involvement. However, it does so in a manner that tends to compromise and diminish religion's character as a *distinctive* culture-forming force. This development is a consequence of both the nature of the public/private nexus (hence raising separation of church and state issues) and of the exigencies of joint, religiously motivated public activity in a highly pluralistic society. These structural factors permit mainline religion a role in the public sphere, but they also contribute to the weakened visibility and influence of mainline religious institutions and values on American society. This diminishing is readily accommodated by individuals immersed in a cultural ethos that relegates the religious impulse to the purely private and subjective realm.

A project like that of ST thus points, paradoxically, to both the enduring role of religion and the independent sector on American life and public policy and to the dynamics of secularization, especially as the latter is associated with the social differentiation and segmentation of religion.

William D. Dinges

---

36. James Beckford, "The Sociology of Religion and Social Problems." *Sociological Analysis* 51, 1 (Spring, 1990): 1–13.

THE CATHOLIC BISHOPS AND THE NUCLEAR DEBATE: A CASE STUDY OF THE INDEPENDENT SECTOR

J. Bryan Hehir

The purpose of this paper is to examine the role of the Catholic bishops in the nuclear debate as a case study of a religious actor in the independent sector. To define the topic this way is to acknowledge but not to pursue two broader questions: a survey of other religious actors in the independent sector and an evaluation of the war and peace issue in non-nuclear terms. While this paper can allude to these issues, it cannot analyze them.

This analysis will proceed in three steps: first, locating the role of the Catholic bishops in the independent sector; second, analyzing their participation in the nuclear debate; and third, assessing trends which will shape the nuclear question—for church and state—in the coming decade.

I. The Catholic Bishops and the Independent Sector: Defining a Religious Role

In this paper the "independent sector" is understood as the arena of non-governmental organizations. More specifically, the participants in the independent sector are organizations or institutions which have the objective of influencing public debate and public policymaking in the United States but are not themselves part of the government or affiliated with any political party.

Religious organizations are one type of participant in the independent sector. As public institutions they share many of the characteristics of other participants. But the public role of religion is both a persistent theme of American history and a continually debated topic in the American political and legal system.[1] In this opening section I will comment generally on the place of religious institutions in the American political system and then I will examine the way the Catholic bishops define their role in that system.

---

1. Cf.: J. C. Murray, *We Hold These Truths: Catholic Reflections on the American Proposition* (N.Y.: Sheed and Ward, 1960); R. J. Neuhaus, *The Naked Public Square: Religion and Democracy in America* (Grand Rapids, MI: Wm. B. Eerdmans Publishing Co., 1984).

A. *The Setting for Religious Actors:*
A Secular State in a Pluralistic Society

The public role of religious institutions in American culture is framed in terms of the relations of church and state. The two principal characteristics of the church-state relationship are the secular character of the state and the religiously pluralistic nature of American society.

The church-state relationship in the United States is governed by the First Amendment. Although the word "separation" is never mentioned in the text of the Amendment, the shorthand description of its meaning is that it upholds "the separation of church and state". The description is accurate if it is precisely defined. The combination of the "no establishment" clause and the "free exercise" clause means that religious institutions should expect neither favoritism nor discrimination from the state in the performance of their public roles. This church-state phraseology is designed to regulate the relationship of the institution of the church and the institution of the state. It is a narrow, precisely defined and critical question. But it leaves much unsaid about the public role of religion in the United States. This larger public role falls not within the ambit of church-state relations but in the context of church-society relations.

No idea is more centrally located in the American political tradition than the distinction of society and state. The state is only part of the society; it is constitutionally limited to fulfill specific functions, but it is never to be identified with the society as such. Such an identification is the essence of a totalitarian state. To accept the separation of church and state does not mean accepting any notion that the church should be separate from the wider civil society. It is precisely in this wider ambit of freedom that religious communities exercise a public role through preaching, teaching, educational and social institutions and the specific voices they bring to wider public policy debates.

The role the churches play in the societal order is that of a voluntary association. While the phrase is not a theological term and does not capture the inner meaning of a religious institution, it is a very accurate description of the public role of religious bodies in the United States. Like other voluntary agencies in the independent sector—unions, cultural organizations, professional societies—the religious institutions are social groups organized for public purposes and they are expected to shape and contribute to the public life of the nation.

There is no indication in history, law, or policy that the separation clause was meant to silence the voices of organized religion. The secular character of the state is assured by the content of the First Amendment, but a secular state does not mean the advocacy of a secularist society which in principle would seek to exclude religious insight, values, or activity in the public life of the society. A secular state leaves the religious institutions free to function in their congregations and in the public arena.

The second characteristic of the religion-state relationship in the United States is the challenge posed by an explicitly religiously pluralistic society. Religious pluralism is the native soil from which the American experiment grew: the society defined itself as religiously plural; it was not something imposed on the nation in the style of the religious wars of the sixteenth century. The constitutional guarantee of freedom of religion for every citizen and each religious institution is designed to produce religious pluralism as a societal fact. Fr. John Courtney Murray, the Jesuit theorist of religious pluralism, provided a working definition of its meaning:

> The coexistence within the one political community of groups who hold divergent and incompatible views with regard to religious questions—those ultimate questions that concern the nature and destiny of man within a universe that stands under the reign of God. Pluralism therefore implies disagreement and dissension within the community. But it also implies a community within which there must be agreement and consensus.[2]

The Murray definition provides a starting-point for examining the particular challenges of religion and the state in the American setting. First, the fact of religious pluralism means that there is no one religious institution confronting the state in American society but a vast variety of religious forces. The terms "church" and "state" often convey the sense of a bipolar dynamic. This does not fit the American reality. Secondly, the specific political-moral challenge facing the U.S. political system is the need to fashion from religious pluralism some coherent moral framework for public policy. This is a necessity at any time in society, but it is particularly urgent at the present time when the moral factor of the public debate is often the most contentious. From abortion to nuclear policy, American society in the 1980s divided less along technical lines than in terms of the moral quality of the action proposed. On an increasing range of questions, it is becoming very difficult to make "good policy" without some sense of what is "right policy".

In the 1980s the Catholic bishops entered the public debate (not for the first time, but in a more visible manner than previously) over what constituted "right policy" in four areas: nuclear strategy, equity in the economy, U.S. policy in Central America and the abortion issue.[3]

---

2. Murray, cited, p. x.

3. Cf. J. Castelli, *The Bishops and the Bomb* (N.Y.: Image Books, Doubleday and Co., 1983); K. Briggs, "Catholic Bishops Oppose Administration on Central America," *New York Times* (Feb. 21, 1982); B. Van Voorst, "The Churches and Nuclear Deterrence," *Foreign Affairs* 61 (1983) p. 827–852.

The next section seeks to set forth the perspective and principles in light of which the bishops defined their role in the public arena.

B. A *Religious Institution in the Secular Arena:* *Perspective and Principles*

The U.S. bishops' involvement in the nuclear debate of the 1980s is an example of an "independent sector" institution at work. It is also an example of the wider social ministry of the church. On each of the four issues cited above the bishops not only had to propose and defend a specific position but also had to explain to their own congregations and others how they understood their religious and civic responsibilities in the public arena. A summary of how the Catholic church sees its role in the public order can be grasped by examining three questions: constitutional, theological, and pastoral.

The *constitutional* question is how the church understands its relationship with the state. I have outlined above an interpretation of the First Amendment which leaves religious organizations free to function but also free of any state support or privilege. If this accurately portrays the political intent of the Amendment, Catholic teaching on church and state will agree in both principle and practice. Acceptance of this interpretation of the church-state relationship would not have been so clear-cut prior to the Second Vatican Council. The conception of church-state relations in possession in Catholic teaching up through the 1950s was that the normative position was "the Catholic state" while other constitutional arrangements (like the one in the United States) could only be tolerated and never approved in principle.[4]

The Council's *Declaration on Religious Liberty* (1965) displaced the notion of the Catholic state with a conception of church-state relations based on three principles. The first was the acceptance of religious pluralism as the expected condition in relation to which the church would pursue its ministry. Pluralism was neither to be resisted nor repressed: within the framework of religious pluralism, the right of every person to religious freedom was affirmed as a demand of the natural law. The second principle was the acknowledgment of the secularity of the state: the state envisioned in the conciliar text is not "the Catholic state" of the post-Reformation era but the constitutional state whose powers are limited by law. The third principle was the freedom of the church: it affirms that the church seeks only one objective from the state, the freedom to function and to fulfill its ministry. Pluralism, secularity, and freedom—these three ideas make it possible for the church to maintain its independence of the state, to affirm the state's limited but

4. J. C. Murray, The Problem of Religious Freedom, *Theological Studies* 25 (1964) p. 503–575.

essential role in society, and to endorse a constitutional order which protects and fosters religious liberty for individuals and communities.

At the same time the acceptance of the separation of church and state embodied in the American constitutional system does not extend to a separation of the church from the society. John Courtney Murray used the liberal distinction of state and society as part of the argument he made prior to and during Vatican II to overturn the normative status of the Catholic state.[5] To accept the separation of the church from the state does not mean accepting a passive or marginal status for the church in society. The church-state question governs the juridical relationship of these two institutions; it does not control the activity of the church in the wider fabric of society. The church's social activity is exercised, in part, in and through "the independent sector," where the church joins other participants in the public argument.

In summary, the Catholic Church finds the American constitutional framework in accord with contemporary Catholic teaching. The teaching endorses the independence of church and state, sees the Church's principal forum of witness in the wider society, and accepts as a social (not theological) description of the Church that of a voluntary association with a specific capability to assess social policy and issues in light of religious values and moral principles.

The *theological* question is how the Church understands and establishes the basis for its social ministry—its participation in the public life of society. In Catholic teaching the foundation of the social ministry is its religious conviction about the dignity of the human person. The reason why the Church addresses issues of a political or social significance is to protect and promote the transcendent dignity of the person. The pivotal text on this theme is found in Vatican II's document, *The Pastoral Constitution on the Church in the Modern World* (1965):

> The role and competence of the church being what it is, she must in no way be confused with the political community, nor bound to any political system. For she is at once a sign and safeguard of the transcendence of the person.[6]

The decisive contribution of Vatican II to the social ministry of the Church was to locate defense of the person—and, by extension, the protection and promotion of human rights—at the center of the church's life and work.

The quotation from the Council, however, highlights a persistent tension in the Church's social ministry. Such a ministry is to maintain the transcendence of the Church from any particular political system, and yet to engage the Church in issues directly affected by the political process. *The*

5. Ibid.

6. Vatican II, *The Pastoral Constitution on the Church in the Modern World (Gaudium et Spes)* 1965, #76.

Pastoral Constitution has been the fundamental reference point for the universal church in keeping the balance of an engaged public ministry without compromising the Church's religious origin, nature, and destiny. The key texts are paragraphs 40–42 in *The Pastoral Constitution* which affirm the following principles:

1) the ministry of the Church is religious in origin and purpose; the Church has no specifically political charism;
2) the religious ministry has as its primary objective serving the reign of God; the Church is, in a unique way, the "instrument" of the Kingdom in history;
3) as the Church pursues its religious ministry it should contribute to four objectives which have direct social and political consequences; these objectives are protecting human dignity, promoting human rights, cultivating the unity of the human family, and contributing a sense of meaning to every aspect of human activity.

These three principles define a role for the Church in the world which is religious in its nature and finality but politically significant in its consequences. The mode of the Church's engagement in the political arena is "indirect". Since the Church has no specifically political charism, its proper competence is to address the moral and religious significance of political questions. This indirect address to political issues also sets limits on the means the Church should use in pursuing its four designated goals. Means which are expected and legitimate for properly political entities are not necessarily legitimate for the Church. The casuistry of keeping the Church's engagement in the political order "indirect" involves an endless series of choices and distinctions. But the effort must be made precisely because the alternatives to an indirect engagement are equally unacceptable: either a politicized church or a church in retreat from human affairs. The first erodes the transcendence of the gospel; the second betrays the incarnational dimension of Christian faith. The Catholic Church is engaged in the public arena on the basis of this "activist" but "indirect" understanding of its public ministry.

The *pastoral* question concerns how the church should fulfill this indirect role. The church has three principal assets to use in the independent sector: ideas, institutions, and a constituency.[7]

In order to participate in the public arena of a complex bureaucratic democracy like the United States, these three resources are necessary. The ideas represent a systematic tradition of reflection about the relationship of

---

7. For a fuller elaboration, cf. J. B. Hehir, *Religion and Politics in the 1980s and 1990s: Evaluating the Catholic Position and Potential* (Lansing, MI: Michigan Catholic Conference, 1989).

religious values and moral principles to social institutions and public policy. The tradition may stand in need of testing and development in order to address contemporary questions, but it acts as a bridge, providing a point of comparison and contact with the wisdom of other times. The institutions provide a means of projecting ideas and positions into the public dialogue. Institutions—social and educational—allow the church to match its words with deeds; they also allow the church to be present where the public contention on issues takes place—from hospitals to shelters for the homeless, from parishes to universities, from schools to legislatures. The constituency of the church, its membership taken as a whole, is the pivotal element in the church's presence in society. The "power" of religious organizations lies significantly in their capacity to share a vision, a set of values, and a perspective on personal and public life with their members.

The U.S. Catholic Bishops' two pastoral letters on peace and the economy[8] were designed to relate its ideas, institutions, and constituency. By projecting ideas into the public arena, by articulating a framework for assessing social policy, and by encouraging reflection and debate within the community of the church, the pastoral letters were one way for a religious community to contribute to the religion, morality, and politics debates.

The experience was an attempt to speak to both the ecclesial and civil communities simultaneously. While the pastoral letters provoked response within both forums, it has been the discussion within the church which has raised pastoral questions about the relationship of the voice of the institution and the views of the community. Contending in the civil arena will undoubtedly catalyze some contending within the church. For a church with as strong a tradition of authority as Catholicism has, the pastoral letters provoked a debate about the limits and binding power of episcopal documents as well as about the scope and limits of freedom of conscience on matters of social policy.[9] This specific form of the conscience and authority relationship has been analyzed within the context of a wider debate on the same topic touching the role of theologians in the church, the role of Catholic universities, and the nature of pluralism within a Catholic context.

The pastoral letters, therefore, provoked a double debate. The principles and policy conclusions were discussed widely in the secular academic and policy communities. Within the church, the same discussion took place, but it had this added note of "conscience and authority" themes. The link

8. National Conference of Catholic Bishops, *The Challenge of Peace: God's Promise and Our Response* (Washington: U.S. Catholic Conference, 1983); same, *Economic Justice for All: Pastoral Letter on Catholic Social Teaching and the U.S. Economy* (Washington: U.S. Catholic Conference, 1986).

9. For a summary of the literature cf. J. Langan, "Notes on Moral Theology 1984," *Theological Studies* 46 (1985) p. 80–101; D. Hollenbach, "Notes on Moral Thology 1985;" same, 47 (1986) p. 117–34; also, G. Weigel, *Tranquillitas Ordinis* (N.Y.: Oxford University Press, 1987); M. Novak, *Moral Clarity in the Nuclear Age* (Nashville, TN: Thomas Nelson, Inc., 1983).

between the two arenas of discourse is the fact that the shaping of a consensus within the church is a key test of how religious communities witness in the public arena. Consensus can be shaped at different levels of specificity; agreement on broad themes of social policy may be possible even if consensus on specific recommendations is not present.

The Catholic church's teaching on war and peace has always had two functions—to inform the individuals' consciences within its own constituency about moral choices and to help shape public policy in light of moral principles.

II. The Catholic Bishops and the Nuclear Question: Describing a Position

The reception accorded the Catholic bishops position on nuclear policy in the 1980s must be seen in light of the context of the nuclear debate itself and the content of the moral teaching. The bishops spoke to the nuclear question twice in the last decade: in the pastoral letter, *The Challenge of Peace*, and in a subsequent analysis, *A Report on The Challenge of Peace and Policy Developments 1983–1988*. While the first document received the greatest amount of attention and commentary, the second text illustrates the on-going role in the nuclear debate which the bishops seek to play in the independent sector. Both documents, of course, were part of the broader nuclear argument of the 1980s.

A. The Shape of the Nuclear Argument: The 1980s

The 1980s produced significant shifts in the way the nuclear question was analyzed and argued in the United States. During the course of the decade, the discussion moved from what was called the "New Cold War" of the early 1980s to predictions about "the end of the Cold War" in 1989.[10] Similarly, the arms-control agenda moved from a stalemate on negotiations in 1980–84 to the first nuclear arms reduction treaty of the era in 1987. These broad shifts overshadow more specific moves in the nuclear debate, but these were hardly passing details. The 1980s saw a change in *who* talked about the nuclear danger and *how* responses to it were evaluated. These changes created a receptivity to the Catholic bishops statements, and the statements, in turn, helped to shape the wider argument.

The early 1980s manifested a change in the constituency and character of the public debate about nuclear weapons.[11] In their pastoral letter the

---

10. Cf.: S. Hoffmann, *Dead Ends: American Foreign Policy in the New Cold War* (Cambridge, MA: Ballinger Co., 1983); M. Mandelbaum, "Ending the Cold War," *Foreign Affairs* 66 (1988) p. 16–36.

11. R. Tucker, "The Nuclear Debate," *Foreign Affairs* 63 (1984) p. 1–32.

bishops referred to a "New Moment" in the nuclear argument which was marked in the first instance by an expanding circle of participants in the nuclear discussion. The nuclear danger had been a threat to all people, but those who analyzed and debated the danger had hitherto been confined to small groups of highly specialized professionals.[12] The public was not prevented from entering the discussion, but for most of the nuclear age they have not been inclined to enter the circle. In 1980–1985, the specialists were joined by physicians, religious leaders, and a substantial corps of citizens who espoused some version of the Nuclear Freeze. The broadening of the debate inevitably changed the shape of the questions. The wider public was interested in the detailed assessments of crises stability, windows of vulnerability and assured destruction, but it also wished to raise the human costs and consequences of the nuclear relationship, the chance of human error even in the most stable nuclear regime, and the need for more far-reaching efforts of control and disarmament than the technical debate usually addressed. The public's emphasis on the human dimensions of the nuclear issue in turn opened the way for a serious moral assessment of the nuclear relationship.

But the changes of the 1980s were not limited to who was in the nuclear discussion. The character of the nuclear debate shifted even in the elite community of experts, and nothing symbolized the shift of tone and themes in the nuclear debate more clearly than the way deterrence itself was analyzed. For thirty years deterrence had been the cornerstone of nuclear policy; it was the common assumption and ground for the nuclear debate. The other issues were about how much was needed to deter, what kind of deterrence was most stable, or how to relate deterrence to arms control. By the mid-1980s, in both the popular and the professional debates, deterrence itself was under review, and in some places under attack. The critique of deterrence came from the left and the right of the political spectrum, and both sides lodged political and moral arguments against this organizing idea of nuclear strategy for the previous three decades.[13] Even in the technical and professional community of scientists and strategists, one could find discussion of "going beyond deterrence".[14] The rhetoric surrounding President Reagan's plan for a Strategic Defense Initiative (SDI) appealed to the these critiques of deterrence. But the arguments about deterrence were broader than the supporters of SDI. By the end of the 1980s deterrence remained securely in place; all sides found it was easier to criticize the

12. F. Kaplan, *The Wizards of Armaggedon* (N.Y.: Simon and Schuster, Inc., 1983).

13. M. McGwire, "Deterrence: The Problem—Not the Solution," *SAIS Review* 5 (1985) p. 105–124; J. Nye, *Nuclear Ethics* (N.Y.: Free Press, 1986) for catalogue of critics of deterrence; R. Reagan, "Launching the SDI," in Z. Brzezinski, ed., *Promise or Peril: The Strategic Defense Initiative* (Washington: Ethics and Public Policy, 1986).

14. J. Nye, G. Allison and A. Carnesale, eds., *Fateful Visions: Avoiding Nuclear Catastrophe* (Cambridge, MA: Ballinger Co., 1988) p. 1–11.

concept than to replace the reality. But the debate about "beyond deterrence" continued, and the nuclear argument had been modified if not transformed.

The modification involved a willingness to examine the nuclear question in all of its dimensions. It involved a shift from stressing the success of deterrence over the last forty years to a stress on the possible vulnerabilities over the next forty years. This open probing of the nuclear question, like the change in the constituency of the debate, provided a receptive setting for the bishops moral assessment of the nuclear age.

B. The Substance of the Bishops' Position

In May 1983 the bishops adopted *The Challenge of Peace* as their policy statement on nuclear arms. The document was a pastoral letter, a form of teaching used regularly by the bishops to elaborate a major policy position. This letter had been three years in preparation, however, and had attracted national attention. While it was addressed to the Catholic community, it was read at least as widely outside the church. The preparation of the letter involved three drafts, each of which had been circulated for public comment. The drafting committee of five bishops and five staff persons had met with a wide range of experts in strategy, technology, politics, ethics, theology, and scriptural studies. A series of meetings, running from the Cabinet level (Defense and State) to working staff level, had been held with the Reagan Administration. James Reston wrote of the Second Draft that it was "an astonishing challenge to the power of the state".[15] Stephen Rosenfeld, writing two days after Reston, in the *Washington Post* spelled out the challenge of the bishops more fully: "Their logic and passion have taken them to the very foundation of American security policy. And they are doing so on a basis—a moral basis—that admits of little compromise once you accept it".[16]

There were three distinct reasons why the pastoral letter generated this kind of assessment from experienced political observers. First, while the subject matter of the pastoral was war and peace in the nuclear age, the core topic was an assessment of nuclear deterrence in principle. This set the letter apart from even highly visible peace protests like the Nuclear Freeze which presupposed deterrence and then sought to limit it. The pastoral letter in the end did not condemn deterrence, but it exposed its well known but seldom discussed vulnerabilities. For some, this was the most significant contribution of the process; for others it was the fatal flaw—to criticize a strategy for which there was no foreseeable substitute.

15. J. Reston, "Church, State and Bomb," *New York Times* (Oct. 27, 1982).
16. S. Rosenfeld, "The Bishops and the Bomb," *Washington Post* (Oct. 29, 1982).

Second, the "in principled" assessment was cast in moral terms. The letter used political, strategic and technological resources, but its fundamental purpose was moral argument. There existed a whole body of ethical analysis of nuclear strategy from the 1960s and 1970s,[17] much of it used by the pastoral, but the moral argument has not been given much space in the public arena. A combination of factors—the drafting process used, the size of the institution sponsoring the process, and the tenor of the times—combined to give this rather intricate moral critique high public visibility. Casting the policy question in moral terms—right/wrong, legitimate/illegitimate—gave the debate a different tenor than asking whether deterrence was stable/unstable or whether we had too much/too little. Moreover, the bishops wrote from within a moral tradition that acknowledged legitimate uses of force by the state. A "just-war" critique of nuclear policy added a distinct edge to the conclusions.

Third, the critique arose from an unexpected group in the political spectrum—from Roman Catholic bishops, often regarded, wrote Reston, "as a militantly anti-Communist organization".[18] There had not been much shift among the bishops on communism, but they were driven by their own moral tradition to test the *means* of policy in the nuclear age, a fact which placed them squarely in the face of the nuclear dilemma.

The bishops brought to the dilemma a long tradition of moral argument about ends, means, intention, and proper authority which is found in the just-war ethic. This intricately crafted set of moral categories had been honed in centuries of church-state debate—Augustine with the Roman Empire, Thomas with the medieval prince, Vitoria with the Spanish King—and it provided the bishops with a tested resource when confronting the policy of a nuclear nation-state. The policy section of the letter, its most widely read part, involved a three-step assessment of U.S. policy. The premise of the evaluation was that nuclear weapons constituted a qualitatively new challenge to the classical moral argument: the categories were still valid, but the bishops did not see their task as simply a linear extension of the work of Augustine and Thomas. Part of the drama of the letter was the expectation it created that the moral tradition, which had often been used to justify the state's resort to force (this Bishops' Conference had been a vocal supporter of World War I and World War II), was now about to be used to set stringent limits on state policy.

This expectation was met. From its premise, the letter moved to an assessment of three cases of nuclear weapons. First, it ruled out, absolutely, directly intended attacks on civilian centers even if American cities had been

17. Cf. P. Ramsey, *The Just War: Force and Political Responsibility* (N.Y.: Scribners, 1968); W. Stein, ed., *War and the Christian Conscience* (London: Merlin Press, 1961).

18. Reston, cited.

hit first. Second, it opposed the existing NATO policy of threatened "first-use" of nuclear weapons to stop a conventional attack. Third, on the question of possible limited second use, the letter did not rule it out but expressed the most severe doubt about the possibility of keeping such attacks within moral limits.[19] The ambiguity about use in this third category, deliberate choice, is what stopped the text just short of a complete nuclear pacifism.

The assessment on use led, by the logic of policy, to an evaluation of deterrence. The judgment on deterrence was neither condemnation of it nor consecration of it. The bishops judged existing policy to be just barely justifiable; the phrase used was "strictly conditioned moral acceptance".[20] The conditions were two—that deterrence be seen as a transitional policy, i.e., there should be movement toward a more stable system of security, and that the "character" or component elements of the deterrent be kept under constant review, e.g., whether to deploy MX or not, whether to move toward strategic defense or not. The nature of this assessment of deterrence constituted an open-ended challenge to the legitimacy of existing policy since the bishops will have to remain in the nuclear debate to illustrate the meaning of their "conditional approval" of deterrence.

It was the logic of conditional acceptance which governed the positions taken by the bishops after 1983. They opposed the MX missile on the basis that the characteristics of the MX would move the deterrence posture of the United States in the wrong direction. In contrast, they supported the Inter-mediate Nuclear Forces Treaty of 1987 as the kind of step toward disarma-ment which the pastoral letter and papal policy has called for. The commentaries on the 1983 letter also pressed the bishops to specify how their "conditions" applied to the deterrence debate. Some, like Professor Susan M. Okin, argued that strict application of the bishops' conditions should lead them to condemn all existing deterrence policies.[21] Dr. Albert Wohlstetter, a patriarch of the strategic debate, argued that the bishops' principles should lead them to endorse more accurate small nuclear weapons which could effectively destroy Soviet military forces.[22] In addition to this kind of policy debate surrounding the pastoral there was the question posed for the bishops by President Reagan's SDI proposal. As critics of deterrence, how did the bishops evaluate the proposed modification (or transformation) of deterrence proposed by Mr. Reagan?

The SDI posed a particular challenge for the bishops. Since the Presi-dent's proposal was announced shortly before the vote on the pastoral letter, there was no treatment of SDI in *The Challenge of Peace*. Moreover, advo-

19. *The Challenge of Peace*, cited, #146–161.
20. Ibid., #186.
21. S. M. Okin, "Taking the Bishops Seriously," *World Politics* 36 (1984) p. 527–554.
22. A. Wohlstetter, "Bishops, Statesmen and Other Strategists," *Commentary* (June, 1983) p. 15–35.

cates of the system were arguing that it constituted a moral method of moving away from the deterrence relationship.

In response to the changed situation of the late 1980s, the bishops developed *A Report on The Challenge of Peace* in 1988. Reviewing their criteria and conditions, they refused to move either in Okin's direction— condemning deterrence—or in the direction of a technological fix *a la* Wohlstetter. But the response to SDI was the major theme of the *Report*. The essential judgment of the bishops was to distinguish between the intensions of the SDI program (which in fact were not always easy to specify) and the consequences of the program: "The SDI debate is less a dispute about objectives or motives than it is about means and consequences. To probe the moral content of the effects of pursuing SDI is to raise issues about its risks, costs and benefits."[23] The *Report* pursued the consequence questions through the SDI debates about technological feasibility, impact on strategic stability and economic costs. In the end the bishops concluded that "proposals to press deployment of SDI do not measure up to the moral criteria outlined in this report".[24]

The Challenge of Peace (1983) and *The Report* (1988) provide a summation of the Catholic bishops' contribution to the nuclear debate of the 1980s. But the logic of conditional acceptance does not stop with the eighties. The bishops and other participants in the nuclear debate of the past decade will now need to assess the changes which are shaping the political, strategic and moral questions of the 1990s.

III. The New Questions of the 1990s: A Framework

The foreign policy arguments of the 1980s gave ample attention to the nuclear question in terms of both strategic doctrine and arms control issues. There are good reasons to expect that a strong interest in strategy and arms control will continue well into the 1990s but with some significant shifts in the context of the public and the policy debates. For actors in the interdependent sector who have been interested in the nuclear question, it is time to assess the direction and likely content of the policy questions emerging for the 1990s.

As I have elsewhere written,[25] I believe there are three major shifts likely in the nuclear debate of the 1990s. The effect of each of these transitions will be to locate the nuclear question in a broader context of argument than in the 1980s. In the past decade, the nuclear issue was often the

23. National Conference of Catholic Bishops, *Building Peace: A Report on the Challenge of Peace and Policy Developments 1983–1988* (Washington: U.S. Catholic Conference, 1988), #99.

24. Ibid., #106.

25. J. B. Hehir, "There's No Deterring The Catholic Bishops," *Ethics and International Affairs* 3 (1989) p. 277–296.

centerpiece of the foreign policy agenda. In the next decade, that will be important, but it will likely share the spotlight with other, more broadly political, questions. The three shifts in the wider argument mean that it will be political *and* strategic, conventional *and* nuclear, and finally, a systemic *and* a superpower question.

The catalyst for the first change, enhancing the *political* dimensions of the nuclear question, is the changing superpower relationship. The discussions about Soviet "New Thinking," the "End of the Cold War," and the redefinition of superpower relations hold the potential to recast the logic of the nuclear strategy and arms control problems.[26] The prevailing assumption of the nuclear age has been that of an abiding conflict between the superpowers which could not be changed politically. The logic of the nuclear debate was then cast in terms of stabilizing a hostile competition. Hence, the goals of arms race stability and crisis stability were to be pursued through a mix of strategic doctrine and arms control. In brief, since political change was deemed impossible, the best one could plan for was a stable nuclear balance.

Beginning with the 1990s, sober assessments of the U.S.-Soviet relationship are being made which point in the direction of seeking to change and "normalize" the superpower relationship. To pursue this goal is not to dispense with the need for the nuclear debate, but it is to place such discussions in subordinate status to more foundational questions. To shift the superpower relationship—even a bit—will open possibilities for arms control previously judged too risky or too radical. Furthermore, to open the political questions in the superpower relationship is to engage issues which extend beyond the nuclear relationship: the future of Europe, the superpowers and regional conflicts; and the structure of international politics as a whole all would surface even more dramatically in the 1990s.

Within the category of arms control, the second shift will require a much closer linkage of *conventional* and strategic negotiations. This will give a new status to conventional arms control which has been in a marginal position for almost twenty years.[27] There are distinct but related forces pushing to give conventional arms control a different status. First, the changing dynamic of the superpower relationship includes a Soviet willingness to accommodate key Western pre-conditions for serious negotiations on conventional forces. The content of recent Soviet proposals on Conventional Forces in Europe (CFE) show a significant shift in searching for common ground with NATO proposals. Second, from the perspective of the West, a post-INF and possibly post-START would require movement on conventional arms control.

26. Cf. Mandelbaum, cited; S. Bialer, "New Thinking and Soviet Foreign Policy," *Survival* (July/August 1988) p. 291–309.

27. K. Kaiser, "After INF: Objectives, Concepts and Policies for Conventional Arms Reduction," *Atlantic Community Quarterly* (Spring 1988) p. 9–22.

(Indeed, one of the debates of the 1990s will be how the United States should relate its negotiating position on START with negotiations on CFE.) Third, changing conditions in Eastern Europe as well as developments in Western Europe will force both the political futures of Europe and the role of military forces in Europe onto the agenda of both superpowers.

The third shift moves beyond the NATO-Warsaw Pact and U.S.-Soviet relationships. The 1990s will require that the superpowers address the systemic dimensions of the nuclear question. The catalyst here will be the need for renewal of the Nonproliferation Treaty in 1995. This will bring the proliferation issue back into the nuclear discussion; it too has been treated as a secondary issue in the 1980s. In the 1990s, nuclear proliferation will have to be analyzed in conjunction with other forms of proliferation, like ballistic missiles and chemical weapons.

This broadened and intensified proliferation debate will inevitably surface the political questions which are at the root of proliferation. On this issue, the superpowers need the cooperation and support of middle powers and small states upon whom they are seldom dependent. These other states are asked and encouraged to commit themselves to nuclear (or chemical) abstention for the sake of global order and safety. The validity and necessity of this objective, however, cannot erase the fact that the states being asked to pledge restraint have a whole range of other concerns about global order which they can seldom get the powers of East or West to address. Returning the nuclear debate to the proliferation question will likely require joining the political-strategic agenda of world politics to the political-economic issues which affect most states in the system on a daily basis more directly than nuclear weapons.

Each of these shifts (toward the political, the conventional and the systemic) would need to be explored in greater detail to illustrate how they may shape the public and policy arguments of the 1990s. None of them will diminish the centrality, significance and urgency of the nuclear question, but each of them will make analysis of it more complicated. The complexity should be welcomed for it opens the possibility of broader developments in world affairs than we have been accustomed to hope for in the nuclear age.

Participants in the independent sector will find much in the wider debates to address and advocate. Engaging the issues, however, will require, in many instances, a recasting of the categories in which the nuclear debate has been argued. Everything surely will not change, but enough is already changing to require a broader framework for addressing world politics in the 1990s.

The Catholic bishops have been called by Pope John Paul II to think in these broader categories about the moral questions involved. In his last encyclical, *On Social Concerns* (1987),[28] the Pope called for an effort to join

28. John Paul II, *On Social Concern (Sollicitudo Rei Socialis)* 1987, p. 36ff; p. 76ff.

the East-West issues to the North-South questions of world politics. All three of the changes outlined in this section fit within this dual frame of reference. The bishops can use their nuclear documents of the 1980s, but they, like others, will have to paint on a broader canvass in the next decade.

HEALTH, HOSPITALS, AND ETHICS COMMITTEES: THE VOICES IN THE CONVERSATION.

James F. Smurl

In beginning a conversation about religion, health, and the third sector in American culture, an invitation should be extended to the voices of hospitals and ethics committees, for they appear to be more than compatible. After all, they too are familiar with ambiguity and misunderstanding, and, like religion and voluntarism, they have proved culturally adaptive. Like others in the conversation, their voices are largely metaphorical. They acquire substantive, but shifting, content only in and through the cultural narratives and practices of specific times and places. And, like those already participating in the conversations about health, hospitals and ethics committees have shown themselves capable of talking about more than power and profit. They appear to be comfortable with the major conventions Americans live by and seem equally uncomfortable with—perhaps even crankier about—the contrived abstractions by means of which the voices of power and profit change the subject. They just might relish a sustained conversation about what is good for humans and their communities. They might even help other participants in the conversation stick to the subject. If so, they may help keep the voice "for-people" from being drowned out by those speaking mainly "for-profit" or "for-power."

In this essay, I will describe three illustrative health-care conversations: one in a late twentieth-century Chicago neighborhood; another in an historical account of the changing social and cultural contexts of voluntary hospitals in the United States; and a third in the relatively new, but potentially significant, context created on a hospital ethics committee. From those illustrative conversations I will then infer that, in interactions between religious forces and activities in American culture and the impulses and practices associated with the independent sector, human health and well-being can be weakened as well as strengthened. What that suggests, I will contend, is that, if voluntary association is undertaken for the sake of people's well-being (in this instance, health), then this aim, and our studies of steps taken toward it, can be accomplished better by attending to *what* is being expressed in the conversations and the practices begun for that purpose—

more so than by asking *who* is speaking and *to whom*, or by simply asking which socially designated roles or sectors they represent. I hope to show that studying the voices in, and the dynamics of, these conversations is more illuminating than is sector analysis for at least three reasons. First, what is truly religious is not always best represented by the persons and practices conventionally associated with religion. Next, voluntary associationalism may be proto-typically American, but the conversations and practices in those alliances are not always independent of coercive governmental and commercial business interests. Finally, caring for health and other qualities important to human prospering can be derailed either by changing the subject of the conversations begun for those purposes or by paying too little attention to *what* is being said. This, then, is an ethical inquiry—in that it investigates the character of the voices involved in three illustrative conversations about morally right and the morally wrong ways to care for human health at a few specific times and places in a nation where the voices speaking for religion and voluntarism are generally taken to stand for people's best interests.

I. Health Before and After The Hospital

Before proceeding to the first illustrative case study from Chicago, there are a few important reminders necessary to set the stage for that conversation. First, it should be noted that some metaphorical expressions of health point to delicate and vulnerable *equilibria* within and between the animate and inanimate beings on and about our planet. If these are not culturally dominant metaphors in America, that is not to say they should not be, nor that conversations about such harmonies are unimportant. They are simply not culturally dominant. More conventional metaphors emphasize animate life. In fact, they narrow the meaning of health even further, restricting considerations to human animals and depicting health as a state of equilibrium between forces which either enhance or detract from physical and mental well-being.

At bottom in conventional conceptions is a paradigm of health called the "germ theory", which holds that health prevails when the antibodies in a person's immune system are sufficient to tame the bacteria and viruses which otherwise would overwhelm one. To the degree that dominant American cultural convictions about health are so shaped, to that same degree American conversations tend to be less inclusive than others which are shaped by the paradigms used by public and world health organizations. Though the standard notion of health in the U.S. is more restrictive than public health models, it seems unable, nonetheless, to curb some rather expansive, even peculiar, usage—as in references to "sick" buildings, "healthy" cities, and a range of "diseases" demonized as "addictions". Ironically, reductionist notions of health are accompanied by reduced expectations of the adequacy and appropriateness of our public discourse about such matters—and at a time when we desperately need to learn how to live well on a complex planet.

Fortunately, however, we at least seem to agree that health is influenced for better or worse by several factors—physical and social environments, lifestyles, heredity, and the quality of whatever health care one receives. But we seem unable to take all of these factors into account regularly and comprehensively. Were we to do so and were we to rank them in terms of their degree of influence, I suggest it would be something like the following. Physical and social environments would be in first place because, taken together, these two are far more influential than anything lifestyle, heredity, or health care, taken singly, can do to counteract their impact.

This ranking suggests how much human health and well-being are influenced *before and after the voice of the hospital* enters in any meaningful way. Quite apart from ideologies upholding the value and/or necessity of voluntary, private, and independent actions and spaces in social life, the nature and character of the health-maintaining and health-promoting factors just mentioned are such that they cannot do what they might for people unless the voices for-profit and for-power are kept in check. Ideologies aside, the very nature of the social goods we create to promote health requires that they enjoy a large measure of independence from business and government. As Michael Walzer puts it, our shared understandings of basic provisions and securities—like food, shelter, health care, and the like—make it imperative that they not be dominated by politics or business.[1] Stated more positively in terms of a Roman Catholic social-ethical principle of "subsidiarity", the creation and allocation of the social goods entailed in caring for human health should be conducted at the lowest social level possible, without overreaching from larger, more powerful domains. At bottom, however, the reason these health-influencing factors need a large measure of independence has little to do with ideology, political science, and social ethics, and everything to do with what they are and how they work.

To illustrate the nature of these factors and how they invite religio-cultural conversations about health, ethics, and independent action, consider what happened in a South-Side Chicago neighborhood during the 1960's and 1970's.[2] Neighborhood leaders, including some pastors, invited a community organizer to help make their local hospital more attentive to the

1. *Spheres of Justice: A Defense of Pluralism and Equality.* N.Y.: Basic Books, 1983. See also William A. Galston, *Justice and the Human Good,* Chicago: University of Chicago Press, 1980, pp. 55–59 and Richard Sennett, *Authority,* N.Y.: Alfred A. Knopf, 1980, pp. 77–83, on metaphors which illegitimately join domains of life.

2. The following story was told by John McKnight in an address presented at the Primary Care Conference (IV, October, 1981) of Indiana University's School of Nursing, sponsored primarily by the Department of Community Health Nursing, with support also from the School of Liberal Arts and other campus and community groups.

needs of residents in the area.[3] They began by doing some fact-finding about what was putting people in the hospital. They discovered that auto accidents at several intersections and at the entrance to a local shopping mall were the principal causes, followed by personal injuries, caused either by neighbors or by unsafe stairs and other hazardous conditions in apartment buildings. Next on the list was bronchitis, which they attributed to a dietary insufficiency of fresh fruits and vegetables. Last on the list were dog bites from a pack of unfriendly canines roaming the neighborhood.

How might those people have maintained good health before and after, perhaps even without, the services of a hospital? They began first by dealing with the problems putting them in what Germans call the "Krankhaus." Several of their problems were not soluble through the "tried-and-true" methods of rapidly mobilizing technical resources. They required slower, more indirect, and more cooperative forms of private-public action. This meant tackling some seemingly intractable social problems, the likes of which Americans more regularly address by declaring "war" on, say, drugs, poverty, infant mortality, and other "diseases" not well handled by the short-term repair shops hospitals have become. The health problems in South Chicago had to be addressed in ways more like what the public health service once did through sanitation and vaccination, more like what neighborhoods today are doing by shutting down crack houses, and more in the style many self-organized Americans employ in order to stem the tides of garbage, pesticides, and violence in homes and on the streets.

Somewhat ironically, the first steps in Chicago were to put a price on the heads of wild dogs and to organize a posse of young bounty hunters on bicycles. Eventually, Mayor Daley sent help in the form of traffic lights for the problematic intersections. And, employing what students of health care call "high-level technology"—such as replacing an array of lower-level tech-nologies with a vaccine against polio, for example—the community's leaders constructed a greenhouse on an apartment roof. There they grew fresh vegetables and fruits for their tables, thereby lessening susceptibility to bronchitis and creating meaningful activities for senior citizens who could not resist showing the younger generation how to cultivate crops properly.

For a number of reasons, this is an altogether fetching story. These folks not only learned that their physical and social environments were *the* major

3. Their expectations about the accessibility of hospitals need to be seen in light of the fact that, during the 1950's, hospitals became symbols of community aspirations writ large—hoping to make unlimited technology accessible to and affordable by all citizens (Rosemary Stevens, *In Sickness and in Wealth: American Hospitals in the Twentieth Century*, N.Y.: Basic Books, 1989, p. 255). They also need to be seen in light of the fact that the public service requirements attached, initially and later, to the federal Hill-Burton hospital construction Act of 1946 were more rhetorical than effective, that they winked at racial segregation for a long while, were administered with an eye to several competing political interest groups, and were regularly evaded in the 1970's (*id.*, pp. 201–226, 314–15). See also note 42 below.

causes of hospitalization but also that, while the community actions needed to redress them might be aided by government and business, the remedies for their problems would not long endure if dominated by profit and power. What they also learned, I contend, is what the history of American hospitals shows—namely, that hospitals have demonstrated little interest in changing the social conditions which bring patients to their doors.[4]

As told by John McKnight, the community organizer engaged by these Chicagoans, the story ends on an upbeat note of self-mobilization, aided in part by neighborhood ministers, to improve the health potential of their immediate environments. Implicit in the story are references to lifestyles, but there is no mention whatever of heredity. Yet, no conversation about health can be adequate without mentioning both of these factors.

Lifestyles are blends of what people are taught and what they do with that. Through familial, educational, and religious pores, people absorb what health care studies confirm—namely, that the way one deals with eating, sleeping, exercise, stress, and the like, is important. There is general agreement that, if *most* of these behaviors are within certain parameters, then a person can be expected to live longer. So qualifying such conclusions, health-care studies implicitly acknowledge that risk-budgeting is a necessary feature in a healthy life. But they rarely say so, much less pay heed to the moral and spiritual qualities of lives or, for that matter, to the matter of passing on the price tag for prolonged living to succeeding generations.

Today, as in previous eras, religious and other cultural zealots regularly change the subject in health care conversations by introducing moralizing jeremiads, refusing to consider all that is relevant and introducing some wrongheaded priorities. Lifestyle jeremiads recently have become both more popular and more puzzling. As the likelihood of making substantial progress on the health front by relying heavily on technology began to fade, lifestyle seemed to represent a promising arena in which to make some major strides. Unfortunately, leading ideologues in movements emphasizing lifestyle developed a dual myopia, becoming nearsighted both about the degree to which changes in lifestyle can offset the effect of physical and social environments and heredity and about the fact that people have to draw up "risk-budgets" if they are to be humanly fit as well as disease-free, to develop coherent, meaningful, and responsible, as well as long-lasting, ways of life.

Clearly, I am not sanguine about the salvific potential of self-help movements which count on the power of will to overcome nature and society. In fact, I believe we have been euchred by their ideological zealots and their

---

4. *id.*, p. 27. As Stevens demonstrates, this disinterest may be attributable, in part, to what hospitals learned early on in a 1912 survey of the reasons why people were admitted to a New York hospital (in the Hudson River Valley). Nearly a tenth of the patients in that hospital were there because of "illnesses" like unsatisfactory homes, poor santiation, ignorance, shift-lessness, and poverty (*id.*, p. 33).

profiteers. We ought to be able to keep the conversation more on track, without changing the subject and without making other health-influencing factors seem irrelevant. Nonetheless, all sorts of religious and cultural voices must be welcomed—so long as they speak predominantly "for-people" rather than "for-power" and so long as Aristotelian and other voices of moderation are welcomed as well. Conversations about health should be open, but not to being derailed by ostracizing either fatties or beanpoles, or by stigmatizing either workaholics or couch potatoes, or, finally, by way of bogus equations of health, productivity, and economic well-being, with moral and religious virtue.

John McKnight might have been thinking of those conversational sleights-of-hand and decided not to say much about the lifestyles of the people in his story. Or he might have been persuaded that lifestyles have to be viewed in light of a person's range of effective freedom and not in terms of neo-Platonic models of human nature in which a person's freedom is studied apart from environing material factors such as one's companions, recreations, and educations. No amount of such "essential" (as opposed to "existential" or "effective") freedom can make people effectively free without help from their environments as well as from their friends. And no one is free to do what contravenes the fate-like, unbargained-for pattern of nucleic acids received through parents, which constitutes the third most influential factor in human health and illness.

Genes set important limits to one's chances for health, and they qualify personal moral accountability for maintaining and promoting it. A recent study of peoples' inherited levels of the cholesterol-dissolving enzyme, lipoprotein lipase, suggests that a person tends to be either fat or skinny less by one's choices and more by one's enzymatic endowment. The folk wisdom in the illustrative Chicago neighborhood no doubt had that straight long ago and taught those people to settle for what they got. But, as the checkered history of eugenics attests and as the tendency of late to peg hopes on finding and regulating one or another gene confirms, some people seem intent on forever inventing and reinventing human life in ways which bespeak a series of struggles with nature. And, in some of the uses to which science and technology are put, one can discern an effort to dominate the molecular versions of the molar sides of life vanquished long ago in arrogant crusades against the beings Adam was commissioned to name in one version of the creation story but told to dominate in the other, more widely reported version.[5]

5. *Genesis* 1 and 2. Daniel Callahan contends that the problems of our health care system lie ultimately in the realm of values, not in the realm of economics or management. We have become victims of our own goals and achievements, victims of our faith in medicine, of our political attachment to individual choice, and of our unwillingness to set limits—to expenditures on health care versus education, housing, and the like, for example (*Setting Limits: Medical Goals in an Aging Society*, N.Y.: Simon & Schuster, 1987; *What Kind of Life: The Limits of*

The voice of heredity in conversations about health calls for a moral maturity which recognizes and voluntarily accepts unbargained-for obligations. It reminds us that there is only so much a Ryan White can do for his health, born, as he was, with homophilia and in need of the transfusion through which he contracted AIDS. The voice of heredity helps assure that the communitarian and intergenerational character of health will be mentioned as a relevant consideration, and it helps assure also that lifestyle and conventional health care will not be permitted to set all of the priorities.

But that is what happens when, like the Chicagoans in the above illustration, people see nothing but hospital doors in their search for the portals of health. All too few recognize that, in order to meet the health-care needs of the vast majority of humans, what are needed are primary, basic levels of preventive, educational, and ordinary care. Those are not newsworthy levels in the U.S., however. The "televangel" of health care proclaims mainly a message of adventurous, acute, restorative, and technologically sophisticated treatments more than the kinds of actions associated with the word "care".

And that is the rub! How is it that some of the least influential forces for good health have become the most visible and most widely-acclaimed symbols of health care? Could it be because the centerpiece of the hospital movement throughout this country—namely, the voluntary, private, and religiously-connected hospital—was not only a voice in the conversation but was speaking in ways which made it difficult to hear its utterance "for-people" amid the din of its co-present utterances "for-profit" and "for-power"?

II. Hospitals as Mirrors and Shapers of Culture

That is part of the thesis in Rosemary Stevens' recent book *In Sickness and in Wealth: American Hospitals in the Twentieth Century*. Stevens recounts the reasons why not-for-profit hospitals became cultural icons, mirroring the brighter sides both of science and of the religious and voluntary forces which shaped their sense of public service. By the same token, however, they also mirror and beam back to Americans some distortions caused by flaws in the sometimes too perfect image we project of ourselves.[6]

Medical Progress, N.Y.: Simon & Schuster, 1989). Callahan might also have noted that many of the high expectations we have of medicine stem primarily from the time of the 1940's when sulfa, and later penicillin, were discovered (Stevens, *id.*, p. 204). These facts should also be taken into account by Bruce Jennings who, when commenting on Callahan's proposals, argues that our goal should be to raise substantive questions about such matters in public discourse, where bioethics is at its best ("Bioethics as Civil Discourse," pp. 34–5 in *Hastings Center Report* 19:5 [September–October, 1989]).

6. Like so many cultural icons and symbols of cultural pride, the successes of hospitals have helped balance failures elsewhere in American society—becoming, for example, "depres-

American hospitals are regarded, variously, as the best in the world, as myopically biased toward high-technology medicine, as riven with problems of cost and accessibility, and as mirroring the social divisions of contemporary America. There is serious concern about a "two-class" or multitiered system of medicine. One out of every eight Americans has no hospital insurance. Investor-owned hospitals have established a strong, if minor, presence; and the idea that hospitals are charities, or even elements of a welfare state, has diminished almost to extinction. The appropriate roles for government, commercial enterprises, and voluntary nonprofit organizations in the provision of hospital service are all being questioned simultaneously. . . . [T]he fundamental attributes of the U.S. hospital system, . . . [its] organizational, professional, political, and economic contexts . . . [tell] a story of medicine, money, and power—of change [in] and the continuity of conflicting ideals.[7]

Some elements in that story are very old, while others are quite new. Older elements in the story echo voices from Benedictine-style hospices, with volunteers working cheerfully for the love of God and neighbor, welcoming the infirm and endangered to be cared for. The newest elements in the story come from the world of business. These are expressed in the fact of an almost entirely salaried staff, for example, and are most inhospitably uttered by those who ask first for an impression of an insurance card before one can be admitted. Subplots in this tale of transition tell of equally radical and overlapping transformations in science, in the professions, in business, in universities, in the changing faces of benevolence and philanthropy, and in the balances struck between political, economic, and social powers over the last century.[8] The principal characters in these subplots bear much of the burden of the hospital story in this century. In fact, they often are responsible for tragic flaws in the heroic tale of a movement which emerged between 1870 and 1917 and led to the development of this distinctively American institution. As a consequence, to paraphrase Richard Rorty's indictment of modern

---

sion cures" comparable to Hollywood movies and movie palaces during the 1930's. So too, however, medical and hospital successes have been intertwined with social failures with respect to health. While their achievements multiplied, public health went begging—despite the fact that, as mentioned in note 4 above and part II, below, public health problems are major causes of hospitalization—while Americans continue to value hospitals more than schools and to pay their practitioners far more handsomely (Stevens, *id.*, p. 356).

7. *id.*, pp. 3–4.

8. For an illustrative instance of these transformations, see the alliances between scientific medicine and "scientific" philanthropy (Stevens, *id.*, pp. 19, 129–30, 226 and Gerald Jonas, *The Circuit Riders: Rockefeller Money and the Rise of Modern Science*, N.Y.: W.W. Norton & Company, 1989). For others, including the wide-ranging professionalization which occurred at the turn of the century, see Robert H. Wiebe, *The Search for Order: 1877–1920*, N.Y.: Hill and Wang, 1967.

philosophy, the hospital became the subject of, rather than a voice in, the broader human conversation about health.[9] Nonetheless, in so doing, it also became a cultural icon, which, now as then, exhibits some distinctively American traits.[10]

First, the hospital has been *segmented and diverse*. From the start, hospitals were ethnically, racially, and religiously pluralistic, and competitive. Depending on the ethnic and religious character of local populations, hosptials came to be known, for example, as Baptist, Black, Catholic, Episcopalian, German, Lutheran, Jewish, Methodist, and Swedish. Private, charitable, or "voluntary" hospitals were especially strong in the Northeast and became the flagships of the movement,[11] while profit-making hospitals tended to be more firmly established in the South and West. Private hospitals not only remained numerically dominant; they also became cultural icons, mirroring the ideology that weds the well-being of communities to a voluntarism considered a major political antidote against an overreaching government intent on making aid to others compulsory. The resultant interdependence of social, cultural, and political ideologies for which the hospital became an icon proved useful in turn for hospitals when they had to adapt to frequently changing social, economic, and political conditions over the century.[12]

9. *Philosophy and the Mirror of Nature*, Princeton, N.J.: Princeton University Press, 1979, p. 389 (Rorty notes that the conversation metaphor alludes to Michael J. Oakeshott's "The Voice of Poetry in the Conversation of Mankind," as found in his *Rationalism in Politics, and Other Essays*, London: Methuen, 1962).

10. Stevens, *id.*, pp. 3, 8–13.

11. Heralding this trend, the 1904 census reported that of nearly 1500 hospitals 800 were private-charitable-nonsectarian, some 400 were "ecclesiastical," and only 200 were operated by local, state, and federal governments (*id.*, 23).

12. *id.*, pp. 9, 338. People often have tried to reforge that chain in periods when hospitals needed desperately to recapture public trust and a measure of the autonomy which the rhetoric of voluntarism so successfully achieved at previous points in history—both when voluntarism meant private initiative without selfish gain or public responsibility without government compulsion and when this essentially apolitical idea was used instrumentally in the service of economic and political ideologies (*id.*, pp. 14–15, 153, 156, 161, 165, 170, 192–3, 213, 218, 252, 339).

One should recall, however, that voluntary hospitals often were given direct government subsidies, enjoyed tax exemption, and, through to mid-century, were legally exempt from tort liability (*id.*, pp. 163, 223, 249, 334). Furthermore, their ideology of community service often translated, in reality, to partnerships with vested interests in communities—alliances evident on boards of trustees, between them and organized philanthropy, and between all of these and the advocates of free enterprise (*id.*, pp. 213, 226, 252, 319–20).

For an indication of the power of these alliances and the links in the chain of voluntarism—even in a time Paul Starr characterizes as witnessing the "decomposition of voluntarism" among hospital leaders (*id.* pp. 291, 310, 314; and Starr's *The Social Transformation of American Medicine: The Rise of a Sovereign Profession and the Making of a Vast Industry*, N.Y.: Basic Books, 1982, p. 436)—see, for example, a 1989 Virginia Conference for hospital executives in which they were urged to reorient policy to focus more on social responsibility and community

Social stratification has been a second trait of hospitals—more in urban areas than in generally more communitarian, rural settings.[13] Urban American hospitals both reflected and reinforced prevalent definitions of social class and of race, among other warts on America's cultural visage, including those which equated indigence with failure. City and county hospitals originally were organized like almshouses, with grim, barracks-style wards, reeking distinctly unpleasant odors, and containing isolation "cells" (for punishment?). They were, and generally remained, necessary props for the modest, but morally unjustifiable, forms of discriminatory charity which successful private hospitals practiced. City and county hospitals became the residual caregivers for the very poor and for those stigmatized as social failures—namely, those deemed unproductive, unwanted, and unworthy.[14] As professional and scientific medicine made headway, creating a companion need for teaching centers and clinical "material," these hospitals, though always more socially inclusive, took on the character of factories in what today might be called the health-care "industry."[15]

In sharp contrast, private, urban hospitals were stratified according to patients' purses—with paying patients in better quarters, with better food and fewer regulations, and with far fewer chances of exposure to hospital-induced disease.[16] Even germs were not allowed to climb the social ladder. Discrimination held sway in the laundry room as well, so much so that one hospital administrator recommended the use of cream and white blankets for private, white patients, slate-colored for Negroes, and, of course, red for emergency room patients.[17] By the 1920's, private and voluntary hospitals resembled stratified multi-class hotels and ocean liners, well on the way to today's "VIP" suites. As Stevens says, "[w]here you . . . [are] treated—in which kind of hospital, in which kind of bed— . . . [confirms] your social status in the general population."[18]

The prevalent American belief that *money signals success* is a third mirror image found in hospitals. This follows in part from their stratification and in part from their preoccupation with paying patients. Although most

---

needs (*Hastings Center Report* 19:6, p. 2) but, notably, with no mention of the ways in which debt and income from regulatory government agencies have made hospitals interdependent with government and business (Stevens, *id.*, p. 338).

13. The notion of, and the rhetoric associated with, community was not very persuasive in cities, not even when these became watchwords in the wake of Hill-Burton legislation during the 1950's and 1960's (*id.*, pp. 131, 236).

14. *id.*, pp. 25, 27.

15. *id.*, p. 29.

16. *id.*, pp. 9–10, 28. Note that suggestions for sorting laundry to avoid contaminating private patients came from, among other sources, the *Journal of the American Nursing Association*.

17. This blanket plan was proposed by a Macon, Georgia hospital administrator (*id.*, pp. 42–3).

18. *id.*, p. 108.

were established on a shoestring, no hospital—not even the private or religiously related—was able to survive without attracting paying patients, and it often survived through elaborate, if not always reputable, forms of advertising and marketing.[19] One of the byproducts was that they became some of the nation's most luxurious and costly expressions of "conspicuous consumption."[20]

In America, showy waste often has been taken as a signal of wealth and power—indeed, even of moral and spiritual worth. To the extent that the nexus between fiscal success and paying patients in the hospital equation grew tighter over the century, to that same extent hospitals became still more socially stratified, rather than representative, public spaces. Luxurious care became available for upper socio-economic classes, while often inadequate "charitable" care was provided those from lower classes—but only for those deemed "deserving," that is, indigent persons, deemed worthy because, though temporarily economically needy, they generally had been productive persons.[21] The unproductive and thus "undeserving" or unworthy poor

19. On and off again over the century, marketing has been socially and morally problematic, but it became more of a sticking point in the 1980's when it became a "must" conducted in spite of attacks from the Federal Trade Commission (*id.*, pp. 33, 36–7, 284, 297, 301–2, 336). In a recent article on that topic in the *Hastings Center Report* (L. J. Nelson, *et al.*, "Taking the Train to a World of Strangers: Health Care Marketing and Ethics," pp. 36–43 in 19:5, September/October, 1989), the authors claim it is time to evaluate health care marketing, especially since health care has become increasingly commercial, involves transactions between strangers, and has been likened to commodity exchanges—rather than fiduciary relationships—and thus evokes no standards higher than negative prohibitions on deceit, fraud, and the like. The authors contend that health care relationships are fiduciary for several reasons and are to be governed by the moral and legal standards appropriate to such relationships. They are fiduciary because patients are more vulnerable and dependent than are ordinary consumers, because the human goods at stake are nothing short of life itself or one's selfhood and destiny, and because the very nature of the healing relationship is fiduciary, as recognized hitorically [but, on that point, see Stevens' nuances, *id.*, p. 37] and is so marketed today even by for-profit health care providers. Accordingly, say Nelson and company, health care providers should act so as to deserve and to maintain the trust of patients. They not only should avoid deceiving them; they also should avoid what could be misleading.

In this connection, we should note the ubiquity of provider-driven strategies in several categories of medical service. As such, they and their pricing structures—Milton Friedman notwithstanding—tend to offer little of the information needed for persons to transact freely in the market transactions. In fact, as Larry Churchill argues in his *Rationing Health Care in America* (Notre Dame, Indiana: Notre Dame University Press, 1987), the reality of health care in the U.S. today is that it is rationed by pricing tactics, among other devices.

20. This is Thorstein Veblen's phrase. For the historical record, see Stevens, *id.*, pp. 105–139 on the "Flowering of Consumerism" in the 1920's, and pp. 256–7 on the "Drive for Reimbursement," especially the fact that what became reimbursable—usually very expensive kinds of care—provided an incentive for hospitals to favor those, rather than other, potentially more adequate and, overall, more effective treatments. The reimbursement pattern established by Blue Cross and Blue Shield, for example, set a still dominant trend toward paying for higher, rather than for primary, levels of care (*id.*, p. 190).

21. See *id.*, pp. 10–11, 25, 27, and pp. 256–7 for evidence that the stigma of indigence

became the responsibility of government. But, whether assigned to private charity or to government, they were considered not to have a right to "relief" and, in order to drive that point home, some hospital administrators argued that accommodations for paupers ought to be less comfortable than those for persons considered self-sufficient.[22]

In order to grasp the religio-cultural significance of these developments, one might note that, in this public-private arrangement, the worth of patients is defined in terms of their ability to pay. Such an estimate of worth is also reflected in the facts regarding which brands of clergy were visiting which kinds of parishioners, in which kinds of hospitals, and in which parts of those hospitals over the century. With these facts in mind, it becomes possible to understand why and how religious traditions, not always able to be at their best in living up to ideals, have, like hospitals, both reflected and sustained morally dubious forms of social stratification and have done so with something other than a prophetic attention to the many voices with which "money speaks".

Until recently, a comparably uncritical stance has been evident in America's religions and hospitals with respect to the salvific potential of technology. Hospitals have been mobilized for acute care and the performance of technologically sophisticated repairs on serious physical ailments. In this fourth way, then, hospitals mirror a general and prevalent image of scientific medicine as a form of daring entrepreneurship. According to this image, surgeons worked in technically sophisticated and arcane spaces far from home, while, closer to home, physicians fought wars on disease. Hospitals developed accordingly. Though designed more like efficient industrial workshops, they advertised themselves as "hygienic sanctuaries" in battles against "surgical sins," waged from shining citadels on hills.[23]

High-level technical skill served to distinguish generally male physicians from the all-purpose, female, service workers which nurses became in times when hospitals emphasized "charity" as one of their major purposes. Some of those women were as maternalistically authoritarian as were their paternalistic counterparts. But public relations seemed to require that they be portrayed as eminently compassionate. Even proprietary hospitals, like the renowned Mayo clinic, relied on the sisters of St. Mary's to polish the rough edges of a for-profit, male enterprise with a pumice provided by female, virginal, but "nursing," sisters.[24]

---

perdured through the 1950's. Note, too, that stratification created a string of different "victims"—blacks and veterans earlier in the century, the poor and the elderly in the 1950's, and the uninsured in the 70's and 80's (*id.*, pp. 228, 345).

22. See Amos Warner's 1919 version of this doctrine, which has been implemented at least in wards overseen by economically-minded government budget officers (*id.*, pp. 47–8).

23. See *id.*, pp. 34, 37, 63, and 162 for a reference to a 1935 hospital organization textbook which used the imagery of the citadel on the hill.

24. See *id.*, pp. 11–12, 63 for descriptions of the self-sacrificial and dutiful character of

That is not to say that the then male-dominated medical profession has fared all that well in hospitals over the century. Hospitals have always been extensions of physicians' private practices, and, thus, from their point of view, the issue has been how to retain access in order to succeed as private practitioners. From the point of view of the internal power structure of hospitals, however, while doctors have always been essential, they have never been deemed essential players in the internal organization—even after hospitals became scientific, technological, and educational centers for the medical profession.[25] In fact, when academic health-centers eventually became formidable, multi-million-dollar arrays of vested interests, their relationships to sheltering universities became more problematic than they had been previously.[26]

Over the last three decades, conversations in hospitals and in some of their sheltering university health-centers came to be dominated by the voices of profit and power, with government and business speaking as if with one voice. The "Drive for Reimbursement" throughout the 1950's and 1960's and practices of "Pragmatism in the Marketplace" between 1965 and 1980 put hospitals and some of their academic hosts increasingly at the mercy of the federal government (by way of Medicare, Medicaid, and cost-containment measures like DRG's). Marketplace pragmatism also placed hospitals at the beck and call of those commercial forces controlling their capital, loans, and bonds.[27]

The hospital's voice speaking for public and community-service for the sake of people and their needs has never been either the only or the only dominant utterance to be heard in hospitals.[28] But their recourse to more overtly capitalistic practices in the last few decades and their reliance on federal guarantees for income—ironically, even during the recent, highly touted, "deregulatory" period—have made even the flagships of the hospital movement (namely, those which were voluntary and religiously-affiliated) at

---

nurses as "sisters"—as they are still called in Britain. See *id.*, p. 22 for the story of the Mayo clinic subserved by the independent charitable hospital of St. Mary's and p. 238 for the ways in which many nursing burdens were shifted to LPN's and Aides during the sixties. For background information on the nature and functions of metaphors correlating nurse, mother, earth, and the medicinal properties of minerals during the Renaissance and Age of Science see Carolyn Merchant, *The Death of Nature: Women, Ecology, and the Scientific Revolution*, N.Y.: Harper & Row, 1980, pp. 27–8.

25. Stevens, *id.*, pp. 12–13, 21.

26. *id.*, pp. 13, 318.

27. *id.*, pp. 256–320, esp. 294–302. Note that, despite the fact that hospitals' response to increasing demands of debt payments was to raise rates during the 1960's, doctors were widely, and mistakenly, perceived as primarily responsible for cost increases (*id.*, pp. 243, 299). The guarantee of Medicare income created incentives for hospital spending, in turn creating a new round of debt assumptions and increased costs to meet them, and giving rise to the anomaly entailed in the fact that the Hospital Corporation of America received one-third of its 1975 income from Medicare (*id.* pp. 284, 303, 319–20).

28. See note 12 above and Stevens, *id.*, throughout, but especially chapters 2, 5, and 11.

once both more competitive and more regulated than previously.[29] The social and cultural fallout from these recent chapters in the story of American hospitals is illustrated in a set of questions posed by Rosemary Stevens:

> Are hospitals primarily useful to U.S. culture as embodiments of the values of money, organizational success, and utilitarianism— and no longer important for suggesting cultural, religious, and altruistic aspirations? Do we need hospitals to articulate social class and to create community cohesion and a sense of common purpose? Are patients purely customers, hospitals machine shops, and doctors mechanics?[30]

III. Continuing the Conversation on Hospital Ethics Committees.

At first blush, it would seem that all of these questions should be answered in the affirmative. But it is heartening to note that, despite the personal toll it takes on them, at least some of the people working in hospitals have refused simply to play the role of gatekeepers for cost controllers, especially when that entails putting patients at risk.[31] Neither should it be forgotten that, although voluntary hospitals have always been better at creating services than they have been at distributing them equitably, they have a history of adapting successfully to adverse circumstances. In fact, if private, voluntary (though almost always for-profit) hospitals did not exist, they probably would have to be invented in order to assure the continuing presence of socially viable alternatives to government-run medicine in the U.S. In this late, jaded 20th Century, such hospitals bear the burden of some seemingly unresolvable contradictions. Still, at least one of the several voices in which hospitals have spoken has been a culturally appealing voice which expresses social ideals like voluntarism, charity, and community.[32] For the

29. In order to enhance their financial positions vis-a-vis federal reimbursements calculated in terms of diagnostically related groupings (DRG's), hospitals have had to become more competitive, and were given ample federal incentives to do so. Paradoxically, that kind of competition—for federal income—requires *more* regulation than did earlier systems built more on trust in voluntary hospitals and the medical profession (*id.*, pp. 256–327, esp. 294–302). Paradoxically, too, the incentives entailed in these reimbursement strategies have encouraged hospitals to launch new ventures which, ironically, have the potential for making them multipurpose institutions—including among those purposes, more programs for preventive healthcare measures (*id.*, p. 349).

30. *id.*, p. 350.

31. *id.*, pp. 328 and 341–2.

32. Hospitals' recent "affairs" with the commercial ethos, with centralized government policymaking, with third-party payment schemes, and with the assumption that the commercially competitive "product" is somehow better, have muted their voice "for people," allowing the voices "for-profit" and "for power" to become shrill in their conversations. In the end, however, they probably cannot meet the idealistic expectations Americans hold them to, will have to be accepted warts and all, and someday may be regulated more like the public utilities they so resemble (*id.*, pp. 338, 354–5, 351–2, 360–1).

remainder of this discussion, then, attention will be drawn to a voice which continues to speak for people's interests in a small, but potentially significant, corner of today's hospitals—namely, the hospital ethics committee.[33]

Ethics committees are not the only place you might hear this voice "for people"—as my colleagues in medical genetics, nursing, obstetrics-gynecology, and hospital administration demonstrate regularly.[34] But this voice has a distinctively different, indeed even ritually significant, modulation on a hospital ethics committee—one which needs to be uttered more widely in hospitals and other social and cultural spheres where it is important to have moral character as well as highly developed technical proficiency.

A hospital ethics committee is a somewhat special gathering of conversation partners assembled by a net cast broadly across the culture, and it is charged with considering how to apply the spectrum of human values pertinent to health care—including values which can be ambiguous and antithetical. Something significant can occur, then, in a modern hospital if the voice "for-people," conventionally associated with representatives of the humanities, should be used regularly and predominantly by the conversation partners on an ethics committee, irrespective of whatever other "voices" their jobs may require of them. Together with a commitment to stick to the subject of ethics committees' conversations, making the voice "for people" prominent would augur well for the future. It would serve to suggest that, even within today's hospitals, there may be some spaces not preempted by power, some places less riven by social stratification and less taken with technological wizardry, places where money speaks only softly, if at all, some gathering in which people with somewhat differing interests can forge mutual accommodations of often competing interests.[35]

The hospital ethics committee is a relatively new phenomenon, little more than a decade old, occasioned in part as a response to regulatory

33. See *Ethics Committees: Core Resources*, a collection of materials prepared by The Hastings Center, Briarcliff Manor N.Y., 1989. Included in this set of resources are Judith Wilson Ross's *Handbook for Hospital Ethics Committees*, selected chapters from *Institutional Ethics Committees and Health Care Decision Making*, edited by Ronald E. Carnford and Edward A. Doudera, and more tha a dozen key articles on the history of these committees, their goals, procedures, pitfalls, and the like.

34. The third voice can be heard also in ethics discussions in grand rounds and in clinical conferences. Chaplains and social workers also regularly speak in this voice—though primarily in one-on-one conversations—but at least more so than do the voices of courts and regulatory agencies when they intrude, invited or not, on conversations within hospitals. The third voice is less likely to be heard on hospital boards of trustees, which we have never been broadly representative, composed, as they were, of the persons hospitals took to be the movers and shakers in communities (*id.*, 72, 213, 357). In fact, of late, these boards seem unable to decide whether they want to be businesses or public services, but, since they spend two-thirds of their time on financial restructuring, competiton, and public policy, they in fact seem to have resolved that issue for the moment (*id.*, p. 341).

35. On mutual accommodations see Stevens, *id.*, p. 362.

intrusions in hard-case health care scenarios like those which prompted the "Baby Doe" regulations from the Department of Health and Human Services. These committees were also occasioned by the increasing reluctance of judges to accede to the requests of interested parties for legal directives either to initiate or to cease specific medical treatments. At least since the Karen Ann Quinlan decision, but also in more recent obstetrical cases involving court-ordered treatments favoring the interests of prospective children, judges have urged that difficult health-care cases be adjudicated in less adversarial ways by more appropriate decision-makers who represent a fuller range of the interested parties and are closer to the relevant particulars.[36]

In addition to service on Indiana University's Committee for the Protection of Human Subjects in research, for several years I also have been a member of the University's Infant Care Review Committee which was formed in part to respond to the legal quandaries and pressures noted above. The objectives of this latter committee, its composition, and its standard operating procedures are fairly typical of what one finds across the land, by now in almost every major hospital. The charge of such committees is to hear the details of especially problematic cases, to discuss them until all participants are satisfied that every pertinent point has been raised, and then to reach a consensus about the advice to be offered patients, families, health care practitioners, hospital administrators, and sometimes judges—most commonly, however, to all of these persons simultaneously.

The cultural value and significance of such committees consist less in the advice they give and more in the way they arrive at that point. Their cultural worth derives in part, of course, from their composition but, in still greater measure, from the content and the ritual form of their conversations. Hospital ethics committees typically include representatives from attending health care teams—doctors, nurses, and social workers—as well as chaplains, ethicists, hospital administrators, lawyers, and representatives of the general public. On first blush, that may sound like little more than yet another group of pertinent "experts". But, what they talk about and how they do so makes the group distinctively inexpert. Theirs is anything but a trite conversation among specialists from different fields who want only to discuss professional subjects rather than the matter at hand.[37]

In my experience, there is an unexpected cultural vitality in these conversations. Perhaps it stems from the nature of the problems faced. But perhaps it owes more to what happens even to highly credentialed persons who encounter each other in search of ways to live with sometimes ironic,

36. See, for example, the case of Angela Carder (In re A.C. 533 A.2d 611 (D.C. App. 1987). For related cases, see Veronika E.D. Kolder, et al, "Court-Ordered Obstetrical Interventions," in The New England Journal of Medicine 316:19 (May, 1987), 1192 ff.

37. This view, and several others in this section, owe much to Howard Brody's "Applied Ethics: Don't Change the Subject," pp. 105–122, in Clinical Ethics: Theory and Practice. ed. by Barry Hoffmaster, Benjamin Freedman, and Gwen Fraser. Clifton, NJ: Humana Press, 1989.

often tragic, but always common, human dilemmas, for which there are no easy technical solutions.[38] The vitality of these encounters also may be due to the fact that members of ethics committees have to perform a task infrequently required today in health care—namely, to stand beside the puzzled parties as friends and to keep their well-being uppermost in mind.[39] One would expect chaplains, ethicists, and social workers to uphold the importance of such a stance. On hospital ethics committees, however, it is upheld just as regularly by physicians and nurses, by lawyers as well as by the representatives of the public.

Whatever prompts members of ethics committees to set aside customary masks of professional expertise in these conversations, the phenomenon is encouraging. In fact, the experience of a conversation about an important human concern while setting aside the veils of social roles is enough to motivate members to attend even when their senses of duty are flagging. Often, too, what happens among the members represents a hospital version of the ritual process Victor Turner characterized as the discovery of *communitas* among persons separated from their status worlds and conjoined on more common grounds, whereon, as Hannah Arendt would have it, they can meet each other in public as equals.[40]

Howard Brody elaborates on that process in his description of how *communitas* is imagined by two hypothetical hospital ethics committees. He compares two hospital ethics committees: one at Man's Greatest Hospital and the other at St. Elsewhere's. Their objectives and constituency are similar to, in fact, identical with, those of the committee I know best. Their standard operating procedures are radically different, however, and in some important ways. Brody contends that only one of these procedures best sustains a conversational voice "for-the-benefit-of-people," which is the voice which we commonly associate with religion and public service in American culture. Since that point is central to the burden of this essay, it merits fuller elaboration.

When first established, the committee at Man's Greatest Hospital held an in-service training session, inviting experts in ethics and law to school them in the basic vocabulary, theory, and major principles set forth in those disciplines and which the committee might later apply to cases coming before it. The committee at St. Elsewhere's decided to forgo such training—except, perhaps, to do some relevant reading in books and journals—and agreed that their only operational rule would be "don't change the subject". The St. Elsewhere's committee further resolved that every point of view and

38. As Rosemary Stevens puts it, individual cases bring home the hardships (*id.*, p. 349).

39. By comparison, as Stevens notes, the well being of patients is nearly invisible in the institutional policy processes of contemporary hospitals (*id.*, p. 348).

40. See Victor Turner's *The Ritual Process* (Ithaca, N.Y.: Cornell University Press, 1969) and Hannah Arendt's *On Revolution* (N.Y.: Viking 1956) and *The Human Condition* (N.Y.: Doubleday, 1959).

every consideration which might be relevant to a particular case would be put on the table in the depth necessary for each member of the committee to understand it. Only then would they try to reach closure and only after having been willing to reopen the discussion if a committee member felt something relevant had not been considered or that something previously considered had been given the wrong priority.

The committee on which I serve has behaved more like the one at St. Elsewhere's. Others I know were launched more like that at Man's Greatest Hospital. They began with the premise that, after hearing from all the experts, the final decision would fall to the health-care practitioner in charge—despite the fact that, on difficult cases these days, there are always several pertinent practitioners on the case and often less than consensus among them. Which kind of committee is likely to offer the better advice and why? Whatever its shortcomings, and despite the possibility it could be affected by local bias, St. Elsewhere's committee seems more exemplary. Its commitment is to sustain a particular kind of conversation in a voice "for-people." If it should live up to that commitment, the results would not be simply chitchat, bull sessions, or mere exchanges of opinions and preju-dices—in all of which changing the subject is quite acceptable and requires no justification. St. Elsewhere's conversations require that all the relevant considerations be on the table before the subject is changed and that com-mittee members stay with the subject until they are able to determine which considerations are the weightiest and which represent biases or pet theories to set aside. Too much is at stake to do otherwise since the topics of the conversation are the interests of patients, families, caregivers, and, in de-creasing order of importance, the social and financial risks which might accrue to legally-fictive corporate persons.

Those stakes, together with what it takes not to change the subject, are probably the reasons why everyone on my committee—including the ethicist and the chaplain, but also the specialists from law and medicine—finds little reason to hide behind a professional mask or, alternatively, to protect one's self from being offered by strangers. Keeping such a conversation going rehumanizes and recommonizes all its partners, even those charged with representing the general public. Theories from all quarters are important, but they are welcomed only if they promote and do not change or dominate conversations among equally human persons. Principles of all sorts also are welcome, even when they are largely uninformed or uninformative. What is most needed, and what most invites committee members to express their voices "for-people" in ways which the best religious and community service representatives can bring to cultural conversations, can be summarized in the creed of the St. Elsewhere's committee.

At St. Elsewhere's they believe that the diversity of views and back-grounds represented on the committee will lead each member to meet all others in public as equals. Given members' backgrounds and the diverse cultural conversations in which they have been reared and in which their lives and work involve them, the conversations will necessarily be as segmented and pluralistic as in America. But it is highly unlikely that an extended conversation will fail to produce a range of considerations comparable to what would have been put on the table by experts from relevant social and cultural professions. For example, in dealing with a specific case, legal issues are on every one's mind, irrespective of whether it is the lawyer on the committee who introduces them. The same is true with respect to ethical considerations. Whether or not the ethicist brings them to bear, it is highly unlikely that no one will mention benefits and harms or that all will fail to raise concerns about human rights or, finally, that none will question the justice of certain courses of action.

In sum, hospital ethics committees have some of the same attributes Rosemary Stevens associated with American hospitals and culture. They are diverse and segmented, and stratified—at least at the beginning of a conversation—and they know how to speak "for-profit" and "for-power". But they also are able to set aside such concerns. They know why wealth should not always be the bottom line,[41] and they know better than to ask that nurses, social workers, and chaplains play the "good guys" while putatively tough-minded realists get on with what are perceived, and often exaggerated, as experiences requiring compromise, as opposed to approximations, of ideals. The masks are off, but, to mix metaphors, so too are the gloves, when committee members meet as equals to deal with human quandaries which require them to speak in voices not always accredited as pertinent in many of their jobs. But America is a country which provides the space and the warrant for conversations dominated by a voice which the persons and the practices associated with religious, voluntary, private, and mediating action can make eloquent indeed, when at their best.

This voice in question is a human voice calling people to live life well. It seemed to dominate in the Chicago neighborhood conversations wherein people discovered that they needed each other and a whole lot more than hospitals to make them healthy. It was the voice that rose above the chorus of the American hospital movement and earned for voluntary and private hospitals, when they were at their best, a leading role in vocalizing it. And that is the voice to be heard frequently and heeded most on hospital ethics committees today. One probably should not be as sanguine as a Jeffersonian might about the likelihood that such a voice will "out" eventually in a health-care system today driven as much by governmental and economic interests as

---

41. In this, they are quite different than many of the hospitals in which they are housed. As Stevens notes, "the secularization of hospitals as images of science and charity and their relegation to the realm of mammon" represents an important cultural shift—one, I might add, which is being addressed, if not yet fully countered, by ethics committees (*id.*, p. 357).

it is by humanitarian impulses.[42] It may be more prudent to heed the wisdom entailed in the sober Pennsylvania Dutch axiom that "Ve grow too soon oldt, und too late schmart."[43] And like Brody, one well might worry that the common sense shared on some committees might be equal parts wisdom and nonsense. But the alternatives to keeping such conversations going are unacceptable. Particularly unacceptable would be an alternative that did not require some ritualized practice through which the voice "for people" (or what might be called the voice which warrants a so-called "third sector") might become more eloquent within the modern American hospital.[44]

Throughout this essay, I have sought to show that examining the identity and nature of this voice can yield more illuminating inferences than can comparable investigations intent on identifying the status of speakers and the sectors they represent. Among these inferences—some of which may be applicable to other spheres of interaction between religious and ethical values in American culture—there are three which seem especially significant.

The first is a seemingly necessary recognition that, notwithstanding

42. The economic and political realities of the arena at present suggest that Callahan's call for transformations in cultural beliefs and expectations (note 5 above) is sufficient without what Charles E. Rosenberg calls for in his review of Callahan's recent book—namely, a concomitant engagement with political and economic systems, with the beliefs and practices which have the power of the purse and the legislature as well as imaginative and persuasive power (*NY Times Book Review* Sunday, December 24, 1989, pp. 1, 21). Stevens' history strongly supports Rosenberg's contention. Witness her history of the lobbying done by professional and hospital associations (*id.*, p. 330, plus chapter 12 on the subtle sanctions market-place metaphors provide for hospital misbehavior) See also note 3 above on the role of politics in the Hill-Burton legilsation, and Stevens' p. 327 regarding the ironies entailed in the role of government as a contractor of hospital services, but in such a way that it becomes an influential economic rule-maker—even in times when deregulation has been the watchword of federal administrations.

43. Consider the possibility that ethics committees might be coopted, as some believe was the case with tissue and utilization committees (Stevens, *id.*, p. 292). They would coopt themselves by breaking "St. Elsewhere's covenants." They could be coopted by elitism in their composition, by vested-interest reasoning in their deliberations, or by being called only when health care professionals or administrators deem it necessary. They also could undercut their own effectiveness by hewing too rigorously to the sometimes pseudo-scientific conventions of present forms of "applied ethics." Finally, even if they should be legally mandated, they may not escape some of the above pitfalls. For example, the possibilities of being co-opted may not be averted completely by the terms of an interesting new bill in the U.S. Senate, sponsored by John C. Danforth and Daniel Patrick Moynihan. Called the "Patient Self-Determination Act of 1989," it would require hospitals to inform patients about all sorts of rights—to living wills, autonomy and self determination with respect to the way they die. This bill also would require all hospitals receiving Medicare and Medicaid funds to have an ethics committee as a forum for such issues, but it makes no provision to avert any of the hazards mentioned above (*Medical Ethics Advisor* 6:1, January, 1990, pp. 7–8).

44. This voice is needed even if the nonsense spoken in its name stands to be corrected from time to time by voices from broader conversations of mankind, as discussed in note 43 above.

America's understandably proud, two-hundred-year celebration of freedom from coercion, affirmations of *in*dependence may open, but should not be allowed to close, conversations about important basic human provisions and securities like health care. As one discovers in any sustained discussion of health care—not to mention education, law, economics, and peace-keeping—the most applicable prefix to describe what is involved in those spheres is *inter*dependent. Similarly, the social and cultural choices and practices which best sustain activities in those areas are *con*versations and *commit*ments, in both of which the prefix signals what is needed to effect social policies designed to develop, enhance, and protect human life in communities.

A second insight which can be inferred from this examination of three illustrative conversations about health may be as sobering for scholar-teachers in ethics as it might be for practitioners in religions, in the independent sector, and in any of the several professions entailed in health care, education, law, government, business, and the like. Irrespective of who is saying what to whom, *what* they say and *how* they say it may be the most decisive indicators of whether or not their voices really speak for people, or for profit, or for power, or some other nonmoral value. Profit and power can, of course, benefit people and prevent harm to them. Conversely, whether or not an emphasis on people in a conversation truly stands to help them depends to a great extent both on *what* is said in their behalf and on *how* it is expressed. Discernment is required. Does the voice in the conversation really speak of, and for, people or does it simply appear to be doing so? Does it exhibit a commitment to meet people as equals in public and to promote practices which help transcend narrowly imagined self-interests—as some of religion's more important ideals encourage—or does it tend to exaggerate differences between people and cater to isolated and competing social and political interests? These are not readily answerable questions: now should they be, if public conversations on such matters are to be remain civil. Nonetheless, answers should be sought if American and other cultural conversations on basic human provisions and securities are to continue to approximate their goals. But this raises a sobering question for ethicists as well as for other professionals who participate in these conversations: how does one learn this art of discernment, much less help others to acquire it?

There is a third, and probably cheerier, insight to be drawn from this exploration of the voices in an illustrative set of conversations about health, hospitals, and ethics committees. People often learn as much when they associate somewhat involuntarily to deal with issues for which there are no ready solutions as they do when they launch more purely voluntary affiliations for the sake of quick, technical "fixes" for human problems. In either case, people stand to learn more of what is of value in human life—and of how to promote and defend it—through conversations in which closure *must* be reached, albeit often with a remainder of nagging and perplexing doubt about the outcome. Rituals which sustain and renew that kind of experience—as do the cultural rituals on hospital ethics committees, among others—are critically needed in a nation in which the interactions of religion and voluntarism need to be better understood lest one or another uncritically accepted paradigm of those interactions be so promoted that it has the unintended effect of harming the very people it envisioned as beneficiaries.

WHETHER PIETY OR CHARITY: CLASSIFICATION ISSUES IN THE EXEMPTION OF CHURCHES AND CHARITIES FROM PROPERTY TAXATION

John Witte, Jr.

The law governing tax exemption of church property illustrates the problem of classifying institutions and activities of the independent sector along religious lines. The "independent sector"[1] is comprised of a variety of institutions, like families, schools, charities, churches, corporations, clubs, and others. Religion assumes a variety of forms and functions within these institutions, ranging from the incidental to the indispensable. The law, however, requires that sharp distinctions be drawn between "religious" and "non-religious" institutions and activities.

Such distinctions are required by state statutory law.[2] Historically, two separate bodies of state law governed tax exemption of church property: (1) a

---

1. For purposes of this essay, I am using the term "independent sector" to describe those institutions that fall between the "private individual" and the "public state," such as churches, families, schools, unions, and others. These institutions have also variously been called "voluntary associations," "mediating structures," and "spheres of justice," and the theory of the independent sector has (also been called a theory of "social pluralism" or "structural pluralism." For samples of different perspectives on the independent sector, see Alexander, "Beyond Positivism: A Theological Perspective," in J. Witte and F. Alexander, eds., *The Weightier Matters of the Law: Essays on Law and Religion* (Atlanta: Scholars Press, 1988), 251; P. Berger and R. Neuhaus, *To Empower People: The Role of Mediating Structures in Public Policy* (Washington: The American Enterprise Institute, 1977); H. Dooyeweerd, *A Christian Theory of Social Institutions*, M. Verbrugge, trans.; J. Witte, ed. (La Jolla, CA: The Herman Dooyeweerd Foundation, 1986); R. McCarthy, et al., *Society, State & Schools: A Case for Structural and Confessional Pluralism* (Grand Rapids, MI: Eerdmans, 1981); J. Maritain, *Man and the State* (Chicago: University of Chicago Press, 1951); J. Skillen, *The Scattered Voice: Christians at Odds in the Public Square* (Grand Rapids, MI: Zondervan Publishing House, 1990), 181ff.; M. Walzer, *Spheres of Justice: An Argument for Pluralism and Equality* (New York: Basic Books, 1983).

2. Property taxation and exemption have always been the exclusive prerogative of state and municipal governments, except in times of war and emergency. See Benson, A History of the General Property Tax, in G. Benson, H. McClelland & P. Thomas, *The American Property Tax: Its History, Administration and Economic Impact* (Claremont, CA: Institute for Studies in Federalism at Claremont, 1965), 11–12.

body of common law, which accorded such exemptions to church properties based upon the *religious* uses to which they were devoted; and (2) a body of equity law, which accorded such exemptions to church properties based upon the *charitable* uses to which they were devoted. Currently, only one body of state statutory law governs such exemptions, yet exemptions remain based on either the religious uses or the charitable uses of a property. State officials are thus required to distinguish between piety and charity, religion and benevolence, to determine whether and on what basis a petitioner's property can be exempted from taxation.

Such distinctions are also required by federal constitutional law. The Constitution of the United States permits government regulations of various non-religious institutions and activities, provided such regulations comply with generally applicable constitutional values. It permits governmental regulation of religious groups and activities, only if they comply with the specific mandates of the establishment and free exercise clauses of the first amendment. State tax exemptions for religious institutions and religious uses of property, therefore, require separate constitutional treatment.

The religion clauses of the first amendment, as currently interpreted, appear to offer conflicting directives on the tax status of church property. The establishment clause has been interpreted to forbid government from imparting special benefits to religious groups. The free exercise clause has been interpreted to forbid government from imposing special burdens on religious groups. Neither the exemption nor the taxation of church property appears to satisfy the principles of both clauses. To exempt church property, while taxing that of other non-religious groups, appears to violate the "no special benefit" principle of the establishment clause. To tax church property, while exempting that of other charitable groups, appears to violate the "no special burden" principle of the free exercise clause.[3] In *Walz v. Tax Commission* (1970), the United States Supreme Court held that tax exemptions of church property, while neither proscribed by the establishment clause nor prescribed by the free exercise clause, are constitutionally permissible. In more recent cases involving federal income taxation and state sale and use taxation, however, the Court has called this precedent into serious question.[4]

This Article retraces the history of tax exemption of church property in America and analyzes current patterns of tax exemption litigation and legislation in light of this history. Part I analyses the common law and equity law sources of tax exemption law, the challenge posed to these laws by early state constitutional provisions, and the rise of the modern theory and law of tax

---

3. I have treated the Supreme Court's multiple interpretations of the religion clauses in Witte, "The Theology and Politics of the First Amendment Religion Clauses," 40 *Emory Law Journal* 677 (1991).

4. See, e.g., Bob Jones University v. United States, 461 U.S. 574, (1983); Texas Monthly v. Bullock, 489 U.S. 1 (1989); Jimmy Swaggart Ministries v. Board of Equalization, 110 S. Ct. 688 (1990).

exemption of church property that emerged in response to these challenges. Part II analyzes briefly new trends in litigation over the tax exemption of church property, particularly in cases raised by new religious groups, which have sought to avail themselves of the same protections enjoyed by traditional religious groups. Part III poses an alternative to the current reforms of tax exemption law now being debated and analyzes this alternative provisionally in light of historical exemption laws and current constitutional interpretations.

I. Tax Exemptions of Church Property in the Past

Modern American laws of tax exemption of church property are rooted in two traditions, each of considerable vintage: (1) a common law tradition, which accorded such exemptions to established churches that discharged certain governmental burdens; and (2) an equity tradition, which accorded such exemptions to all churches that dispensed certain social benefits.[5] These two traditions have contributed to the widespread development of colonial and, later, state laws that exempt church property from taxation. There are, however, strong tensions between these two traditions as well, which manifest themselves in both historical and contemporary property tax exemption laws. This section analyzes the development of these two traditions in the colonies and illustrates their manifestations in the theory and law of church property exemptions in the nineteenth and early twentieth centuries.[6]

A. Sources of Tax Exemption at Common Law and Equity

1. *Tax Exemptions at Common Law.* The common law that prevailed in most seventeenth century American colonies treated religion as an affair of

---

5. I am using the term "common law" not as an antonym for "statute" but as a generic term to describe the English and endemic customs and statutes enforced by common law courts. I am using the term "equity" not as a synonym for fairness and justice, but as a generic term to describe the English and colonial American customs and statutes enforced by equity or chancery courts.

6. Two related distinctions that are currently commonplace were not so clear historically. First, the line between property taxation and income taxation was not always sharply drawn. Particularly in rural areas, the income of a person was often so inextricably tied to his property that taxation of one was tantamount to taxation of the other. Second, the distinction between taxation of the property itself and of the person (whether real or fictional) occupying the property was not always sharply drawn. Tax liability sometimes ran with the land and sometimes followed the prior holder. The discussion that follows must thus necessarily intrude on matters of personal income taxation as well. See generally, Jerome R. Hellerstein and Walter Hellerstein, *State and Local Taxation*, 5th ed. (St. Paul, MN: West Publishing Co., 1988), 115–123; Claude W. Stimson, "The Exemptions of Property from Taxation in the United States," 18 *Minnesota Law Review* 411 (1934).

the law and the church as an agency of the state. In the course of the English Reformation a century before, the Tudor monarchs had consolidated their authority over religion and the church and subjected them to comprehensive ecclesiastical laws enforceable by common law and commissary courts.[7] Many of these laws were adopted or emulated in the American colonies— both in the Anglican south and, by the end of the seventeenth century, in the Puritan north.[8] The exemption of church property from taxation was part of this broader set of ecclesiastical regulations.

The common law established orthodox doctrine, liturgy, and morality and proscribed various forms of heathendom, heresy, and hedonism. Communicant status in the established church was a condition for citizenship status in the commonwealth. Religious dissenters, if tolerated, were fore-

---

7. For a comprehensive treatment of post-Reformation ecclesiastical law in England and a convenient collection of relevant ecclesiastical statutes, see R. Burn, *Ecclesiastical Law*, 6th ed. (London: A. Strahan for T. Cadell and W. Davies, 1787). For other discussion, see E. Coke, *The Second Part of the Institutes of the Lawes of England* (London: The Assigns of R. Atkins and E. Atkins for C. Wilkinson, 1642; repr. ed. 1797), chap. 1; J. Godolphin, *Repertorium Canonicum: or, An Abridgement of the Ecclesiastical Laws of this Realm, Consistent with the Temporal*, 3d ed. (London: n.p., 1687); J. Paterson, *The Liberty of the Press, Speech, and Public Worship* (Littleton, CO: F.B. Rothman, 1985; reprint of 1880 ed.), 349–550. Unless otherwise indicated, citations to English Statutes are from the *Statutes at Large of England* (London: 1787–1867).

8. The following summary is drawn principally from the ecclesiastical laws of the southern Anglican colonies of Virginia, North Carolina, and South Carolina, and the northern Puritan colonies of Massachusetts, Connecticut, and New Hampshire. For much of the seventeenth century at least, the middle colonies of Rhode Island, Pennsylvania, New York, and Maryland went their own way. I have drawn on the following collection of colonial laws and other documents: W. Hening, ed., *The Statutes at Large: Being a Collection of all the Laws of Virginia from . . . 1619* (New York: R. & W. & G. Bartow, 1809–1823) [hereinafter Hening]; T. Wynne and W. Gilman, eds., *Colonial Records of Virginia (1619–1680)* (Richmond, VA: n.p., 1874) [hereinafter Wynne and Gilman]; W. Saunders, ed., *The Colonial Records of North Carolina* (Raleigh, NC: State Printer of North Carolina, 1886–1890) [hereinafter Saunders]; T. Cooper and D. McCord, eds., *The Statutes at Large of South Carolina* (Charleston, SC: State Printer of South Carolina, 1836–1841) [hereinafter Cooper]; J. Easterby, ed., *The Colonial Records of South Carolina* (Columbia, SC: Historical Commission of South Carolina, 1951–1953) [hereinafter Easterby]; M. Farrand, ed., *The Laws and Liberties of Massachusetts . . . 1647* (Cambridge, MA: Harvard University Press, 1929) [hereinafter Farrand]; *The Acts and Resolves, Public and Private, of the Province of the Massachusetts Bay, 1692–1780* (Boston: n.p., 1869–1922) [hereinafter Massachusetts Acts]; N. Shurtleff, ed., *Records of The Governor and Company of the Massachusetts Bay in New England, 1628–1686* (Boston: Free Press of J. Hein, 1853–1854) [hereinafter Massachusetts Records]; J. Trumbull and C. Hoadly, eds., *The Public Records of the Colony of Connecticut, 1636–1776* (Hartford, CT: n.p., 1850–1890) [hereinafter Trumbull]; *Connecticut Historical Society, Collections* (Hartford, CT: Connecticut Historical Society, 1860–1878) [hereinafter Connecticut Collection]; *New Hampshire Historical Society, Collections* (Concord, NH: New Hampshire Historical Society, 1824–1939) [hereinafter New Hampshire Collection].

closed from most political and ecclesiastical offices and various social and economic opportunities.[9]

The common law governed the form and function of the established church polity. It delineated the boundaries of the parishes and the location of the churches. It determined the procedures of the consistories and the prerogatives of the vestries. It defined the duties of clerics and the amount of their compensation. It dictated the form of the church corporation and the disposition of its endowments.[10]

The common law regulated the acquisition and maintenance of established church properties. Magistrates were authorized to purchase or condemn private properties within their domains and to convey them to the established church for meetinghouses, parsonages, cemeteries, and glebe lands.[11] Stern criminal laws sanctioned interference with the enjoyment of these properties. Special property laws prohibited parties from gaining prescriptive or security interests in them.[12] Magistrates levied taxes to maintain the property and the clergy of the established church—"tithe rates"

9. See, e.g., Farrand, 1–2; *Massachusetts Records*, 142ff., 168ff.; *New Hampshire Collection*, 1:326–327; Hening, 1:121ff., 155ff., 532ff.; Saunders, 1:634–644, 885; Cooper, 236ff. For English antecedents and analogues, see 16 Car. 2, ch. 4; 25 Car. 2, ch. 2; 35 Eliz. ch. 1, 2; 31 Hen. 8, ch. 14. The famous English Toleration Act of 1688/89, 1 W. & M. ch. 18, entitled Protestant dissenters to worship without interference, provided they swore oaths of allegiance to the Trinity, Scripture, and the Crown. Roman Catholics and Jews, however, were denied such privileges until well into the nineteenth century. See 10 Geo. 4, ch. 7; 10 Vict., ch. 59. The Toleration Act was made binding on most of the colonies through the colonial charters, that required respect for English liberties, rights, and privileges. See, e.g., Third Charter of Virgina (1611–1612), reprinted in F. Thorpe, ed., *The Federal and State Constitutions: Colonial Charters and Other Organic Laws of the States, Territories, or Colonies* (Washington: Government Printing Office, 1909), 7:3802 [hereinafter, Thorpe]; Charter of Massachusetts Bay (1629), reprinted in id., vol. 3, 1853. The Toleration Act was sometimes also specifically adopted by colonial statute. See, e.g., Hening, at vol. 3, 171.

10. See, e.g., Hening, 1:122ff., 155ff., 204ff., 240ff., 250ff., 433ff.; Cooper, 236ff.; Saunders, 207ff. Prior to the eighteenth century, magistrates in Puritan New England accorded the congregational churches far greater freedom to govern themselves, though no new churches could be formed "unless they shall acquaint the Magistrates . . . and have their approbation therein," and the magistrates were authorized to exercise "their coercive power [against] schismatical and heretical churches." Farrand, 18; Cambridge Synod and Platform (1648), reprinted in W. Walker ed., *The Creeds and Platforms of Congregationalism* (Boston: Pilgrim Press, 1960; reprint of 1893 ed.), chap. 17. See further discussion in Witte, "How to Govern a City on a Hill: The Early Puritan Contribution to American Constitutionalism," 39 *Emory Law Journal*, 41, 55–64 (1990).

11. See, e.g., Hening, 2:261, 3:152.

12. See, e.g., Farrand, 19–20; *Massachusetts Records* 99–101; Hening, 2:121. See the rich historical discussion in R. Tyler, *American Ecclesiastical Law: The Law of Religious Societies, Church Government and Creeds, Disturbing Religious Meetings and the Laws of Burial Grounds in the United States* (Albany, NY: W. Gould, 1866). For English antecedents and analogues, see Burn, *Ecclesiastical Law* 3:180–97, 216–260; Coke, *Institutes* 2–5; Godolphin, *Repertorium*, 134, 142; Paterson, *The Liberty*, 434.

to meet general ecclesiastical expenses, "church rates" to repair or improve existing properties, and a host of minor parish fees.[13] These ecclesiastical taxes, though paid to the established church alone, were levied on all taxable persons in the commonwealth, regardless of their church affiliation. Baptists, Quakers, Catholics, Jews, and other non-conformists were thus forced to pay for the support of churches and clerics that they considered heretical or even heathen.

It was in this broader context of ecclesiastical regulations that the common law governed the taxation of church properties. As in England, so in the colonies, the common law afforded no automatic and unrestricted tax exemption to church properties. All property that lay within the jurisdiction of the Crown and its colonial delegates, including church property, was considered presumptively taxable at common law, unless it had been specially and specifically exempted by legislative act.[14] Colonial legislatures readily accorded such privileges to the properties of political officials and to

13. See, e.g., Farrand, 9–10; *Massachusetts Records*, 1:240ff.; *Connecticut Records*, 1:59ff.; Trumbull, 1:111ff., 6:33ff.; Hening, 1:122, 128, 207, 220, 401.

14. The importance of this new presumption—first articulated after the Protestant Reformation—was noted by Richard Burn:

> The traditional presumption that churches and clergymen are not to be charged with the same general charges as the laity of this realm; neither to be troubled or incumbered, unless they be specifically named and charged by some statute [is no longer accepted.] Now the contrary doctrine prevails, that churches and clergymen are liable to all charges by Act of Parliament, unless they are specially exempted.

Burn, *Ecclesiastical Law*, 3:204, quoting, in part, Godolphin, *Repertorium*, 194–195. See also Coke, *Institutes*, 4 (arguing that because "in times past ecclesiastical persons [sought] to extend their liberties beyond their true bounds, [they] either lost or enjoyed not that which of right belonged to them"); Web v. Bachellor, 3 Keb. 476 (1653) (holding that a "[p]arson is not exempted from any new charge for repairing highways.") 4 W.& M. ch. 1 (declaring that taxes are to be levied on "every person spiritual and temporal of what estate or degree soever" with no "manner of Liberties, Privileges, or Exemptions" granted). See further S. Dowell, *A History of Taxes and Taxation in England* (London: Longmans, Green, 1884), 2:32ff.; P. Adler, *Historical Origin of Tax Exemption of Charitable Property* (Westchester, NY: Chamber of Commerce, 1922), 45ff.; S. Morgan, *The History of Parliamentary Taxation in England* (New York: Moffat, Yard & Co., 1911), 224–227.

Colonial legislatures seem to have accepted this new presumption. They started their tax provisions with instructions to "tax all the lands in the several plantations" (Trumbull, 2:294) or to raise "publique leavies and county leavies . . . by equal proportions out of all the visible estates in the colonies" (Hening, 1:305–6). They then listed copiously the properties and persons "immune" or "exempt" from its payment, including the properties of the government and political officials. See, e.g., Hening, 1:242; Cooper, 3:409ff.; Saunders, 1:185; B. Pruitt, ed., *The Massachusetts Tax Valuation List of 1771* (Boston. G. K. Hall, 1978) [hereinafter Pruitt]. There is little evidence to support the conventional assumption that church properties "were exempt from taxation as public property by the nature of things, and not by the constitution or by statute." C. Zollmann, *American Civil Church Law* (New York: AMS Press, 1969), 239; see also W. Torpey, *Judicial Doctrines of Religious Rights in America* (Chapel Hill, NC: University

those of immigrants, indigents, and incapacitated persons.[15] Three restrictions, however, limited the availability of these privileges to colonial church properties.

First, only certain types of church property were considered exemptible at common law. The properties of incorporated established churches that were devoted to the "religious uses" prescribed by the ecclesiastical laws, such as chapels, parsonages, glebes, and consecrated cemeteries, were generally exemptible. Established church properties, however, that lay vacant, that were devoted to non-religious uses, or that were held by unincorporated religious bodies were generally taxable.[16] Properties of dissenting religious groups were taxed, regardless of their use.[17] Properties held personally by ministers were taxed in some colonies but exempted in others, particularly in the later colonial period.[18] These latter colonies also exempted the properties held personally by political magistrates.

---

of North Carolina Press, 1948), 171; D. Robertson, *Should Churches Be Taxed?* (Philadelphia: Westminster Press, 1968), 51. Zollmann's assertion, widely accepted as authoritative, is based upon the undocumented dicta of a few nineteenth century state supreme court cases which upheld church property exemptions against constitutional challenges. See, e.g., Franklin Street Society v. Manchester, 60 N.H. 342, 346–351 (1880); Yale Univ. v. New Haven, 71 Conn. 316, 329–339 (1899); All Saints Parish v. Inhabitants of Brookline, 178 Mass. 404, 411–416 (1901).

15. See, e.g., Saunders, 1:185, 3:409; Hening, 1:242; Pruitt, passim. Exemptions for new immigrants was sometimes required by the founding colonial charter. See e.g., Charter of Massachusetts Bay (1629), reprinted in Thorpe, 3:1859.

16. The statutes often exempted property "under improvement" (that is, those that were built up and occupied). See, e.g., the Massachusetts Taxation Act of 1767, reprinted in Pruitt, 3; *Massachusetts Records,* 4:486. On the restriction of incorporation, see generally, Kauper and Ellis, "Religious Corporations and the Law," 71 *Michigan Law Review* 1499, 1505–1507 (1973) and sources cited therein. For English antecedents and analogues, see Burn, *Ecclesiastical Law,* 3:204; Coke, *Institutes,* 4; Godolphin, *Repertorium,* 194.

17. By the middle of the eighteenth century, legislatures in the northern colonies had exempted Protestant dissenters (though not Catholics or Jews) from these ecclesiastical taxes. In both Puritan Connecticut and Massachusetts, for example, Anglicans were exempted in 1727, Quakers and Baptists in 1729 See W. McLoughlin, *New England Dissent: The Baptists and the Separation of Church and State* (Cambridge, MA: Harvard University Press, 1971), 1:225–243, 263–277; F. Jones, *History of Taxation in Connecticut, 1636–1776* (Baltimore, MD: The Johns Hopkins Press, 1896), 60–64, and the literature cited therein. Such exemptions were not always readily accorded, however, despite the statutes. See, e.g., the case of Green v. Washburn (1769), reported in L. Wroth and H. Zobel, eds., *Legal Papers of John Adams* (Cambridge, MA: Belknap Press, 1965), 2:32–47. The southern Anglican colonies, by contrast, granted no such exemption until after the Revolutionary War. See, e.g., Hening, 9:164.

18. See, for example, Farrand, 10; *Massachusetts Records,* 4:486; *New Hampshire Collection,* 8:33; Hening, 2:359–360. Such personal exemptions to ministers, however, were strictly limited to "such estate as is their one proper estate, & vnder their one custody & improovement." Such exemptions were also conceived as forms of compensation to ministers. Ministers and their families could "by special contract with the toune . . . consent" to the payment of taxes in return for other forms of compensation. *Massachusetts Records,* 4:486; see also Jones, *History of Taxation,* 61–62. For ministers with modest personal estates this was an attractive option.

Second, these established church properties were usually exempted only from the ecclesiastical taxes that were levied for their own maintenance and use. To impose these taxes on established church properties would have been but "an idle ceremony."[19] Other property taxes, however, such as the quit-rents, poll taxes, land taxes, special assessments, hearth taxes, window taxes, and a variety of other rates on realty and personalty were often collected from the properties of the established church as from other properties.[20] A universal exemption for these established church properties from all property taxes appears to have been the exception, rather than the rule, in the colonies.[21]

Third, these tax exemptions could be held in abeyance in times of emergency or abandoned altogether if the tax liability imposed on remaining properties in the community proved too onerous. Thus in times of war, pestilence, poverty, or disaster, established churches and their clergy were required to contribute to the public coffers regardless of their eligibility for exemption.[22]

This common law pattern of tax exemption and subsidy could be readily rationalized when the state was responsible to propagate and protect one established religion to the exclusion of others. Established church corporations were effectively state agencies, their clergy effectively state officials. By devoting their properties to the religious uses prescribed by the common law, church corporations and their clergy were discharging the state's responsibility for the established religion. In return, they received tax support, tax exemptions, and other protections and privileges, like other state agencies. Occasionally the clergy themselves also received such privileges, like other state officials. These privileges could be accorded, however, only if and to the extent that churches adhered to right religion and devoted their properties to prescribed religious uses. Thus the properties of dissenting or wayward

19. Zollman, *American Civil Church Law*, 239.

20. See, for example, Benson, 21–29; B. Bond, *The Quit-Rent System in the American Colonies* (New York: Charles Scribner's Sons, 1919), 221, 255, 300; A. Smith, *The Quit-Rents of Virginia 1704*, 13, 68, 75, 98 (Baltimore, MD: Geneological Publishing Co., 1957). Even a cursory glance of some of the records of the Anglican parishes and Puritan congregations demonstrates such payments were made (or at least budgeted). See, for example, G. Chamberlayne, ed., *The Vestry Book of Saint Peter's, New Kent County, Virginia* (Richmond, VA: n.p., 1905), 170, 175, 222; *Records of the Congregational Church of Hartford* (Hartford, CT, n.p. 1876), 34, 56, 99. 109.

21. In 1702 Connecticut granted exemption to all properties devoted to "ecclesiastical, educational, and charitable uses." *Connecticut Collection*, 8:133. In 1739, South Carolina exempted the properties of churches and "free schools." *Statutes at Large of South Carolina* (1836), 3:528.

22. For example, during King Philip's War in New England the congregational churches were heavily taxed to support the authorities and during Bacon's rebellion in the south, substantial property was taken from the glebes and substantial taxes were imposed on the vestries. See H. Chadworth, *Ecclesiastical Regulations* (New York: C. Pebble Printers, 1839), 12ff., 53ff.

churches and those devoted to non-religious uses were taxable. These privileges also could be accorded only in modest proportion, lest the church grew ostentatious and opulent at the expense of the state and society, as it had prior to the Reformation. Thus the common law limited closely the scope of exemptions once granted.

2. *Tax Exemptions at Equity.* The law of equity, applied by English Chancery courts and their colonial analogues,[23] accorded tax exemptions to church properties with a rather different rationale. Consistent with the common law courts, equity courts treated all church property as presumptively taxable unless specially exempted by statute. Contrary to the common law courts, however, equity courts exempted church properties from taxation not because of the "religious uses" but because of the "charitable uses" to which they were devoted. Church properties could be exempted at equity only if and to the extent that they were used "charitably."

A definition of charity was derived from the famous Elizabethan Statute of Charitable Uses of 1601.[24] The Statute regarded as charitable all activities that supported orphans, apprentices, or scholars, that sustained public works (like highways, prisons, and bridges), that subsidized schools and universities, or that succored indigent, ill, incapacitated, elderly, or "decayed" persons. Through interpretation and application of the Statute over time, equity courts developed a more general definition of charity as any activity that redounded

> "to the benefit of an indefinite number of persons, either by bringing their hearts or minds under the influence of education or religion, by relieving their bodies from disease, suffering or constraint, by assisting them to establish themselves in life or by erecting or maintaining public buildings or works or by otherwise lessening the burdens of government."[25]

23. On the development of equity in the colonies, see Wilson, Courts of Chancery in America—Colonial Period, 18 *American Law Review* 226 (1884); J. Story, *Commentaries on Equity Jurisprudence as Administered in England and America,* 7th ed. (Boston: Little Brown, 1857), 1:56ff. The southern and middle colonies generally established chancery courts very early in their development and exercised jurisdiction over similar subjects and persons to that of the chancellor of England, though the general courts often heard equity cases as well. See O. Chitwood, *Justice in Colonial Virginia* (New York: Da Capo, 1971), 48; Wilson, Courts of Chancery, 239–255. The Puritan New England colonies resisted the establishment of separate courts of equity until well into the eighteenth century, but vested equitable jurisdiction in the governor and/or deputy-governor and sometimes also the General Court. See W. Davis, *History of the Judiciary of Massachusetts* (Boston: The Boston Book Co., 1900), 47–48, 55, 68–72. I use the generic term "equity court" to refer to both these equitable institutions.

24. 43 Eliz. ch. 4, repealed ultimately in 1888, 51 & 52 Vict. ch. 42, 13.

25. Jackson v. Phillips, 96 Mass. (14 Allen) 539, 556 (1867). This definition, which distilled numerous early definitions offered by English and American equity courts, has remained standard until well into the twentieth century. See generally Holland, "The Modern Law and

The effect, not the intent, of the activity was critical to determining its charitable character. The charitable activity could be motivated by either piety or pity; it could be meant to serve religious or secular persons or causes—so long as it yielded a distinctly "public benefit" to a sufficiently "indefinite number of persons."[26] Religion and piety were considered acceptable species, not necessary sources, of charity or benevolence.[27]

Those institutions that devoted their properties to one or more such charitable uses, or that had property entrusted to them for such charitable uses, received a variety of equitable privileges. Special trust and testamentary doctrines, like the *cy pres* doctrine, enabled them to receive property by deeds and wills that were defective in form and generally unenforceable at common law. Special property rules enabled them to transfer goods and lands to beneficiaries, free from liens, fees, and excises. Special procedural rules allowed them to bring actions that were otherwise barred by the statute of limitations or by the doctrine of laches.[28] Special tax rules afforded them both tax subsidies and tax exemptions. These charitable institutions received subsidies from the "poor rates," "education rates," and "charity taxes" that the authorities occasionally levied on the community. They received exemptions from taxes on those portions of their property that were "devoted to

Charities as Derived from the Statute of Charitable Uses," 52 *American Law Register* 201 (1904). On comparable definitions by English Chancery courts that had influence in America, see C. Crowther, *Religious Trusts: Their Development, Scope and Meaning* (Oxford, G. Ronald, 1954), 19ff.

26. See generally, J. Pomeroy, *A Treatise on Equity Jurisprudence as Administered in the United States*, 4th ed. (San Francisco, CA: Whitney Bancroft Co., 1918), SS. 1019–1020; Story, *Commentaries*, S. 1164 and the numerous sources cited therein. See also Crowther, *Religious Trusts*, 29: "The shift from a religious to a public benefit rationale for charity change the focus of the inquiry. Whereas it was previously assumed [before the Statute of Charitable Uses] that any gift of land or money was automaticallly a charitable act, now it was to be decided whether the gift served a proper public purpose. Where the property was used only privately, it could be declared non-charitable."

27. See G. Jeremy, *A Treatise of the Equity Jurisdiction of the High Court of Chancery* (New York: Halstead and Voorhies, 1840), 237; Pomeroy, *Treatise on Equity*, SS. 1021–1024; Story, *Commentaries*, S. 1164. This disassociation of piety and charity was precisely the intent of the drafters of the Statute of Charitable Uses in 1601. See generally, G. Jones, *History of the Law of Charity 1532–1827* (London: Cambridge University Press, 1969), 29ff., 57ff., 76ff.; M. Chesterman, *Charities, Trusts, and Social Welfare* (London: Weidenfeld and Nicolson, 1979), 16ff.; W. Jordan, *Philanthropy in England 1480–1660: A Study of the Changing Patterns of English Social Aspirations* (London: G. Allen & Unwin, 1959), 112ff.

28. See, e.g., White v. White, 28 Eng. Rep. 955 (1688); Moggridge v. Thackwell, 32 Eng. Rep. 15 (1803); Mills v. Farmer, 35 Eng. Rep. 597 (1815), which summarize early modern precedents. See generally, G. Cooper, *A Treatise of Pleading on the Equity Side of the High Court of Chancery* (New York: I. Riley, 1813), xxvi–xxvii, 218–222; L. Shelford, *A Practical Treatise of the Law of Mortmain and Charitable Uses and Trusts* (Philadelphia: John S. Littell, 1842), 512ff., 672ff.; Story, *Commentaries*, SS. 1165–1173; and G. Jones, *History of the Law of Charity*, 57–104. The colonial equity courts based many of these privileges on the authoritative English source G. Duke, *Law of Charitable Uses*, R.W. Bridgman, ed. (London: n.p., 1805; reprint of 1676 ed.), which enjoyed wide circulation and authority.

charitable uses and other public concernments."[29] Both the amount of the subsidy and the scope of the exemption received by these charitable institutions were calculated on a strictly case-by-case basis. Overseers, visitors, or commissioners regulated by the equity courts periodically visited each charitable institution to assess its performance and to determine its needs. Thereafter the regulators recommended to the equity court each charity's entitlement to subsidy and exemption. It was not unusual for the equity court to afford well-established and well-endowed charities only modest subsidies and minimal exemptions but to afford new and impoverished charities plentiful subsidies and plenary exemptions from tax.[30]

This law of equity provided colonial churches with a second basis for receiving tax exemptions and tax subsidies. As religious institutions, they could receive the ecclesiastical tax exemptions and subsidies afforded by the common law. As charitable institutions, they could receive the charitable tax exemptions and subsidies afforded by equity law. While the exemptions and subsidies afforded by the common law were restricted only to established churches, those afforded by equity were available to all churches.

Colonial established churches often served as charitable institutions. Church meetinghouses and chapels were used not only to conduct religious services but also to host town assemblies, political rallies, and public auctions, to hold educational and vocational classes, to maintain census rolls and marriage certificates, to house the community library, and to discharge a number of other public functions. Parsonages were used not only to house the minister's family, but also to harbor orphans and widows, the sick and the handicapped, and victims of abuse and disaster. Glebe lands were farmed not only to sustain the minister and his family but also to support widows, sojourners, and elderly and incapacitated members of the community. Moreover, charitable societies sponsored by the established churches, such as the famous Society for the Propagation of the Gospel in Foreign Parts, helped to found schools, orphanages, hospices, and almshouses throughout the colonies. These acts of public charity were vital parts of the established church's ministry and mission in the colonies. In return, the established churches and the charitable institutions that they founded were entitled to receive charitable tax exemptions and subsidies from the equity courts.[31]

29. Trumbull, 3:158.

30. See generally Shelford, *A Practical Treatise*, 204–282; G. Jones, *History of the Law of Charity*, 39ff.

31. See generally Adler, *Historical Origin*, 76ff.; R. Kelso, *The History of Public Poor Relief in Massachusetts, 1620–1920* (Montclair, NJ: Patterson Smith, 1969; reprint of 1922 ed.); P. Bruce, *Institutional History of Virginia in the Seventeenth Century* (New York and London: G. P. Putnam's Sons, 1910), 1:73–93, 163–193. In the Anglican south, primary responsibility for social welfare fell to the established churches. See, e.g., Hening, 1:242. The annual budgets of the vestries thus included large expenditures for poor relief, education, and other forms of welfare for both members and non-members. See, e.g., the C. Chamberlayne, ed., *Paris*

Established churches, however, held no monopoly on charitable activity. Non-conformist churches and private philanthropic groups under their sponsorship were equally active. The non-conformists often used their meetinghouses and parsonages for night shelters, relief stations, and refuge places. Pennsylvania Quakers and Maryland Catholics were famous for their diligence in establishing day schools, hospitals, hospices, almshouses, orphanages, poor farms, and workhouses all along the Atlantic seaboard, particularly in the middle colonies. Scottish Presbyterians and Irish Catholics helped to form philanthropic groups, like the Scot's Charitable Society and the Charitable Irish Society, which sponsored and subsidized the families of new immigrants and newly emancipated indentured servants. Various religious groups contributed to the establishment and support of some of the great eastern colleges. In return, these non-conformist churches, and the charitable organizations that they established were entitled to receive tax exemptions and subsidies from the equity courts.[32]

These twin traditions of church property exemptions stood sharply juxtaposed on the eve of the American Revolution. Equity courts accorded tax exemptions to any church properties that were devoted to charitable uses. Common law courts accorded tax exemptions to established church properties that were devoted to prescribed religious uses. In some colonies, the sharp contrasts between these two traditions had begun to soften. Equity courts, following English precedents on superstitious uses, had occasionally prevented the formation of charities by religious non-conformists.[33] Colonial

---

Register of Christ Church, Middlesex County, Virginia, 1653–1812 (Baltimore, MD: Geneological Publications Society, 1975); C. Chamberlayne, ed., Paris Register of St. Peter's, New Kent County, Virginia, 1680–1787 (Baltimore, MD: Geneological Publications Society, 1975); C. Chamberlayne, ed., Vestry Book of St. Peter's Parish, New Kent County, VA, 1682–1758 (Baltimore, MD: Geneological Publications Society, 1975); C. Chamberlayne, ed., Vestry Book of Petsworth County, Virginia, 1677–1793 (Baltimore, MD: Geneological Publications Society, 1974). In the Puritan north, primary responsibility for social welfare fell to the municipalities and families. See generally L. Wright, The Cultural Life of the American Colonies, 1607–1763 (New York: MacMillan & Co., 1957), 23ff.; Kelso, History of Public Poor Relief, 89ff. Where churches did engage in social welfare, it was often restricted to congregant members. See, e.g., Records of the Congregational Church in Suffield, Connecticut, 1710–1836 (Boston: Boston Book Company, 1949).

32. On the charitable activities of dissenting churches in the colonies, see generally Adler, Historical Origin, 76ff.; H. Miller, The Legal Foundations of American Philanthropy, 1776–1844 (Madison, WI: State Historical Society of Wisconsin, 1961), 3–8; D. Schneider, The History of Public Welfare in New York State, 1609–1866 (Montclair, NJ: Patterson Smith, 1969; reprint of 1969 ed.); A. Jorns, The Quakers as Pioneers in Social Work (Montclair, NJ: Patterson Smith, 1969; reprint of 1931 ed.).

33. On the English background to superstitious use doctrine, see G. Jones, History of the Law of Charity, 11–15, 82–87; Story, Commentaries, S. 1164; Pomeroy, Treatise on Equity, S. 1021. On the American development of the doctrine, see H. Desmond, The Church and the Law, With Special Reference to the Ecclesiastical Law in the United States (New York: n.p., 1898), 49–56. In general, however, American courts, both before and after the Revolution, spurned the doctrine.

legislatures, responding to widespread popular agitation, had granted to some Protestant dissenting churches the right to exemption from the ecclesiastical taxes levied for the established church—though formidable administrative obstacles often obstructed the exercise of this right, and the ecclesiastical tax revenues were still paid to the established church alone.

B. State Constitutional Challenges to the Tax Exemptions of Church Property

The colonial law of tax exemption of church property continued largely uninterrupted in the early decades of the American republic. This conservatism was constitutionally conditioned. The United States Constitution included no provision on tax exemption, and the religion clauses of the first amendment were binding only on the federal government ("Congress"), not the state governments.[34] The early state constitutions provided simply that "[a]ll the laws which have heretofore been adopted, used, and approved . . . and usually practiced on in the courts of law shall still remain and be in full force, until altered or repealed by the legislature."[35] The states legislatures and judiciaries were further instructed that "all religious societies or bodies of men heretofore united or incorporated for the advancement of religion or learning, or for other pious or charitable purposes, shall be encouraged and protected in the enjoyment of the privileges, immunities, and estates, which they are accustomed to enjoy."[36] Thus, in most states religious bodies that were previously united or incorporated received the traditional exemptions afforded by common law and equity law courts.[37]

Three provisions in the new state constitutions and their amendments, however, provided the ground for challenge to these colonial laws of tax exemption of church property.

1. *Disestablishment of Religion.* The first challenge was posed by state constitutional prohibitions on religious establishment. These prohibitions

34. On the restricted scope of the first amendment religion clauses, see Handy, "Why it Took 150 Years for Supreme Court Church-State Cases to Escalate," in R. White and A. Zimmerman, eds., *An Unsettled Arena: Religion and the Bill of Rights* (Grand Rapids, MI: Eerdmans, 1990), 52; Witte, Theology and Politics.

35. Mass. Const. pt. II, ch. VI, art. VI (1780). Similar language appears in the constitutions of other states. See, e.g., De. Const. art. 25 (1776); N.H. Const. art. XC (1792); N.J. Const. S. 22 (1776); R.I. Const. art. 14, s. 1 (1842); S.C. Const. art VII (1790). On the initial conservative attitude of the states toward colonial and English law, see generally E. Brown and W. Blume, *British Statutes in American Law 1776–1836* (Ann Arbor, MI: University of Michigan Law School, 1964), 47–200.

36. Penn. Const. S. 45 (1776). See similar language in Mass. Const. pt. I, art. III (1780).

37. A convenient summary of the state laws on tax exemption of church personalty and realty is provided in Wolcott, Report on Direct Taxes Communicated to the House of Representatives, December 14, 1796, reprinted in *American State Papers (Finance)* Class 3, 1:414–441 (1858).

undercut the authority of government officials to endorse one religion over another, to prescribe religious beliefs, to mandate church attendance, to levy ecclesiastical taxes, and to govern ecclesiastical polities and properties. Religion was no longer an affair of government and law. The cleric was no longer a political official. The church was no longer a subsidized state agency. The meetinghouse was no longer a public property.[38]

These disestablishment provisions rendered the traditional common law of church property exemptions vulnerable to attack. The establishment rationale on which these exemptions had been based was no longer available. No other rationale had as yet been offered. A small, but persistent group of critics from the 1810s onward thus challenged these common law exemptions as vestiges of religious establishment. Their arguments lie at the heart of the anti-exemption case still today.

Tax exemptions of church property, the critics charged, favor religious groups over non-religious groups. To exempt religious properties from their portion of the cost of state services and protections is not only to subsidize them but also to penalize non-religious properties within the same tax base whose tax burdens are proportionately increased. This form of religious support and subsidy, albeit indirect, cannot be countenanced under the disestablishment clauses of the state constitutions.[39]

Furthermore, such exemptions favor well-vested, traditional religions over struggling, newer religions. Since properties are taxed according to their value, the "humble congregation in a small wooden church," can enjoy only a fraction of the tax savings enjoyed by "the same-sized congregation in the beautiful hewn palace, with painted windows, frescoed ceilings, and silver mounted pews."[40] The disestablishment clauses, if they permit any government supports of religion, mandate uniformity in government treatment of all religious groups. The "inequality and disparity" in the benefits afforded religious groups under exemption laws, therefore, cannot be countenanced.[41]

Finally, the critics argued, such exemptions encourage the conflation of

38. New Jersey was the first of the former colonies to disestablish religion by constitutional provision. See N.J. Const. S. 19 (1776). Massachusetts was the last. See Mass. Const. art. 11 (1833).

39. See, e.g., Orr v. Baker, 4 Ind. 86, 88 (1853); Commonwealth v. Thomas, 119 Ky. 208, 213–214 (1904); Rep. Pettit, in *Official Records of the Indiana Constitutional Convention* (Indianapolis, IN: State Government Printing Office, 1851), 1287–1289; Rep. Buckner, in *Official Report of the Proceedings and Debates of the Kentucky Constitutional Convention* (Lexington, KY: State Government Printing Office, 1890), 2:2402ff. [hereinafter Kentucky Records]; J. Morton, *Exempting the Churches: An Argument Against this Unjust and Unconstitutional Practice* (New York: n.p. 1915), 11ff., 63ff.; J. Parton, *Taxation of Church Property* (n.p., 1873), App., 17; E. Tarr, *Upon the Subject of the Laws Exempting Church Property From Taxation*, quoted and discussed in Robertson, *Should Churches be Taxed*, 67–69.

40. Rep. Sachs in *Kentucky Records*, 2:2425.

41. See especially J. Quincy, *Tax Exemption: No Excuse for Spoliation* (n.p., n.d.), 8.

church and state. The "silent accumulations of [church] property" occasioned by tax exemption and religious corporation laws, James Madison warned, will inevitably result in "encroachments by Ecclesiastical Bodies" upon the public square and the political process.[42] Several decades later, President Grant similarly cautioned that tax exemptions had allowed churches to accumulate such "vast property" and to aggregate such "vast political power" that "sequestration without constitutional authority" and "bloody" confrontation would eventually ensue.[43] "The separation of Church and the State" required that all "legal instruments encouraging ecclesiastical aggrandizement of wealth and power," including tax exemptions, be "expunged."[44]

These criticisms of the traditional exemptions of church property were not just isolated pedantic musings. In the middle decades of the nineteenth century they appeared rather regularly in editorials, pamphlets, and petitions.[45] Legislative assemblies and constitutional conventions in several states debated bills and proposed amendments that would have outlawed such exemptions.[46] President Grant proposed a similar amendment to the United States Constitution that was only narrowly defeated.[47] State and federal courts occasionally faced similar constitutional arguments.[48]

2. *Truncation of Equity.* The second challenge to the colonial law of tax

42. Fleet, "Madison's 'Detached Memoranda'" 3 *William and Mary Quarterly*, 3d. ser. 554–560 (1946). See similar sentiments in G. Hunt, ed., *The Writings of James Madison* (New York: G. P. Putnam's Sons, 1900), 8:132–133.

43. U.S. Grant, State of the Union Message of 1875, in F. Israel, ed., *The State of the Union Messages of the Presidents, 1790–1966* (New York: Chelsea House, 1966), 2:1296.

44. Ibid. President Garfield likewise commented: "The divorce between church and state ought to be absolute. It ought to be so absolute that no church property anywhere, in any state, or in the nation, should be exempt from equal taxation; of if you exempt the property of any church organization, to that extent you impose a tax upon the whole community." Quoted by Morton, *Exempting the Churches*, 63.

45. See the collection of quotations in id., 63ff., Robertson, *Should Churches be Taxed*, 69ff.

46. For a detailed state-by-state account, see C. Antieau, P. Carroll, & T. Burke, *Religion Under the State Constitutions* (Brooklyn, NY: Central Book Co., 1965), 120–172; B. Moll, *Zur Geschichte Vermoegenssteuren* (Berlin: 1911), 33ff.

47. On the debates over the proposed Sixteenth Amendment to the United States Constitution, which would have included provisions concerning church property and taxation, see or at least i on tax exemptions, see 4 Cong. Rec. 5190ff. 5453ff. (1876). See discussion in Meyer, "The Blaine Amendment and the Bill of Rights," 64 *Harvard Law Review* 939 (1951); Witte, Theology and Politics.

48. Though critical of exemptions, none of these opinions held such exemptions unconstitutional under the stage establishment clauses. See, e.g., Congregational Society v. Ashley, 10 Vt. 241, 245 (1838); State v. Collector of New Jersey, 24 N.J.L. 108, 120–121 (1853); Trustees of Griswold College v. State, 46 Iowa 275, 282 (1877). On the other hand, however, courts have persistently treated such exemptions as legislative privileges protected neither by state free exercise nor state impairment of contract provisions. Ibid.; Franklin Street Society v. Manchester, 60 N.H. 342, 349–350 (1880).

exemptions was posed by state constitutional mandates to revise or to revoke English statutes. Most state constitutional conventions had initially ratified such statutes without amendment or emendation, but the state legislatures were empowered to "alter or repeal" such laws as "circumstances demanded."[49] As nationalist sentiment became more strident and judicial criticisms of English law grew more sharp, legislatures began to respond. Several states appointed committees to review English statutes and precedents that had traditionally governed the colonies and territories and to purge that those they found "odious, obsolete, and obnoxious."[50] Many English statutes survived such "purges" only in revised form, if at all.

These constitutional mandates rendered the traditional equity law of ecclesiastical exemptions vulnerable to attack. For one of the casualties of the purges was the English Statute of Charitable Uses of 1601, which undergirded both the charitable jurisdiction of equity courts and the law of charitable institutions that these courts had helped to devise.[51] As a result, several states thus removed charitable institutions from equity jurisdiction and relieved them of their equitable privileges.[52] The special testamentary, procedural, and property privileges previously accorded these institutions at equity were removed. The special tax subsidies and tax exemptions were withdrawn. Courts also developed strict rules for the formation and function of new charitable institutions. Such institutions were required to incorporate, to limit their property holdings, and to divulge in detail their charitable activities. In several cases, donations and devises to religious charities were invalidated, religious groups were denied charitable corporate charters, and religious functions were deemed "inappropriate" as charitable uses.[53]

3. *Universality of Taxation.* A third challenge to traditional ecclesiastical exemptions was posed by state constitutional requirements that property taxes be "universally" applied. In the middle third of the nine-

---

49. See, e.g., Mass Const. pt. II, ch. VI, art. VI (1780); N.J. Const. S. 22 (1776).

50. Z. Swift, *A System of the Laws of the State of Connecticut* (Windham, CT: John Bryne, 1795), 42. See Brown & Blume, *British Statutes,* 9ff.; H. Berman, Comparative Legal History: Course Materials, IV. 46–108 (unpublished).

51. See the excellent discussion in Miller, *Legal Foundations,* 21–39 on the debate between Chief Justice Marshall, who in Philadelphia Baptist Association v. Hart's Executors, 17 U.S. (4 Wheat) 1 (1819) argued that such jurisdiction was based exclusively upon the Statute and Justice Story, who in Vidal et al. v. Executors of Stephen Girard, 43 U.S. (2 How.) 127 (1844) argued that such jurisdiction was based on long standing custom that antedated the Statute.

52. For a careful state-by-state analysis, see Zollmann, "The Development of the Law of Charities in the United States," 19 *Columbia Law Review* 91, 286 (1919).

53. See, e.g., Trippe v. Frazier, 4 Harris and Johnson 446 (Md. 1819); Dashiell v. Attorney General, 5 Harris and Johnson 392 (Md. 1822); Green v. Dennis, 6 Conn. 293 (1826); Janey's Executor v. Latane, et al. 4 Leigh 351 (Va. 1834); Gass & Bonta v. Wilhite 32 Ky. (2 Dana) 170 (1834). This restrictive policy was inspired, in part, by the Hart's Executors case, in part by a sharp jurisprudential reaction to the equitable doctrines of cy pres. See Fisch, "The Cy Press Doctrine and Changing Philosophies," 51 *Michigan Law Review* 375 (1953).

teenth century, many states thoroughly reformed their property taxation laws. The myriad species of special and sporadic taxes on realty and personalty were consolidated into a general annual property tax. The multiple layers of tax officials were merged into uniform state and municipal tax commissions. The antiquated tax valuation lists were thoroughly revised. The long lists of tax exemptions and immunities inherited from the colonies were cast aside as "unwieldly" and "unfair."[54] These revisions were written into the state constitutions. The constitutional conventions started with the new presumption that "[t]axation shall be equal and uniform throughout the State, and all property, both real and personal, shall be taxed in proportion to its value."[55] The presumption was that all property was to be universally taxed, and tax exemptions, including those for church property, were exceptions. These exemptions could be granted only if the "public welfare" would be advanced or other "good and compelling" reasons could be adduced.

C. The Rise of the Modern Theory and
Law of Tax Exemption of Church Property

These three constitutional challenges prompted proponents of ecclesiastical exemptions into action. The establishment argument had to be rebutted. The equitable privileges of churches and their properties had to be restored. The "good and compelling" reasons for exemption had to recited. Later nineteenth century statesmen and churchmen met these constitutional challenges forcefully and developed the core of the modern theory and law of tax exemptions of church property. They did not forsake the common law and equity law traditions of tax exemption in this effort, but fused them. The basic exemption theory of each tradition was preserved but was cast in more generic form. The basic exemption laws of the colonies remained in place but were given more general application.

1. *The Modern Theory of Tax Exemption.* The modern theory of tax exemption of church property was forged in the later nineteenth century in a plethora of judicial opinions, legislative arguments, convention speeches, popular pamphlets, newspaper editorials, printed sermons, and scholarly

---

54. See generally Benson, "A History of the General Property Tax," 34–47. For more specific state studies, see J. Brindley, *History of Taxation in Iowa* (Iowa City, IA: State Historical Society of Iowa, 1911), 260ff.; *Exemption from Taxation in Massachusetts: History and Documentation* (Boston, Little Brown, 1910); C. McLeish, *The Laws of the State of Texas Affecting Church Property* (Washington: The Catholic University of America Press, 1960), 160ff.; M. Welsh, *The Laws of the State of Nevada Affecting Church Property* (Washington: The Catholic University of America Press, 1962), 130ff.

55. Wa. Va. Const. art. VIII, s. 1 (1861/3). See also Benson, at 34–47. By the end of the Civil War, at least 15 states had written comparable requirements into their state constitutions. Id., at 42. Similar language appears in more than 30 state constitutions today. See M. Bernard, *Constitutions, Taxation, and Land Policy* (Lexington, MA: Lexington Books, 1979).

papers. Though these sources varied widely in quality and cogency, their basic premises and principles admit of rather short summary.

"The policy on which the exemption of church property is granted," declared the Connecticut Supreme Court, "is simply the encouragement of religion" and the churches.[56] For churches serve to the advantage of both society in general and the state in particular.

Churches, exemption proponents argued, dispense intangible, but invaluable, benefits to society through their religious activities. Churches cultivate public spiritedness. They induce citizens to "benevolence, charity, generosity, love of our fellowman, deference to rank, to age and sex, tenderness to the young, active sympathy for those in trouble and distress, beneficence to the destitute and poor." Without such acts and dispositions, a truly "civil society . . . could not long endure."[57] Churches inculcate public morality. They teach chastity and continence, temperance and modesty, obedience and obligation, respect for the person and property of another. They have internal structures of authority to punish parishioners guilty of immorality. Such moral discipline is "probably of as much value to society, in keeping the peace and preserving the rights of property, as the most elaborate and expensive police system."[58] Churches enhance neighborhood values. Their "immaculate" buildings and grounds are aesthetically pleasing. They attract respected citizens. They promote stability of neighborhood populations.[59] Churches foster democratic principles and practices. They inspire citizens to vote for candidates and to participate in the political process. They instruct officials on moral principles and social needs. They preach against injustice by the authorities and insurrection by the masses.[60] "Churches and religion, therefore," a Massachusetts Tax Commissioner put it, "make life and property more secure and promote peace, order, and prosperity in the community." Exemptions are thus granted "not that religion may increase . . . but that society may be benefitted."[61]

---

56. Town of Hartford v. First Unitarian Society, 66 Conn. 368, 375 (1895); see similar sentiments in Commonwealth v. Y.M.C.A., 116 Ky. 711 (1903).

57. Trustees of the First Methodist Episcopal Church v. City of Atlanta, 76 Ga. 181, 192–193 (1886), rev. on other grounds sub nom., City of Atlanta v. First Presbyterian Church, 86 Ga. 730 (1890).

58. Commonwealth v. Y.M.C.A., 116 Ky. 711, 718 (1903).

59. See, e.g., P. Schaff, *Church and State in the United States* (New York: Arno Press, 1972; reprint of 1844 ed.), 75; H. Foote, *The Taxation of Churches* (n.p., c. 1870), 27–30.

60. See, e.g., Ward v. New Hampshire, 56 N.H. 508 (1876); T. Brown, *Some Reasons for the Exemption of Church Property From Taxation* (Rochester, NY: Scranton, Wetmore & Co., 1881), 12.

61. Quoted by Foote, *The Taxation of Churches*, 19–20. See also A. Bledsoe, *Shall Georgia Tax Church Property?* (Atlanta, Atlanta Litho & Print Co., 1897), 5: "It is upon this principle . . . that church property has heretofore been exempted from taxation, viz: that the exemption was worth more to the state than the taxation. Churches are not built for the purposes of gain. [T]he church is built for the benefit of the public."

Churches not only dispense social benefits through their religious activities, exemption proponents argued, but also discharge state burdens through their charitable activities. They discharge the burdens of education through their parochial schools and colleges, educational and vocational programs, literary and linguistic societies. They discharge burdens of social welfare through their hostels and hospitals, almshouses and nightshelters, counselling and crisis centers, youth camps and retirement homes. They discharge burdens of foreign aid through their programs for foreign missions and disaster relief.[62] Churches, one exuberant pamphleteer wrote, must be considered the "most charitable of charities."[63] Through such voluntary social services, the church saves the state enormous costs that would "otherwise be imposed upon the public . . . by general taxation."[64] Tax exemption, proponents concluded, is a suitable *quid pro quo* for such services.

This new "state burden" and "social benefits" theory of tax exemption skillfully blended traditional arguments. The traditional common law theory had taught that religious use exemptions were accorded to properties that discharged state burdens for the established religion. The traditional equity law theory had taught that charitable use exemptions were accorded to any properties that dispensed social benefits. These arguments were now reversed and softened. Religious use exemptions, no longer justifiable on establishment grounds, were now justified on the basis of the distinctive social benefits dispensed by all religious groups. Charitable use exemptions, no longer justifiable on unspecified social benefit grounds, were now justified on the basis of the specific state responsibilities discharged by all religious groups. The new theory of tax exemptions thus captured the traditional arguments but recast them to broaden an unduly narrow category of religious use exemptions and to narrow an unwieldily broad category of charitable use exemptions.

2. *The Modern Law of Tax Exemption.* Not only the theory but also the law of tax exemptions of church property was transformed in the latter half of the nineteenth century and the early part of the twentieth. Such exemptions no longer turned on the isolated statutes and equitable customs inherited from colonial times. Nearly one third of the states developed new constitutional provisions that guaranteed such exemptions to all religious groups.[65]

62. See C. Tobin, *The Exemption from Taxation of Privately Owned Real Property Used for Religious, Charitable, and Educational Purposes* (Albany, NY: William E. Hannan & Leland L. Tolman, 1934), 20–27. Among cases, see Seminary of our Lady of Angels v. Barber, 49 N.Y. Sup. Ct. 27 (1886); M.E. Church, South v. Hinton, 92 Tenn. 128 (1893); Y.M.C.A. v. Douglas County, 60 Neb. 642 (1900).

63. Bledsoe, *Shall Georgia Tax Church Property,* 5.

64. Y.M.C.A. v. Douglas County, 60 Neb. 642, 646 (1900).

65. See Ala. Const. art. IV, S. 91 (1901); Ark. Const. art. XVI, S. 5 (1874); Cal. Const. art. XIII, S.1.5 (1875; amended 1900); Colo. Const. art. X, S. 5 (1876); Kan. Const. art. XI, S. 1 (1859); Ky. Const. S. 170 (1890); La. Const. S. 230 (1898); Minn Const. art. XI, S. 1 (1857); N.D.

The remainder of the states developed comprehensive statutory schemes that were either mandated by or validated under state constitutions.[66]

Consistent with the common law tradition, virtually all states exempted properties "devoted to religious uses" or "used for religious purposes." Most states insisted, however, that such property uses be "actual" and "real." Properties that had been abandoned or sporadically used for religious purposes in the past or that were merely purchased or planned for religious uses in the future were generally taxable.[67] Most states also insisted that such properties be owned by a "religious association"; a few states, particularly in earlier decades, insisted further that such religious associations be incorporated under local state law as religious corporations.[68] A few states took no account of the identity of the property owner, so long as the exempt property was devoted to religious uses. This allowed investors to receive property exemptions by leasing their properties to churches.[69]

The definition and delimitation of the phrase "religious use" was the subject of considerable legislation and litigation. Tax assessors and judges could no longer simply look to the uses prescribed by the establishment law, as they had done in colonial and early republican times. They could no longer simply consider the property uses of the one established church. A

Const. art. XI, S. 176 (1889); Okla. Const. art. X, S. 6 (1907); S.C. Const. art. X, S. 4 (1895); S.D. Const. art. X, S. 6 (1889); Utah Const. art. XIII, S. 2 (1896); Va. Const. S. 1902 (1902); Wyo. Const. art. XV, S. 10 (1889).

66. See Ariz. Const. art. X, S. 2 (1912); Del. Const. art. VIII, S. 1 (1879); Fla. Const. art. IX, S. 1 (1885); Idaho Const. art. VII, S. 5 (1889); Ill. Const. art. IX, S. 3 (1848; amended 1870); Ind. Const. art. X, S. 1 (1851); Mo. Const. art. X, S. 6 (1875); Mont. Const. art. VII, S. 2 (1889); Nev. Const. art. X, S. 1 (1864); N.C. Const. art. V, S. 5 (1876); Ohio Const. art. XII, S. 5 (1851); Pa. Const. art. VIII, S. 2 (1873); Tenn Const. art. II, S. 28 (170); Tex. Const. art. VIII, S. 2 (1876); W. Va. Const. art. X, S. 1 (1872); Wyo. Const. art. XV, S. 12 (1889).

67. See, e.g., Gibbons v. District of Columbia, 116 U.S. 404 (1886); Trinity Church v. New York, 10 How. Prac. 138 (N.J. 1854); All Saints Parish v. Brookline, 178 Mass. 404 (1901). Later, courts softened this latter requirement and exempted properties that were clearly intended for, or under construction for, religious uses. See, e.g., Harrison v. Guilford County, 218 N.C. 718 (1940).

68. These requirements of both ownership and use of an exempt property were usually imposed by statute or judicial interpretation, rather than by express constitutional provision. See, e.g., Wisconsin Statutes Annotated, Sec. 70.11. The requirement of incorporation of the religious association was imposed by judicial interpretation. See, e.g., Evangelical Baptist Benevolent & Mission Society, 204 Mass. 28 (1910); Christian Business Men's Comm'n v. State, 228 Minn. 5489 (1949); People ex re. Unity Congregational Society v. Mills, 189 Misc. 774 (N.Y. 1947); Harrisburg v. Ohev Sholem Congregation, 32 Pa. Co. 589, 9 Daugh Co. 184 (1906). The requirement of incorporation of the religious association was imposed by judicial interpretation. See, e.g., Manresa Inst. v. Norwalk, 61 Conn. 228 (1891); Church of Saint Monica v. Mayor of New York, 119 N.Y. 91 (1890); United States National Bank v. Poor Handmaids, 148 Wisc. 613 (1912); Franke v. Mann, 106 Wisc. 118 (1900).

69. See, e.g., Horwell v. Philadelphia, 8 Pa. 280 (1853); Church of Epiphany v. Raine, 10 Ohio Dec. Repr. (n.d.); People v. Salvation Army, 305 Ill. 545 (1922); Willard v. Pike, 59 Vt. 202 (1886).

more generic and pluralistic definition of religious use was required. Over time, a vast spectrum of "religious use" exemptions emerged among the states.

All states exempted sanctuaries, synagogues, and other properties devoted to religious worship services, together with the driveways, walkways, parking lots and other appurtenant lands necessary for the reasonable use of these improvements.[70] Two conditions, however, were often imposed. First, the religious worship that occurred in those buildings had to be "public" in character. Thus secluded cloisters and monasteries, private chapels in hospitals, orphanages, or schools, and the worship facilities of small, exclusive cults or those who engaged in private meditation or family worship were generally not eligible for religious use exemptions.[71] Second, the property usually had to be "improved." Thus agrarian communal religions, youth retreat groups, or naturalist religions that worshipped in crude temporary shelters or in designated regions of the countryside generally did not receive religious use exemptions.[72]

A few states, like Pennsylvania and Illinois, limited their religious use exemptions to these public worship facilities alone. Most states, however—either by express statutory provision or, more frequently, through judicial interpretation—extended the scope of such exemptions well beyond this core.

First, religious use exemptions were generally accorded to the properties that supported the ministry of the exempted church. Church buildings annexed to or near the sanctuary or synagogue and used for catechization, fellowship, weddings, storage, and comparable functions were usually exempted in such states, though acreage and space limitations were sometimes imposed.[73] Separate church properties, however, that housed denominational printing facilities, mission and evangelism centers, administrative and governmental offices, or religious educational and vocational facilities were often not eligible for religious use exemptions, though in some states, they could be eligible for charitable use exemptions. Second, more than half the states accorded religious use exemptions to parsonages and other living quarters of ministers and their families, though strict limitations were often

---

70. There are a few extreme cases, where courts have exempted the building, but not the property that it occupies, but these are exceptions. See, e.g., Lefevre v. Detroit, 2 Mich. 586 (1853).

71. See, e.g., St. Joseph's Church v. Providence, 12 R.I. 19 (1878); Association for Benefit of Colored Orphans v. New York, 104 N.Y. 581 (1887); In re City of Pawtucket, 24 R.I. 86 (1902); People ex rel. Carsen v. Muldoon, 306 Ill. 234 (1923); Layman's Weekend Retreat League v. Butler, 83 Pa. Super. 1 (1924).

72. See, e.g., People ex rel. McCullogh v. Deutsche Evangelische Lutherische Jehovah Gemeinde, 249 Ill. 132 (1911).

73. See, e.g., In re Bond Hill-Roselawn Hebrew School, 151 Ohio St. 70 (1949); Saint Barbara's Roman Church v. City of New York, 277 N.Y.S. 538 (1935).

imposed on the size and value of such quarters.[74] A few states insisted further that such quarters be actually occupied by an ordained cleric serving the church that owned the parsonage, not merely a retired minister, church administrator, or custodian.[75] Third, a small minority of states went even further and extended religious use exemptions to church properties that provided "auxiliary religious services" to their parishioners. In these states, church-run parochial schools, cemeteries, counselling centers, summer camps, retirement homes, retreat centers, restaurants, and even recreation facilities were granted religious use exemptions.[76]

Consistent with the equity tradition, all states also exempted properties that were devoted to "charitable," "benevolent," or "eleemosynary" uses or purposes. The colonial definition of charity remained in effect: any use of property that provided distinctive public services to a sufficiently indefinite number of persons was considered charitable. The conditions that were imposed on religious use exemptions were also imposed on charitable use exemptions. The charitable use had to be "actual" and "public," and the exempt property usually had to be owned by a charitable association.[77]

Religious associations could readily avail themselves of these charitable use exemptions for their properties. Aside from "purely sacerdotal associations," most religious associations were also considered to be charitable associations.[78] Aside from religious worship services, most religious uses of property were also considered to be charitable uses of property. Though the core "religious uses" and core "charitable uses" of church property remained distinctive, most uses of church property could be considered at once

74. A few states interpreted vague constitutional or statutory provisions on "religious use" and "church property" to include parsonages and other clerical residences. See, e.g., Church of Holy Faith v. State Tax Comm'r, 39 N.M. 403 (1935); Wilmington v. Saint Satnislaus Kostka Church, 49 Del. 5 (1954). Most states, however, have consistently denied exemptions for parsonages, arguing that the primary use of parsonages is for room and board, not worship. See, e.g., M.E. Church v. Ellis, 38 Ind. 3 (1871); People ex rel. Thompson v. First Congregational Church of Oak Park, 232 Ill. 158 (1907); State v. Union Congregational Church, 173 Minn. 40 (1927). Courts have insisted on this interpretation, even where the parsonage is used in part for religious services, church meetings, and storage of items used in the sanctuary. Ramsey County v. Church of the Good Shepherd, 45 Minn. 229 (1891); Watterson v. Halliday, 77 Ohio St. 150 (1907); Gerke v. Pucell, 25 Ohio St. 229 (1874); St. Joseph's Church v. Assessors of Taxes, 12 R.I. 19 (1909).

75. Ibid. See also Broadway Christian Church v. Commonwealth, 112 KY. 448 (1902); Saint Matthew's Lutheran Church for the Deaf v. Division of Tax Appeals, 18 N.J. Super. 552 (1952).

76. See generally Zollmann, *American Civil Church Law*, 270–275; Van Alstyne, "Tax Exemption of Church Property," 20 *Ohio State Law Journal* 461, 490–503 (1959).

77. See generally, Zollmann, "Religious Charities in the American Tax Law," 7 *Marquette Law Review* 131 (1922–23); Zollmann, "Tax Exemption," in *American Law of Charities* (Boston: Little Brown, 1924), 16.71.

78. See, e.g., Carter v. Eaton, 75 N.H. 560 (1910); Glaser v. Congregation Kehillath Israel, 263 Mass. 435 (1928); Betts v. Young Men's Christian Association of Erie, 83 Pa. Super. 545 (1924).

"religious" and "charitable" under state exemption laws. Thus a variety of church property uses and improvements were exempted under charitable use categories—the properties occupied and used by church administrative centers, seminaries, Bible societies, missionary societies, religious publishers, church youth camps and retreat centers, parochial schools, Sunday schools, church women's societies, and many others.[79]

Three exemption patterns emerged as a result of these overlapping categories of exempt uses of church property. First, most states allowed religious associations to mix both religious uses and charitable uses of their properties, and to choose either one or both forms of exemption for such uses.[80] Religious use exemptions were often more attractive, since they required only an annual petition for renewal to the local tax assessor. Charitable use exemptions required not only such a petition, but also subjected the association to the supervisory jurisdiction of the attorney general or a charitable commissioner or visitor. Second, several states required religious associations to make one such use of their properties "primary" or "predominant," and to petition for exemption of their property based on that use alone. If an association could demonstrate that most of the property was devoted to one such exempt use for the majority of the time an exemption was granted—even if the property was also put to other incidental exempt and non-exempt uses.[81] Third, a few states required either exclusive religious use *or* exclusive charitable use of the exempt property. Under such a wooden classification system, religious organizations had to choose either to truncate or to bifurcate their activities. Those organizations that resisted such a choice—for reasons of ideology or economics—on occasion were denied exemption altogether.[82]

This modern law of ecclesiastical exemptions reflects both the common

79. See, e.g., Appeal Tax Court v. Grand Lodge of Masons, 50 Md. 421 (1879); Board of Home Missions Church Extension of the M.E. Church v. Philadelphia 266 Pa. 405 (1920); Woman's Home Missionary Society v. Taylor, 173 Pa. 456 (1896); Maine Baptist Missionary Convention v. Portland, 65 Me. 92 (1876); Ferry Beach Park Association of Universalists v. City of Saco, 127 Me. 136 (1928); M. E. Church, South v. Hinton, 92 Tenn. 188 (1893); Y.M.C.A. v. Douglas County, 60 Neb. 642 (1900); Davis v. Cincinnati Camp Meeting Association, 57 Ohio St. 257 (1897); American Sunday School Union v. Philadelphia, 161 Pa. 307 (1894); Catholic Women's Club v. City of Green Bay, 180 Wisc. 102 (1923).

80. See, e.g., Congregational Sunday School & Publishing Soc'y v. Board of Review, 290 Ill. 108 (1919); Commonwealth v. Y.M.C.A. 116 Ky. 711 (1903); Assessors of Boston v. Lmason, 316 Mass. 166 (1944); Association for the Benefit of Colored Orphans v. Mayor of New York, 104 N.Y. 581 (1887).

81. See, e.g., First Unitarian Society v. Hatford, 66 Conn. 368 (1895); In re Bond Hill-Roselawn Hebrew School, 151 Ohio St. 70 (1949); St. Mary's Church v. Trippp, 14 R.I. 307 (1883). See further discussion in T. Cooley, *The Law of Taxation*, 4th ed. (Chicago, IL: Callaghan & Co., 1924), S. 725.

82. See, e.g., People v. Muldoon, 306 Ill. 234 (1922); People ex rel McCullough v. Deutsche Evangelische Lutherische Jehovah Gemeinde Ungeaenderter Augsburgischer Confession, 249 Ill. 132 (1911); Commonwealth v. Thomas, 119 Ky. 208 (1904); Evangelical Baptist Benevolent & Missionary Soc'y v. Boston, 204 Mass. 28 (1910); Evangelical Lutheran Synod & Hoehn, 355 Mo. 257 (1946).

law and equity traditions, and the tensions between them. It reflects the traditional common law concern to exempt property devoted to religious uses, to predicate such exemptions on explicit statutory authority, to limit the scope of exempt religious uses, to restrict the size and value of properties that fall within this scope, and to restrict the discretion of officials who award exemptions. It also reflects the traditional equity law concern to exempt property devoted to charitable uses, to engage in inventive exegesis of exemption statutes, to expand the scope of exemptions well beyond their original core, and to accord broad discretion of officials to make case-by-case determinations of whether, and to what extent, a given property can be exempted.

II. Tax Exemptions of Church Property at Present

Both the theory and the law of ecclesiastical exemptions that emerged in the late nineteenth century remain firmly in place among the states today. Judicial opinions continue to recite faithfully the social benefit and social burden arguments in favor of such exemptions.[83] Many of the constitutional and statutory exemption provisions drafted in the late nineteenth and early twentieth centuries remain the state law today, although they have been heavily amended and subject to broad judicial interpretation. The Supreme Court declared such exemptions laws constitutionally permissible in the landmark case of *Walz v. Tax Commission* (1970).[84] Yet litigation—in both traditional and novel forms—concerning such exemptions has continued apace for the past two decades. Such exemption stems in part from the terseness of state exemption provisions and the ambiguity of judicial precedents interpreting them, in part from the exponential rise of new religious groups that have sought to avail themselves of such exemptions.

A. New Trends in Litigation Involving Tax Exemption of Church Property

The tax exemption provisions adopted by most states are cryptic and often devoid of definitions. Judicial precedents interpreting these provisions are copious and often disconcordant. Churches that have been denied property tax exemptions have not been hesitant to exploit these ambiguities and to seek judicial redress. This has given rise to scores of state court cases on tax exemption of church property in the past two decades. The cases are too few in number and too broad ranging in result to discern any consistent pattern or integrated law. Several trends, however, are apparent in this recent litigation. These trends, taken together, have tended to expand the

83. For a recent case, citing virtually all the arguments for and against exemptions, see Murray v. Comptroller of the Treasury, 241 Md. 383 (1966), cert. den. 385 U.S. 816 (1966).

84. 397 U.S. 664 (1970). See discussion and criticism of the case in Witte, Tax Exemption, 364–368.

availability of tax exemptions for church properties, and to exacerbate some of the abuses inherent in traditional tax exemption laws.[85]

First, the requirement that the property be "actually" used for exempt purposes has been considerably softened. Traditionally, courts did not hesitate to deny exemptions to church properties whose exempt uses were merely planned for the future or were held in abeyance for financial or other reasons. Today the majority of state courts and legislatures have become less churlish. Most states exempt church properties as soon as construction of improvements thereon has begun. In a few states, mere purchase of the property and good faith planning of a religious or charitable use thereon is sufficient to warrant an exemption from property tax. Most states also retain exemptions for properties that churches or charities can afford to use only partly or sporadically; complete abandonment of the property, however, still renders it taxable.

Second, the requirement that the religious use of the property be "public" in nature is not so stringently enforced. Traditionally, courts struck down exemptions for religious or charitable uses of property that did not work a sufficiently "public benefit." Today courts and legislatures have softened this public benefit requirement and have allowed for the exemption of monasteries, convents, religious communes, retreat centers, youth homes, missionary furlough stations, summer camps, and similar secluded and segregated properties.

Third, several courts have come to interpret rather broadly the type and amount of contiguous property that is "reasonably necessary" for the religious or charitable use of a property. Traditionally, many states limited exemptions to improved properties together with the driveways, walkways, parking lots, and other immediately surrounding properties that facilitated the use of the improvement. Today courts in some states grant exemptions for large tracts of unimproved land that surrounding a church or charity on grounds that such lands provide a buffer against residential or industrial encroachment or traffic, enhance the aesthetic appeal of the church, or foster a tranquil setting more conducive to religious worship and spiritual reflection. Courts in other states have exempted convents and communes, residential religious centers, missionary furlough stations, and parsonages with their surrounding properties on grounds that they are "reasonably necessary for the accomplishment and fulfillment of the . . . charitable institution."

Fourth, state courts and legislatures have become sharply split over the requirements regarding the nature of the owner of the exempt property. Traditionally, all but a few states insisted that properties exempted for religious uses be owned by religious organizations and that properties exempted for charitable uses be owned by charitable organizations. Today, a

85. The following paragraphs are a summary of the more detailed treatment of recent case and statutory law in id., 395ff. and the cases cited and discussed therein.

growing minority of states take no account of the identity of the owner of the property so long as the property is devoted to charitable or religious uses. This allows investors and for-profit organizations to receive property tax exemptions by leasing the properties to churches or charities. Though the majority of states still continue to require that property that is accorded a religious use or a charitable use exemption be owned by a religious or charitable organization, the nature of the owner and the use need not match. Religious organizations can receive charitable use exemptions, and charitable organizations can receive religious use exemptions. Indeed, the definition of a "religious" organization often bears little resemblance to the definition of a "religious" use. This permitted asymmetry of ownership and use has invited protracted litigation. Religious groups that are denied religious use exemptions have thereafter sought charitable use exemptions for the same property. New religious groups or well-established religious groups that have added new properties have often spent years litigating the tax status of their properties.

Fifth, virtually all states now grant exemptions based on the primary or predominant use to which a property is devoted. Traditionally, some states allowed parties to mix religious and charitable uses and choose freely their category of exemption. Today courts have become more inclined to deem either the religious use or the charitable use to be primary and determine the exemption status based on that categorization. Traditionally, other states forced parties to devote their properties exclusively to religious uses or exclusively to charitable uses; any mixture of uses was fatal to a claim for exemption. Today such a wooden classification system has been largely abandoned; if either the religious use or charitable use is predominant, parties can make other incidental exempt uses of their properties.

Sixth, many states also permit parties to make incidental nonexempt uses of their properties. Traditionally, many states denied exemptions to church properties that in any way mixed exempt and nonexempt uses. Even incidental profiteering was fatal to a claim for exemption. Today courts and legislatures grant partial exemptions based on the percentage of space or time devoted to such exempt uses.

Finally, the scope of religious use exemptions has tended to narrow while the scope of charitable use exemptions has tended to broaden. Traditionally, courts interpreted both religious use and charitable use exemptions rather broadly, allowing for a considerable amount of overlapping treatment. Today courts have begun to limit religious use exemptions to the sanctuary and the synagogue, the mosque and the meetinghouse, thereby forcing churches to seek charitable use exemptions for many of their properties. Correspondingly, many courts have broadened the definition of charitable uses to include a variety of forms of religious education, catechization, fellowship, liturgy, recreation, mission work, communal living, and auxiliary services in support of religious groups.

These trends in recent cases have tended to expand the availability of tax exemptions for church properties. The softened definition of an "actual" and "public" exempt use has rendered a number of undeveloped and secluded religious properties eligible for exemption. The broadened definition of what property is considered "reasonably necessary" to support the exempt use has allowed religious organizations to surround their developed properties with considerable tracts of unimproved land. The permitted admixture of two or more exempt uses on one property has made exemptions available to the properties of non-profit organizations that offer multiple services.

These trends have also, however, permitted some abuses of exemption laws. The lack of any necessary correlation between the nature of the owner and the nature of the use of an exempt property has allowed nonprofit organizations to gain exemptions through lease of their properties to religious or charitable organizations. The permitted admixture of predominant exempt uses and incidental nonexempt uses has allowed religious and charitable groups to engage in short-term or occasional profiteering with no adverse property tax consequences.

B. Tax Exemptions for the Properties of New Religious Groups

The exponential rise of new religious groups has tested the edges, and the efficacy, of religious use exemptions. In the past two decades, various new religious groups have petitioned state commissioners and courts for the same property tax exemptions enjoyed by traditional religious groups. Such petitioners range from large, highly organized groups like Moonies, Scientologists, and various oriental cults to small, highly selective communitarian religions, faith families, personality cults, and other sects. Courts and commissioners have had few criteria at their disposal to evaluate these petitions for exemption. State property tax laws, unlike federal income tax laws, generally offer no definition of a "religious" association or a "religious" use. State and federal constitutional laws offer only rudimentary and inconsistent definitions of religion. Thus state courts and legislatures have recently developed at least four tests to evaluate these petitions. These can be called the commonsense, deference, minimalist theism, and multifactual analysis tests, respectively. The first two tests guard jealously the independence of the petitioner, and make no inquiry into the petitioner's religious beliefs. The other two tests scrutinize these religious beliefs more closely. Application of these tests has led to widely varying results.

Courts in some jurisdictions have adopted a simple "commonsense" test to evaluate petitions for tax exemption. They view the "objective facts" of the petitioner's property uses but studiously avoid any inquiry into the petitioner's religious inspirations or motivations. They then make a commonsense judgement regarding whether such uses are religious or secular. This test is applied primarily in cases involving seemingly specious petitions for exemption. In *Golden Writ of God v. Department of Revenue*, the Supreme Court of Oregon, for example, was asked to determine the tax status of some 230 acres of largely untilled farmland, occupied by a large house and barn. The property was owned by a nonprofit organization consisting of a dozen members who lived in the house and who had recently conveyed their own property to the organization. Members of the organization regarded the property as a tabernacle, its plants as symbols of divine attributes, its animals as sacred creatures. They also regarded work on the property as a form of spiritual discipline. The court denied the religious use exemption, arguing that the "objective facts demonstrate non-religious use of the property." "The farmland with a house and barn were just that," the court reasoned. "The house was primarily used for living quarters, . . . the untilled farmland was otherwise uncultivated and possessed no unusual attributes other than being a nice place to run horses, to study nature and to meditate and pray."[86] Courts in other jurisdictions have used similar arguments to deny exemptions to open lands that are consecrated as spiritual havens, farms and ranches that are dedicated to spiritual catharsis, or private homes that petitioners deem to be shrines, cathedrals, or other places of religious worship.

While the commonsense test relies heavily on a court's characterization of the petitioner's beliefs and property uses, the "deference" test relies heavily on the petitioner's self-characterization. In *Holy Spirit Association for Unification v. Tax Commission*, the New York Court of Appeals formulated the test as follows:

> In determining whether a particular ecclesiastical body has been organized and [uses its property] exclusively for religious purposes the courts may not inquire into or classify the content of the doctrine, dogmas, and teachings held by that body to be integral to its religion but must accept that body's characterization of its own beliefs and activities . . . so long as that characterization is made in good faith and is not sham.

The court applied this test to determine the tax status of the administrative headquarters, missionary residence, and storage facilities owned and operated by the Reverend Sun Myung Moon. Both the New York tax commissioner and lower state courts had denied the exemption on grounds that the Unification doctrine was "so inextricably interwoven with political motives and activities" that it could not be regarded as religious, regardless of the sincerity of the church's members. The New York Court of Appeals reversed. After quoting at length from the religious organization's own description of its beliefs and purposes, the court concluded that "what have been characterized below as political and economic beliefs and activities are

86. 300 Or. 479 (1986).

in view of the Church integral aspects of its religious doctrine and program."
Because the church's properties are integral to the successful maintenance
and dissemination of its religion, the court felt that the property had to be
exempt from taxation.[87]

Other courts have adopted a "minimalist theism" test to evaluate petitions submitted by new religious groups. Petitioners must at least "exhibit
the minimal requirements of religion." Such requirements are defined as "a
sincere and meaningful belief in God occupying in the life of its possessors a
place parallel to that occupied by God in traditional religions and dedi-
cat[ion] to the practice of that belief."[88] Property used in support of such
religious beliefs is eligible for exemption.

The minimalist theism test has been applied both to affirm and to deny
petitions for tax exemption. In *Roberts v. Ravenwood Church of Wicca*, for
example, the Supreme Court of Georgia upheld the tax exempt status of a
two-storey suburban home owned and operated by the Wiccan church. The
Wiccan church believed in a "primordial, supernatural" force that created
the world and sustained its creatures in a "karmic circle." Members of this
religion were seen as divine sparks of this supernatural force with moral
responsibilities to themselves and nature. The church observed eight formal
Sabbaths per year and celebrated communion, marriage, and other religious
rituals. The two-storey home was used both for weekly services and for the
residence of the church founder, her petitioners, and some non-parishioner
tenants. Convinced that the church was sufficiently and sincerely theistic,
the court concluded that its property was being used for religious worship
and was therefore exempt from taxation.[89] By contrast, in *Religious Society of
Families v. Assessor*, the New York Supreme Court denied tax exemption for
property of the Religious Society of Families, a new cult founded by one
"Calvin of the Universe." The society was professedly this-worldly in orientation, believing in a variety of ecological and political causes, eugenics,
scientific humanism, monogamous relationships, and death by suicide. It
was organized as a neo-monastic community devoted to agricultural production. Upon rehearsing theistic definitions in dictionaries and earlier cases,
the court concluded that the society was "not religious as religion is traditionally defined" and declared its property taxable.[90]

At least one court has developed a rather comprehensive "multifactual
analysis" test to evaluate petitions for exemption. In *Ideal Life Church of
Lake Elmo v. County of Washington*, the Supreme Court of Minnesota
rejected simple litmus tests and dictionary definitions of religion and insisted
that each petition must be subjected to a multifactual analysis. Under this

87. 55 N.Y. 2d 512 (1982).
88. Roberts v. Ravenwood Church of Wicca, 249 Ga. 348, 350 (1982).
89. Ibid.
90. 73 Misc. 2d 923 (1973).

analysis a court or commissioner must consider such factors as the motives for the formation of the religious organization, the presence of a supreme being or something in lieu thereof in the belief system, the presence and sophistication of religious doctrine, the practice and celebration of religious liturgies or rites, the degree of formal religious training required for the religious leaders, the strictures on the ability of members simultaneously to practice other religions, and other factors. Thereafter, the court must make a reasoned determination whether the petitioner is a religious group and/or whether its property is devoted to religious uses. In the case at bar, the court used such an analysis to reject the exemption petition of the Ideal Life Church. The church had been chartered and the minister had been ordained by the Universal Life Church of Modesto, California upon petitioner's payment by mail of 70 dollars. The church was comprised of some 18 members, most of whom were members of the same family and each of whom accepted the principles of freedom, fraternity, and choice. The church was theistic in orientation but professed no formal religious doctrine, celebrated no formal religious rites, and imposed no prohibitions against its members' practice of other faiths. The church building was previously a private home, which family members had donated to the church immediately after its organization. It was used both for the family residence and for the monthly public religious meetings. Regardless of the petitioner's characterization of itself as a sincere, bona fide religious organization, the court denied its petition.[91]

These four tests strike different balances between sophistication of analysis, on the one hand, and intrusiveness of inquiry, on the other. The deference test avoids intrusive inquiry into the beliefs of the petitioner but does so at the cost of analytical sophistication. The multifactual analysis test affords sophisticated and sensitive analysis of each petition, but does so at the cost of intrusion on the independence of the religious organization. The commonsense test is neither sophisticated nor intrusive; the minimalist theism test is both more sophisticated and more intrusive.

III. Tax Exemptions of Church Property in the Future

Opponents and proponents of tax exemption of church property have thus far found little common ground. Opponents insist that such exemptions are subsidies of religion that are proscribed by the establishment clause and its principle of state separation from the church.[92] Proponents argue that

91. 304 N.W. 2d 308 (Minn. 1981).

92. See, e.g., West, "The Case Against the Right to Religion-Based Exemptions," 4 *Notre Dame Journal of Law, Ethics & Public Policy* 591, 600–613 (1990); id., Religious Exemptions, in T. Robbins and R. Robertson, eds., *Church-State Relations: Tensions and Transitions* (New Brunswick, NJ: Transactions Books, 1987), 103–108; Note, "Religious Tax Exemptions: A Challenge to Walz v. Tax Commission," 13 *Southwestern University Law Review* 129 (1982); L. Pfeffer, *Church State and Freedom*, rev. ed. (Boston: Beacon Press, 1967), 210–219.

such exemptions are supports of religion that are prescribed by the free exercise clause and its principle of state accommodation of the church.[93] Opponents look to the future and portend with alarm the further erosion of the municipal tax base and the further aggrandizement of church wealth and power.[94] Proponents look to the past and portray with approval the long tradition of mutual support and cooperation between church and state in serving society. Enmeshed as it is in this dialectic of separatism and accommodationism, the controversy over the constitutionality of tax exemption of church property will not admit of swift or easy resolution.

A fresh understanding of the history of tax exemption of church property suggests a *via media* between the wholesale eradication of exemptions proposed by their opponents and the blanket endorsements of exemptions proffered by their proponents. Neither opponents nor proponents have recognized sufficiently that modern exemptions of church property are rooted in both common law and equity law traditions, that historically they were granted on account of both the "religious uses" and the "charitable uses" to which church properties were devoted. Thus besides the all-or-nothing approaches currently debated in the academies, a third alternative is to remove tax exemptions for church property that are based on religious uses, but to retain those that are based on charitable uses. Church properties would thus be exempted from taxation not because of the internal, cultic, sacerdotal uses but because of the external, cultural, social uses to which they are devoted.

This alternative is less radical than it may initially appear. The term "charity" has always been broadly enough defined to include most aspects of religious life. Most religious institutions, save the most austere and ascetic cults, can thus as be considered charitable institutions. Most religious uses of property, save the most sacramental and ritualistic, can also be considered charitable uses. Most states allow parties to mix two or more exempt uses. Most, if not all, religious organizations would find little difficulty in retaining their property tax exemptions, albeit on different grounds.

93. See, e.g., D. Kelly, *Why Churches Should Not Pay Taxes* (New York: Harper & Row, 1977); *Taxation and the Free Exercise of Religion: Papers and Proceedings of the Sixteenth Religious Liberty Conference* (Washington: 1978).

94. See, e.g., A. Balk, *The Free List* (New York: MacMillan & Co., 1971); M. Larson & C. Lowell, *Praise the Lord for Tax Exemptions: How the Churches Grow Rich—While the Cities and You Grow Poor* (Washington: R.B. Luce, 1969); Bennett, "Real Property Tax Exemptions of Non-Profit Organizations," 16 *Cleveland-Marshall Law Review* 150 (1966).

95. See generally Berman, "Religious Freedom and the Challenge of the Modern State," 39 *Emory Law Journal* 149, 159–164 (1990).

96. P. Kurland, *Religion and the Law* (Chicago: Aldine Publishing Co., 1962), 16–18; Kurland, "The Irrelevance of the Constitution: The Religion Clauses of the First Amendment and the Supreme Court," 24 *Villanova Law Review* 1, 23–27 (1979). See evaluation in Tushnet, "Of Church and State and the Supreme Court: Kurland Revisited," 1989 *Supreme Court Review* 373 (1989).

This alternative has considerable intuitive appeal. First, it stands on firmer historical ground than the current pattern of exemption laws. Religious use exemptions are rooted in an establishment theory that the First Amendment prohibits and in a "social benefits" theory that today often defies reality. Many modern churches simply do not cultivate public spiritedness or public morality and do not promote neighborhood values and democratic ideals as the traditional social benefits theory teaches. Charitable use exemptions, by contrast, are rooted in an equitable theory that still commands assent and a "state burden" argument that the rise of the modern welfare state has rendered even more persuasive. The modern state has come to bear much of the burden of education, poor relief, and other forms of social welfare. Whatever charitable and other services churches and other organizations render relieve the state of a portion of that burden.

Second, this alternative promotes greater governmental neutrality toward, and equality in treatment of, religion. It spares officials the task of distinguishing between religious groups and secular groups in determining whether a party has standing to claim tax exemption. It spares officials the task of distinguishing between piety and charity, catechization and education in determining whether a property is being sufficiently devoted to "religious uses." It removes the disparity in benefits accorded to different churches under current exemption laws. Philip Kurland once wrote that the religious clauses of the First Amendment "should be read as stating a single precept: that government cannot utilize religion as a standard for action or inaction because [the clauses] read together . . . prohibit classification in terms of religion either to confer a benefit or confer a burden." Although Kurland's principle has been sharply criticized in other contexts, it finds ready application to the issue of tax exemptions of church property.

Third, this alternative shifts the economic priorities of the church. Since its tax exempt status would turn not on the religious uses but on the charitable uses of its property, a church would be encouraged to devote its resources not only to building crystal cathedrals, prayer towers, and theme parks, but also to furnishing soup kitchens, youth houses, and night shelters.

This alternative, however, is not free from difficulty.

First, the alternative raises logistical concerns. The value of church property is not always too easy to assess for purposes of taxation. An improved church property can rarely be converted to private use and is not often sold to other religious groups. Traditional market criteria, therefore, cannot be so readily used. Moreover, in states that permit "mixed" religious, charitable, and other uses of church properties, it is not always easy to calculate the percentage of church property use that is charitable, and thus exempt. Tax commissioners, however, would hardly be daunted by such logistical concerns. They regularly assess the values of other properties devoted to highly specialized and unique uses, such as wineries, galleries, and factories. They readily distinguish between the profitable (and thus taxable) uses and non-profitable (and thus exempt) uses of charitable properties. While logistical concerns may have been formidable in earlier decades, they have become less of a concern as the science of tax assessment has grown more refined.

Second, this alternative raises free exercise concerns. Although it may appear neutral on its face, the alternative will inevitably lead to taxation of certain church groups. Religious groups whose faith is world affirmative and socially active can readily receive charitable use exemptions for their properties. Religious groups whose faith is world avertive and socially inactive cannot. Although the Supreme Court has held that tax exemption of a church might be permissible under the establishment clause, it has not yet determined whether taxation of church property is permissible under the free exercise clause.

The United States Supreme Court has developed an array of rather disconcordant lines of interpretation of the free exercise clause, three of which are relevant here.[97] This alternative is consistent with all three lines of interpretation.

In one line of cases, the Court has consistently upheld a variety of general safety and welfare regulations that indirectly burden the religious exercise of some individuals or groups. The government must demonstrate that such regulations promote a compelling or overriding state interest, are narrowly tailored to achieve that interest, and are non-religious discriminatory on their face or in application. Thus the Court has upheld general license, permit, and tax requirements for solicitation, distribution, or sale of religious articles even though such measures indirectly burden the proselytizing efforts of certain groups. It has upheld general criminal laws against the use of child labor or narcotic substances, even though such uses are considered spiritually wholesome by certain religious groups. It has upheld general military dress codes, even though they obstruct a Jewish soldier's wearing of his yarmulke. It has required compliance with social security regulations, even though certain religious individuals are conscientiously opposed to social security. It has sustained the development of federal land, even though portions of such lands are considered sacred by native American Indians. The logic of these cases could be applied to rebut free exercise objections to the alternative proposed here. The charitable use exemptions promote a governmental policy of supporting and encouraging charity and are narrowly tailored to achieve that end. Such regulations scrupulously avoid any facial discrimination.

In a second line of cases involving church property disputes, the Court has distinguished between the "sacred" and "civil" attributes and activities of churches and between the right of free exercise of religion itself and the right

---

97. For citations and further discussion see Witte, "Theology and Politics," 689–698; Witte, "Tax Exemption," 412–414.

to the means and instruments used to facilitate and support such exercise. Church property, it can be argued, is among the civil attributes of the church, among the means used to facilitate and support the exercise of religion. Church property can thus be subjected to a considerable degree of state regulation and control without violating the free exercise clause. Lower courts have used this logic to uphold various onerous zoning, historic preservation, property registration, and other regulations of church property. The Supreme Court has very recently used similar logic to uphold the imposition of sale and use taxes on religous groups and activities. Such logic may also serve to rebut against the alternative tax exemption policy proposed here.

In a third line of cases, the Court has used the free exercise clause to support religiously-based exemptions. In these cases, parties have been exempted from general regulations that compel them to violate their sincerely held religious beliefs. Thus the Amish have been exempted from full compliance with compulsory school attendance laws for children. Petitioners for unemployment compensation have been exempted from regulations that compel them to work on their Sabbath or to participate in the production of military hardware. Conscientious objectors have been exempted from active service in the military. Such cases, however, are distinguishable. Mainline religious groups have no inherent religious aversion to the payment of taxes. The Bible enjoins Christians to "[r]ender . . . to Caesar the things that are Caesar's" and to pay "taxes to whom taxes are due, revenue to whom revenue is due."[98] The Talmud teaches the principle of *dina de-Malkhuta dina*, which, among other things, compels payment of uniformly administered taxes imposed by a recognized sovereign.[99] Arguments for the free exercise right to exemption from taxes, therefore, appear ill-founded.

Finally, and perhaps most importantly, this alternative raises questions of symbolism. Tax exemptions have long been regarded as signs of the state's "benevolent neutrality"[100] toward the church—"a fit recognition by the state of the sanctity of religion," as one official put it.[101] Taxes would be regarded by many as signs of the state's malevolent adversity toward the church—a reminder of earlier eras of religious persecution, and a foretaste of religious repression to come. To give the state the power to tax the church would for

98. Matthew 22:21 (RSV); Romans 13:7 (RSV).

99. Talmud, BK 113a, quoted and discussed in G. Graff, *Separation of Church and State: Dina de-Malkhuta Dina in Jewish Law 1750–1848* (University, AL: University of Alabama Press, 1985), 8–29, 140–141.

100. The phrase is from Walz, at 669.

101. Massachusetts State Tax Commission (1897), quoted by Roberston, *Should Churches be Taxed,* 191. See also Hornell v. Philadelphia, 8 Pa. 280 (1870); J. Bennett, *Christians and the State* (New York: Charles Scribner's Sons, 1958), 234–235 (tax exemptions are "the most remarkable of all forms of aid to religious bodies"); W. Sperry, *Religion in America* (Cambridge: Cambridge University Press, 1963), 60· ("The most important governmental recognition of religion made in America is the exemption of church property from taxation—at least so much of it as is used for purposes of worship and religious education.").

many be tantamount to giving it the power to destroy the church. It was the fear of ecclesiastical condemnation and political retaliation that compelled many nineteenth century legislators and judges to maintain church property exemptions. The same fear may well be what has stayed the hand of contemporary legislatures and courts, including the Supreme Court.

The catalyst for reform of church property exemptions must thus come not from the state but from the church. Churches must consider the costs of exemption—not so much the incremental financial costs to other taxpayers as the important symbolic costs to themselves. For many people—adherents and antagonists alike—tax exemptions and other legal privileges have rendered the contemporary church too mercenary, too opulent, and too self-indulgent. The church's voluntary renunciation of one of its privileges would do much to allay the anxieties of its adherents and to parry the attacks of its antagonists.

RELIGION, THE "CURE OF SOULS," AND THE THIRD SECTOR IN AMERICA: AN HISTORICAL PERSPECTIVE

E. Brooks Holifield

In the American independent sector, religious institutions have often claimed to be the most independent of all. And the courts have tried to keep them that way. Yet when religious groups have sought to promote a common good—as in their efforts to nurture health—they have often established complex links with both business and government. They have created spaces within state-sponsored and commercial institutions and formulated ideas that eventually secured a hearing within the other two sectors of American society. But historically they have also provided alternative sources of health care by assuming burdens that both government and business were unwilling to accept.

Early in the twentieth century, two Episcopal priests from the Emmanuel Church in Boston founded a movement that illustrated the complexity in the relationships among business, government, and the independent sector in America. The two priests, Elwood Worcester and Samuel McComb, called for a renewal of the church's ministry of health. "In short," they wrote, "it is plain to the unprejudiced student of religion that one cause of the Church's present weakness is that the Church has mutilated the Christian religion, retaining with some degree of faith Christ's message to the soul, but rejecting with unbelief His ministry to the body." To recover that ministry, they called for clergy, social workers, and physicians to join together in a venture to offer healing to the sick.[1]

Worcester and McComb became the leading figures in the Emmanuel Movement, a pioneering effort of the churches to appropriate innovations in medical practice as part of their ministry to the suffering. Impressed especially by recent developments in psychotherapy, they joined with local neurologists to launch a program of group therapy modeled on the example

---

1. Elwood Worcester and Samuel McComb, *The Christian Religion as a Healing Power* (New York: Moffatt, Yard, 1909), p. 11; Elwood Worcester, Samuel McComb, and Isador H. Coriat, *Religion and Medicine: The Moral Control of Nervous Disorders* (New York: Moffat, Yard, 1908), p. 380.

of medical practice. Beginning in 1905 with small groups of indigent tuber-culosis patients, they and their physician allies, some of whom came from Massachusetts General Hospital while others worked in private practice, explored the healing powers of the "law of suggestion," first with the poor and then increasingly with middle-class Bostonians suffering from nervous and emotional disorders. The movement soon attracted support from Con-gregational clergy in Baltimore, Presbyterians in Cleveland, Unitarians in Portland, Baptists in Chicago, and Universalists in Brookline. By 1920 it had waned in popularity, but for a decade the Emmanuel Movement embodied a vigorous effort of the churches to find a distinctive place, alongside public hospitals and commercial medicine, in the American system of health care.

The Emmanuel Movement, along with the Protestant pastoral care movement that it foreshadowed, provide lenses for observing relationships both between religion and health and among the three sectors in America. Emmanuel combined three earlier ways of linking religion and health: the tradition of the cure of souls, the tradition of harmonial religion, and the tradition of service and reform. It adapted these to new therapeutic pro-cedures developed by European and American physicians, seeking alliances between the church and the hospital precisely at a time of momentous change in the function and status of the hospital in American medicine. The pastoral care movement that succeeded the Emmanuel experiment often embodied the same three traditions and shared a similar alliance with the hospital. Issues that remained implicit in the Emmanuel Movement later emerged as topics of debate and division within the pastoral care movement. By looking at the relationship between Emmanuel and its successor move-ments, we can both illumine some of the roots of current discussions about religion and health and explore the complexity of the three-sector arrange-ment in American society.

I. Traditions

As an experiment in pastoral care, the Emmanuel Movement continued an ancient function of the Christian churches. The term "pastoral care" often designated the whole range of clerical activity aimed at guiding, nurturing, and sustaining a congregation. In America, as elsewhere, the tradition of pastoral care quite often entailed some measure of attention to physical and mental health, especially since the earliest American pastors made no sharp distinction between some forms of illness and spiritual malaise. Seventeenth-century Puritans in New England, Lutheran Pietists in Pennsylvania, Catho-lic missionaries to Native Americans, and Anglican clergy in Virginia often assumed that spiritual care—ranging from prayer and sacramental action to confession and counsel—could bring healing to a distressed body or distem-pered mind.

They also recognized that some forms of spiritual malaise grew out of physical impediments: Seventeenth-century physicians and clergy could note, for example, the difference between true afflictions of conscience and a melancholy that occurred when gross elements in the blood settled in the spleen and created "vapours" that pressed upward to the brain. The English Puritan casuist William Ames, widely read in New England, suggested that such a problem as scrupulosity might well be rooted in "Melancholy, or some such like constitution of body"; a diseased spleen might on occasion lie at the source of spiritual malaise.[2]

From the early seventeenth century, therefore, more than a few pastors served also as physicians; the practice of medicine formed part of their identity as ministers. Cotton Mather in Boston, whose *Angel of Bethesda* was the first medical book written in the English colonies, referred to the pastoral conjoining of ministry and medicine as the "angelical conjunction," and the assumption that ministers might provide medical care remained strong in America through the 1820s. As late as 1850 complaints could still be heard from physicians about ministers who practiced medicine as part of their agenda of pastoral care.[3]

Pastoral care in antebellum America nonetheless focused far more on the intricacies of conversion and moral guidance than on the ills of the body. When early nineteenth-century pastors expended pastoral energies with the sick and their families, they usually were trying to ensure that the suffering adopt the proper attitudes toward their illnesses—attitudes of submission, resignation, and faith. Pastoral care meant teaching people more how to die well than to live in good health.

After the Civil War, however, a few pastoral theologians found themselves attracted to a new vocabulary of "muscular" Christianity. Impressed by the natural vitalities in which liberal writers found the divine presence, attentive to the pioneers in the psychology of religion, and aware of innovations among European psychotherapists, they began to urge the clergy to promote physical and mental health among their parishioners. It was in this period, for instance, that the evangelical Luther Gulick invoked the dynamism of Christ to persuade the Y.M.C.A. to promote team sports.[4]

The Emmanuel Movement embodied some of these new impulses. Worcester and McComb thought of themselves as transforming pastoral care in the light of new methods of healing that had already been introduced in public and private commercial hospitals. Every minister, they said, practiced "psychotherapy," whether intending it or not, and they wanted the cure of

2. Gail Thain Parker, "Jonathan Edwards and Melancholy," *New England Quarterly* 41 (1968); 195, 197; William Ames, *Of Conscience and the Cases Thereof*, 2 vols. (London, 1643), 1:13.

3. Richard H. Shryock, *Medicine and Society in America 1600–1860* (New York: New York University Press, 1960), p. 154.

4. E. Brooks Holifield, *A History of Pastoral Care in America: From Salvation to Self-Realization* (Nashville: Abingdon Press, 1983), pp. 164–201.

souls to be guided by science rather than tradition. By 1908 the movement published a journal entitled *Psychotherapy*, with articles by neurologists and psychologists, physicians and philosophers, medical materialists and orthodox Freudians, all designed to help ministers apply therapeutic principles to the practice of pastoral care. Emmanuel illustrated one way in which religious institutions appropriated medical views and techniques developed by practitioners in other sectors.[5]

In pushing the churches toward greater sensitivity to questions of health and healing, the Emmanuel Movement collided with other movements that had similar aims. In particular, Worcester and McComb felt the need to counter the growing popularity of Christian Science. They feared that Christian Scientists would sweep tens of thousands away from the Church and, at the same time, undermine faith in doctors. They saw the Emmanual Movement as an alliance of doctors and ministers that would win the people back from "irrational healing cults."[6]

In their frequent references to irrational healing cults. Worcester and McComb had in mind mainly a tradition of "harmonial," or "metaphysical," or "aesthetic" piety that began to attract widespread attention in America during the early nineteenth century. The prophets of the harmonial vision proclaimed that physical health—as well as spiritual peace—resulted from a deep rapport with the powers or energies that undergirded the cosmos. They usually taught techniques of reflection or meditation through which men and women could tap those resources, and they claimed that those techniques brought healing to the sick.[7]

Followers of the eighteenth-century Swedish scientist and seer Emanuel Swedenborg were the first Americans to popularize the harmonial vision. By 1817 the American Swedenborgians reported seventeen societies intent on promoting the view that esoteric patterns of correspondence linked the natural, spiritual, and celestial worlds. By establishing rapport with other cosmic levels, they said, men and women could not only communicate with a hidden world of spirits but also open themselves to the "psychic influx" that brought healing for physical and emotional ailments. Soon after 1843, a few American Spiritualists, intrigued especially by the promise of communication with the spirits of the departed, added that attunement to these higher realities could convey the power to heal others.[8]

5. Worcester and McComb, *Christian Religion as a Healing Power*, pp. 7, 43.

6. Worcester and McComb, *Christian Religion as a Healing Power*, p. 26.

7. Robert C. Fuller, *Alternative Medicine and American Religious Life* (New York: Oxford University Press, 1989), p. 8; Sydney Ahlstrom, *A Religious History of the American People* (New Haven: Yale University Press, 1972), p. 1019–36; J. Stillson Judah, *The History and Philosophy of the Metaphysical Movements in America* (Philadelphia: University of Pennsylvania Press, 1967).

8. Fuller, *Alternative Medicine and American Religious Life*, pp. 50–58; Ahlstrom, *Religious History*, pp. 486–90.

The audience for the harmonial message expanded after 1836, when the French lecturer Charles Poyen began to titillate American audiences by demonstrating the powers of animal magnetism. This mysterious force was the discovery of the eighteenth-century Viennese physician Franz Anton Mesmer, who described it as the invisible substance that transmitted energy from one source to another. He claimed that it provided the explanation for his ability to hypnotize his patients by moving his arms and hands. By 1840, a host of American mesmerists were touting the therapeutic benefits of the somnambulic state, and a few also began to claim that it put them in touch with levels of reality that transcended ordinary consciousness. The healing, they concluded, came from the linkage to that hidden realm of transforming power.[9]

When Poyen lectured in Belfast, Maine, he attracted the attention of a young clockmaker named Phineas Parkurst Quimby, who not only established his own healing practice but also refined the Mesmerist theory. He concluded that ideas and beliefs could control the flow of the vital force. True ideas opened one to its healing power; false ideas blocked the flow, creating both emotional and physical distress. Quimby and his followers began therefore to exploit the healing power of language by literally explaining away the illnesses of their patients.[10]

Quimby's most celebrated patient was Mary Baker Eddy, whose Christian Science combined philosophical idealism, biblical exegesis, and the theory of animal magnetism into another method of attaining health and well-being. But others also explored the healing possibilities of the metaphysical vision. Andrew Taylor Still founded Osteopathy in 1874 on the idea that the manipulation of vertebrae and joints could restore the flow of electrical magnetic energy. After 1895, D. D. Palmer developed Chiropractic, as well, on the theory that misaligned spinal vertebrae blocked the flow of animal magnetism. In their reliance on manipulation, Still and Palmer moved away from Quimby's eventual conclusion that the mind alone could tap the power of healing, but they joined Quimby in promising to restore the natural harmony of the body by opening it to the deeper harmonies that flowed in and under the world of nature.[11]

Quimby stood in the background of the flourishing of what came to be called New Thought or Mind Cure. Such writers as Warren Felt Evans and Ralph Waldo Trine made it clear that harmonial healing was more than simply a therapeutic device; it was a religion with its own distinctive beliefs and rituals. It was a pathway to communion with the Infinite Spirit through

9. Robert C. Fuller, *Mesmerism and the American Cure of Souls* (Philadelphia: University of Pennsylvania Press, 1982), pp. 1–47.

10. Fuller, *Mesmerism and the American Cure of Souls*, p. 137.

11. Catherine L. Albanese, "Physic and Metaphysic in Nineteenth-Century America: Medical Sectarians and Religious Healing," *Church History* 55 (December, 1986), pp. 489–502.

which men and women could exchange dis-ease for ease, weakness for strength, and suffering for health. In some cities and regions—notably in California—such metaphysical themes deeply pervaded Protestant culture. And William James could predict by 1902 that both the medical and the clerical professions would soon open their eyes to the striking results. It was entirely in keeping with the American spirit, he added, that this "original contribution to the systematic philosophy of life should be so intimately knit up with concrete therapeutics."[12]

The founders of the Emmanuel Movement disdained what they saw as the excesses of New Thought, but they also praised the substratum of "sound idealism" in its teachings. Like the advocates of harmonial piety, the leaders of the Emmanuel Movement insisted that the curative power of nature—the *vis medicatrix naturae*—was the true agent in healing. Like the mind curists, they believed that healing could occur through access to depths of reality that lay beneath the reach of the conscious mind. Some proponents of the Emmanuel Movement adopted methods familiar to mental healers. They had their clients practice rhythmic breathing, muscular relaxation, and visual imagery before leading them into "the silence of the quiet mind," through which the power of healing might work. Whatever their reservations about the undiluted ideas of the New Thought movement, Worcester and McComb brought into the mainstream churches some of the prominent themes of harmonial piety. Their movement also foreshadowed later appropriations of harmonial piety by the other sectors, especially by commercial enterprise. Harmonial techniques, especially in their secularized versions, proved profitable, whether in the form of positive-thinking seminars or unconventional health-spas. The expansion of chiropractic provides only one illustration of the way healing techniques originally grounded in harmonial piety could later develop into a commercial health care business.[13]

Finally, the Emmanuel Movement also continued a time-honored tradition within the American churches of encouraging healthful living and helping others to attain it. In this respect, Worcester and McComb were quite conventional. The sixteenth-century Catholic Council of Trent had instructed the faithful to maintain their health for the sake of doing their duty in justice and charity, and the Protestant reformers had no quarrel with that admonition. Martin Luther told his followers that "God created medicine and provided us with intelligence to guard and take care of the body so that we can live in good health"; John Calvin taught that physicians were gifts

12. Sandra Sizer Frankiel, *California's Spiritual Frontiers* (Berkeley: University of California Press, 1988), pp. 59–119; William James, *The Varieties of Religious Experience* (New York: Random House, 1902), p. 94; Fuller, *Alternative Medicine and American Religious Life*, p. 62.

13. Lyman P. Powell, *The Emmanuel Movement in a New England Town* (New York: G. P. Putnam's Sons, 1909), pp. 68, 71, 77, 92; Worcester and McComb, *Religion and Medicine*, p. 134; Raymond J. Cunningham, "The Emmanuel Movement: A Variety of American Religious Experience," *American Quarterly* 14 (1962): 57.

of God, and he encouraged the upgrading of medical care in Geneva's hospitals; Anabaptists promoted medicinal baths and set aside deaconesses to visit the sick; and Anglican clergy often worked also as physicians so that they could bring both spiritual and bodily healing to their parishes. Ursuline nuns embodied this tradition in the colonial Catholic hospitals of Quebec, New Orleans, and Biloxi.[14]

By the early-nineteenth century, Catholic orders of religious women— like the Sisters of Charity and the Dominican Sisters of the Sick-Poor—were conspicuously devoting themselves to care for the sick. By that time, moreover, individual American Protestants had begun to organize for the purpose of promoting public health, distributing medical guidebooks, and encouraging healthful living. Some of the new American religious groups made a healthy diet a matter of religious obligation: Mormons advised their adherents against liquor, tobacco, and excessive consumption of meat, and Ellen White told her Adventist followers that a vision from God prompted her advocacy of health reform and hydropathic therapy.[15]

The main Protestant push toward a health society came in the temperance movement, which intensified with the formation of the American Society for the Promotion of Temperance in 1826. Even in the eighteenth century Methodists and Quakers had opposed the consumption of spirits: after 1826 the temperance cause attracted widespread support in the Protestant churches, which often made their case on medical grounds. The movement had other aims, ranging from social order to economic stability, but medical arguments, taken especially from Benjamin Rush's *Inquiry into the Effect of Ardent Spirits upon the Human Mind and Body* (1815), permeated Protestant rhetoric.[16]

Religious reformers also had little good to say about tobacco. As early as 1833 Joseph Smith told his Mormon followers to lay down their pipes and cigars, and by the 1850s the Adventists included smoking among their proscriptions. Other denominations reached no consensus: in the 1890s, Northern Methodists, who condemned tobacco, and Southern Methodists, who refused to condemn it, found in the cigar another reason for mutual

14. Marvin R. O'Connell, "The Roman Catholic Tradition Since 1545," in *Caring and Curing: Health and Medicine in the Western Religious Traditions*, ed. Ronald L. Numbers and Darrel W. Amundsen (New York: MacMillan, 1986), p. 124; Carter Lindberg, "The Lutheran Tradition," ibid., p. 178; James H. Smylie, "The Reformed Tradition," ibid., p. 212; Walter Klaasen, "The Anabaptist Tradition," ibid., pp. 276–77; John E. Booty, "The Anglican Tradition," ibid., pp. 248–50; Harold Y. Vanderpool, "Medicine and Medical Ethics," *Encyclopedia of the American Religious Experience*, 3 vols., ed. Charles H. Lippy and Peter W. Williams (New York: Charles Scribner's Sons, 1988), 2:1257.

15. O'Connell, "Roman Catholic Tradition Since 1545," *Caring and Curing*, pp. 136–37; Lester E. Bush, Jr., "The Mormon Tradition," ibid., p. 400; Ronald L. Numbers and David R. Larson, "The Adventist Tradition," ibid., p. 451.

16. Joseph R. Gusfield, *Symbolic Crusade* (Urbana, Illinois: University of Illinois Press, 1963), pp. 36–86.

suspicion. But by that time, sentiments against the use of tobacco were intensifying within most Protestant groups.[17]

The helping tradition within the churches found its most enduring expression, however, in the growing inclination to sponsor hospitals. Prior to 1850, most American hospitals were institutions for the mentally ill. Both the mental institutions and the small number of general hospitals depended either on public support or on the sponsorship of voluntary societies, often Protestant in their leadership and motivation but rarely linked to particular religious denominations. The immigration of Irish Catholics and German Lutherans after 1840 brought a change. Isolated from the larger culture, the Catholics and Lutherans constructed their own general hospitals, partly as havens of ethnic familiarity, partly as agencies of care for members of their religious communions, but increasingly also as means of service to the poor regardless of their religious faith. The Lutherans built their first hospital in 1849 in Pittsburg; the Catholics began earlier and expanded faster: By 1880, they operated 119 hospitals in America.[18]

Before long, other denominations began to emulate the immigrant example. Presbyterians in New York built a hospital in 1868 to serve the poor of the city "without Regard to Race, Creed, or Color." Methodists opened Seney Hospital in Brooklyn in 1887 to serve "Jew and Gentile, Protestant and Catholic, heathen and infidel, on the same terms," and in the next half century they built 59 additional hospitals. The Disciples provided Axtell Christian Hospital in 1887 as a humanitarian venture in Newton, Kansas. Baptists constructed the Missouri Baptist Sanitarium in St. Louis, in 1890 and the Samaritan Hospital in Philadelphia in 1892 in order to imitate the "charitable acts" of Christ. The denominations conceived of these hospitals as avenues of service, especially to the needy. They took special pride in what they called "free work" or "gratuitous services" by their physicians and staffs, and they referred to the labors of doctors and nurses as "ministries." The hospitals would fulfill the Christian "duty to the sick and suffering of the land, especially to the poor."[19]

The hospitals drew especially on the service of Protestant and Catholic women. After 1849 the deaconess movement expanded within American Lutheranism: nineteenth-century Quakers sponsored nursing societies;

---

17. Numbers and Larson, "Adventist Tradition," *Caring and Curing*, pp. 451, 459; Timothy P. Weber, "The Baptist Tradition," ibid., 298–300; Bush, "Mormon Tradition," ibid., 411, 413; Harold Y. Vanderpool, "The Methodist Tradition," ibid., 340–41.

18. Lindberg, "The Lutheran Tradition," *Caring and Curing*, p. 194; Jay P. Dolan, *The American Catholic Experience* (Garden City, New York: Doubleday, 1985), p. 324.

19. Smylie, "The Reformed Tradition," *Caring and Curing*, p. 218; E. Brooks Holifield, *Health and Medicine in the Methodist Tradition* (New York: Crossroad, 1986), p. 55; David Edwin Harrell, Jr., "The Disciples of Christ—Church of Christ Tradition," *Caring and Curing*, p. 388; Weber, "Baptist Tradition," ibid., pp. 306–07; George Mains, *James Monroe Buckley* (Cincinnati: Methodist Book Concern, 1917), pp. 201, 205; Charles Jarrell, *Methodism on the March* (Nashville: Methodist Publishing House, 1924), p. 246.

Methodists opened training schools—such as the New England Deaconess Home and Training School, founded in 1889—which promoted the ideal of medical training for women as an expression of a social gospel. The people who made Catholic hospitals possible were the orders of women—the Sisters of Charity, or the Sisters of St. John and All Saints, or the Sisters of St. Margaret—who treated the institutions as their agencies of service to the world. It is symbolically appropriate that the Mayo Clinic in Rochester, Minnesota, opened in 1887 as the result of an alliance between the Mayo brothers and a small group of Franciscan nuns.[20]

The denominations had fallen into step with the new trend in American medicine. In 1873, one government survey counted fewer than 200 hospitals in America; in 1875, another surveyor counted 661. A substantial percentage of these were church-sponsored; almost 20 percent were Catholic (and Catholic religious women also owned 15 percent of the nursing schools in the United States). The pace intensified in the final quarter of the century; by 1900 Americans had built 2,070 hospitals, and they continued to build them during the next three decades at a rate of 200 a year. Increasingly after 1890, however, they built a different kind of hospital: profit-making institutions owned by investors. By 1923 America had 6,830 hospitals—the institutions were becoming the symbolic centerpiece of American medicine—and the market economy increasingly shaped their administration.[21]

The hospitals expanded partly as a result of developments within the medical profession, including new antiseptic and aseptic procedures, new knowledge about clinical pathology, and innovations in the building of diagnostic laboratories. They grew also, because the population changes associated with the mushrooming of American cities multiplied the number of persons who could no longer count on aid from a nearby family in time of sickness. But whatever the reasons for the expansion, the new hospitals also symbolized the rising status of scientific medicine and the burgeoning importance of the market as the mechanism for the distribution of medical care.[22]

For at least some American Protestants, the alliance between the church and the hospital represented an alternative to the sudden preoccupation with

20. Lindberg, "The Lutheran Tradition," *Caring and Curing*, p. 190; O'Connell, "Roman Catholic Tradition Since 1545," ibid., 136; Henry E. Sigerst, *American Medicine* (New York: W. W. Norton, 1934), p. 224; Holifield, *Health and Medicine in the Methodist Tradition*, p. 24; Carlan Kraman, "Women Religious in Health Care: The Early Years," in Ursula Stepsis and Dolores Liptak, *Pioneer Healers: The History of Women Religious in American Health Care* (New York: Crossroad, 1989), pp. 15–38.

21. Goerge Rosen, *The Structure of American Medical Practice 1875–1941* (Philadelphia: University of Pennsylvania Press, 1983), p. 46; Mary Carol Conroy, "The Transition Years," in Stepsis and Liptak, *Pioneer Healers*, p. 148; Paul Starr, *The Social Transformation of American Medicine: The Rise of a Sovereign Profession and the Making of a Vast Industry* (New York: Basic Books, 1982), pp. 169–70; Paul Starr, "Medicine, Economy, and Society in Nineteenth-Century America," *Journal of Social History* 10 (1977): 588–607.

faith-healing that swept through the country after 1870. Various forms of confidence in direct divine healing had long been a part of Christian piety: Seventeenth-century colonial Catholics anointed the sick with oil. So did seventeenth-century colonial Baptists. Christian African slaves, acting in accord with traditional African conceptions of healing by diviners and conjurers, constituted a large subculture that practiced nonphysical means of healing. Nineteenth-century Mormons had faith-healing rituals; some nineteenth-century Adventists also published reports of divine healing. But a renewed preoccupation with gifts of healing emerged in America after 1870 as a result of the holiness revival. A number of Methodists claimed that God's gracious gift of entire sanctification—perfect holiness—could bring healing to the body as well as the soul, and an even larger number of holiness proponents outside Methodism began to see divine healing as an integral part of Christian practice.[23]

Faith-healing became especially a visible expression of a radical holiness theology. An Episcopalian physician, Charles Cullis, began to practice spiritual healing in 1870 after the devotional meetings of the Methodist Phoebe Palmer introduced him to holiness piety, and his admirers—like A. B. Simpson, the founder of the Christian and Missionary Alliance, or the Baptist A. J. Gordon—popularized the notion that the atonement of Christ made possible an instantaneous deliverance from sickness analogous to the instantaneous deliverance from sin about which the holiness movement preached. And a number of faith-healers combined their practice with spirited attacks on both physicians and hospitals.[24]

To some nineteenth-century American Protestants, support for hospitals symbolized an embarrassed repudiation of these faith-healing movements. The Methodist James Buckley, whose editorials spurred the building of Seney Hospital in Brooklyn, argued that the proponents of divine healing threatened to lead the church into the darkness of superstition and magic. The building of hospitals advertised an alternative piety, attuned to the values of a scientific era, consistent with the spirit of progressive reform, and properly mindful of the professional authority of scientists and doctors. Some advocates of the hospitals said explicitly that only through such service to the world could the churches continue to attract the loyalty of laity in an "ethically minded age."[25]

22. Rosen, *Structure of American Medical Practice*, pp. 45–46.

23. O'Connell, "The Roman Catholic Tradition Since 1545," *Caring and Curing*, p. 115; Weber, "The Baptist Tradition," ibid., p. 293; Bush, "The Mormon Tradition," ibid., 401, 403; Numbers and Larson, "The Adventist Tradition," ibid., 449; Albert J. Raboteau, *Slave Religion* (New York: Oxford University Press, 1978), pp. 275–88.

24. Donald Dayton, "The Rise of the Evangelical Healing Movement in Nineteenth-Century America," *Pneuma* 4 (1982): 1–18; Grant Wacker, "The Pentecostal Tradition," *Caring and Curing*, pp. 516–28; Paul Gale Chappel, "The Divine Healing Movement in America" (Ph.D. diss., Drew University, 1983), pp. 87, 145–59, 340–55.

25. James Monroe Buckley, *A History of Methodism in the United States*, 2 vols. (New York: Harper and Brothers, 1898), 2:431; Jarrell, *Methodism on the March*, pp. 244, 246.

The founders of the Emmanuel Movement shared the desire to ally the church and the hospital. The result was an alliance among representatives of the three sectors: ministers, physicians in state hospitals, and physicians operating privately within the market for medical services. Worcester and McComb worked closely with a neurological adviser, Isador Coriatt, an early Freudian at Worcester State Hospital; they joined with Joseph Pratt of Massachusetts General Hospital in applying the "law of suggestion" to patients; they enlisted the support of the physicians Richard Cabot and James Jackson Putnam; they drew on the emerging medical literature in psychotherapy; and they agreed to work under the direction of regular physicians while limiting themselves to moral education or suggestive therapy. Physicians conducted diagnostic sessions at the Emmanuel church each week, and it was the doctors who decided which cases went to physicians and which ones the ministers could safely handle. The Emmanuel Movement thus continued the time-honored helping tradition in American religion, working alongside physicians and medical institutions to promote both health and scientific healing. But it also embodied a tendency for religion to look to the hospital for guidance, and in that respect it anticipated the early twentieth century pastoral care movement.[26]

II. Pastoral Care and the Hospital

The Protestant pastoral care movement represented, in part, the effort to refine ministry by drawing upon the findings of modern medicine, psychotherapy, and the behavioral sciences. It represented one realization of the ideal toward which the Emmanuel Movement pointed, and it embodied the same three traditions that had coalesced at Emmanuel: It modified an older pastoral care tradition, created new forms to continue the helping tradition, and in subtle ways incorporated themes that had found expression earlier in the harmonial tradition. The pastoral care movement therefore became, as it were, an experiment to test whether the synthesis envisioned by Worcester and McComb could endure as the paradigm for relating religion to issues of health and to commerical and state health institutions. In the nineteenth century, the churches had sponsored hospitals; in the twentieth, medicine became a model for ministry, and the hospital, whether state-sponsored or commercial, became a setting for the training of ministers.

The formation in 1909 of the National Committee for Mental Hygiene gave religious leaders a different kind of opportunity to interact with the medical community. Some saw the mental hygiene movement as a means of confirming the association between religion and health. Indeed, some of its clerical recruits assigned to the pastor the "responsibility for the health of his parishioners." The initial aim of the movement was the reform of private and state mental hospitals, but it soon expanded its goal. Its governing theme of

26. Holifield, *History of Pastoral Care in America*, pp. 202–09.

adjustment—to other persons, to society, and to "the whole of things"—suggested a way to prevent serious mental illness and enhance human happiness.[27]

The event that cemented the linkage between the church and the hospital was the formation in 1930 of the Council for Clinical Training of Theological Students. It represented a new program of professional education for clergy, which eventually came to be known as clinical pastoral education—a long-term supervised encounter with men and women in crisis in hospitals, prisons, and social agencies. Its primary locus was the hospital.

Most of the founders of clinical pastoral education had spent their professional careers in hospital settings, and they believed, for various reasons, that the ethos of the hospital could best raise the questions that potential leaders in the churches needed to hear. The Boston physician Richard Cabot helped launch the program with the publication in 1925 of his "Plea for a Clinical Year in the Course of Theological Study." He thought that clinical training should give the clergy a realistic vision and moral toughness that would help them form and shape strength of character in their pastoral work. A hospital chaplain, Anton Boisen, gave Cabot's proposal its first real test when he began in 1925 to train a handful of students at the Worcester State Hospital, an institution in Massachusetts for the mentally ill. Boisen viewed clinical pastoral education as a study of sin and salvation. Because he interpreted mental illness as a chaotic encounter with God, which could lead either to a reintegration of the soul or to a fall into total inner disarray, he considered the patients as "living human documents" through whom students could discern religious truth.[28]

The hospital setting was no necessary condition for the new form of education. William S. Keller, an Episcopal physician in Ohio, had organized in 1923 a summer school in social service, designed to deepen theological education by having students do casework in social agencies. Keller's model might conceivably have prevailed over others. But the future of clinical pastoral education lay, as the name implied, in the hospital. Indeed, one of the primary issues that split the clinical movement grew out of differing perceptions of how hospitals should be used. Under the leadership of the

27. Clifford W. Beers, A Mind That Found Itself (Garden City, New York: Doubleday, Doran, 1944), pp. 275–94; Helen Flanders Dunbar, "The Clinical Training of Theological Students," Religion in Life (1935): 383; Daniel W. LaRue, Mental Hygiene (New York: Macmillan, 1972), pp. 240–46, 262; Edwin Kirkpatrick, Mental Hygiene for Effective Living (New York: Appleton-Century, 1934), pp. 1–21, 225–58.

28. Richard Cabot, Adventures on the Borderlands of Ethics (New York: Harper and Brothers, 1926), pp. 1–55; Anton Boisen, The Exploration of the Inner World (Philadelphia: University of Pennsylvania Press, 1971; 1st ed., New York: Willet, Clark, 1936), pp. 3–111; Robert C. Powell, CPE: Fifty Years of Learning Through Supervised Encounter with Living Human Documents (New York: n.p., 1975), pp. 3–5; Edward E. Thornton, Professional Education for Ministry: A History of Clinical Pastoral Education (Nashville: Abingdon Press, 1970), pp. 49, 52, 100.

psychiatrist Helen Flanders Dunbar, the Council for Clinical Training favored mental hospitals as training sites, partly because they might give students a clearer conception of the place of psychoanalysis in psychotherapy. Richard Cabot, scornful of psychoanalysis and skeptical of other forms of psychotherapy, soon joined with others to form another clinical program, which formed the background for the emergence in 1944 of the Institute for Pastoral Care. Unlike the Council, the Institute initially preferred general hospitals as training sites.

It turned out, however, that both kinds of hospital settings encouraged the students and supervisors to accent the therapeutic dimension of both ministry and religious faith. Boisen soon complained that the clinical programs had wandered from his ideal of treating the mental hospital as a laboratory in the psychology of religion; he regretted, for example, the prevalence of texts in psychoanalytic therapy. Other critics from within the movement also regretted a movement toward the therapeutic: Rollin Fairbanks, one of the organizers of the Institute for Pastoral Care, argued that clinical training should rather develop moral sensitivity—"clarity as to right and wrong"—than therapeutic insight. But the growing use of "verbatims"— verbatim reports of conversations between students and patients—tended to incline the supervisory sessions toward issues in counseling or to focus attention on psychodynamic themes. And the hospital setting itself raised the question of how the chaplain—and by extension, religious faith—contributed to the process of healing.[29]

This theme marked the early literature that emerged from the circle of pastoral theologians who stayed in close touch with clinical education. In 1936, Richard Cabot and the chaplain Russell Dicks collaborated on *The Art of Ministering to the Sick,* which argued that the minister's task in the hospital was to draw patients into an awareness of a purposive healing force at work within them. Cabot and Dicks defined "God" as "the great power in ourselves that makes for health," and suggested to ministers that by learning skills of "good listening" they could help patients discern the "growing edge" of God's presence in their lives. Two years later, the Presbyterian pastor John Sutherland Bonnell published his *Pastoral Psychiatry,* designed to help realize his father's prediction that religion would some day become "one of the extensively used forms of psychotherapy." And Carroll A. Wise, who had been a chaplain at Worcester State Hospital, soon contributed his *Religion in Illness and Health,* presenting a functional view of religious symbols as bearers of value and meaning that "in specific ways affect the health of the

29. Thornton, *Professional Education for Ministry,* pp. 92–93; Anton Boisen, *Out of the Depths* (New York: Harper and Row, 1960), pp. 185–86; Rollin Fairbanks, "Standards for Full-Time Clinical Training," in *Clinical Pastoral Training,* ed. Seward Hiltner (Commission on Religion and Health, Federal Council of Churches of Christ in America, 1945), p. 37; Fairbanks, "On Clinical Pastoral Training," *Journal of Pastoral Care* 17 (1963): 154–55; Fairbanks, "Ministering to the Sick," *Journal of Clinical Pastoral Work* 1/2 (1948): 6.

individual." By 1943, Seward Hiltner, executive secretary of the new Commission on Religion and Health of the Federal Council of Churches, could argue in his *Religion and Health* that the religious communities were now ready to pursue the question of "what religion does for health, concretely and specifically."[30] And these are but four examples of an extensive list of publications that accompanied the spread of the clinical education movement and helped to accentuate the therapeutic dimensions of religion.

By drawing heavily on recent developments in psychotherapy, moreover, the clinical pastoral education movement—and the larger pastoral care movement that was forming around it—also rediscovered some of the themes that once had marked the harmonial tradition in American religion. Far more subtle than the earlier proponents of New Thought, some of the therapists who attracted the attention of pastoral theologians also argued, like the New Thinkers, that healing might occur when the mind, conscious or unconscious, became a channel for an influx of energy from either the inner depths of the person or the surrounding extramundane environment. Rollo May's *Art of Counseling* (1939) and *Springs of Creative Living* (1940) contended that healing occurred when the ego gained the capacity to trust "the structure of reality." Carl Rogers' *Counseling and Psychotherapy* (1942) foreshadowed his later distinction between the inner wisdom of the organism and the internalized distortions imposed by others. Erich Fromm's *Psychoanalysis and Religion* (1950) argued that a humanistic religion could promote health insofar as it helped put people in touch with a "spiritual reality which we can strive to realize in ourselves and yet can never describe or define." In adapting these and other similar conceptions, the pastoral theologians drew into the circle of Protestant theology a set of concepts and images that once had found expression in a harmonial piety that Protestant theologians had deeply distrusted.[31]

It would be far too strong to say that the pastoral care movement redefined religion as therapy, even though a few figures pushed in that direction. A vigorous minority in the movement persistently decried any tendency, however subtle, to see religious symbols as medical concepts in disguise. But the pastoral care and clinical education movements succeeded in impressing upon thousands of theological students the therapeutic pos-

30. Richard Cabot and Russell Dicks, *The Art of Ministering to the Sick* (New York: Macmillan, 1936), pp. 16, 74, 97, 117–18, 130; John Sutherland Bonnell, *Pastoral Psychiatry* (New York: Harper and Brothers, 1938), p. 18; Carroll A. Wise, *Religion in Illness and Health* (New York: Harper and Brothers, 1942), p. xii; Seward Hiltner, *Religion and Health* (New York: Macmillan, 1943), p. viii.

31. Rollo May, *The Art of Counseling* (Nashville: Abingdon Press, 1978; 1st ed., 1939), foreword; Rollo May, *The Springs of Creative Living: A Study of Human Nature and God* (Nashville: Abingdon Press, 1940), pp. 70–97, 200, 208, 232, 257; Erich Fromm, *Psychoanalysis and Religion* (New York: Bantam Books, 1972; 1st ed., 1950), pp. 19, 22, 82, 115; Carl Rogers, *Counseling and Psychotherapy* (New York: Houghton Mifflin, 1942), pp. 38, 40, 114; Fuller, *Alternative Medicine and American Religious Life*, p. 96.

sibilities of ministry. By 1955 more than four thousand Protestant students had undergone some form of clinical pastoral education; by 1960 clinical supervisors had organized at least 117 regular centers for clinical pastoral education, most of them located in hospitals; by 1963 there were 149 independent pastoral counseling centers staffed by people who often called themselves pastoral psychotherapists. And the public turned to religious counselors in large numbers: one survey conducted during the 1950s by the National Institute of Mental Health showed that 42 percent of all people who sought help for emotional problems turned first to their ministers. By the end of the 1960s, it seemed that the Emmanuel ideal had finally begun to flourish in American religion and that the hospital chaplaincy represented one means by which religion secured a niche in both commercial and state health agencies.[32]

III. New Directions

The Emmanuel Movement embodied a synthesis of the pastoral care, harmonial, and helping traditions, and the twentieth-century pastoral care movement refined that synthesis by forging alliances with the agencies of American medical care. But just at the moment when the synthesis seemed secure, a number of critics began to question the precise forms it had assumed in American religious culture.

First came the debate over the equation of pastoral care and psychotherapy. As early as 1955, Wayne Oates of Southern Baptist Theological Seminary, chairing a Commission on the Ministry sponsored by the New York Academy of Sciences, could advise clergy not to think of counseling as a religious or professional "specialty." But by 1963 a number of pastoral counselors, most of them associated with counseling centers, began to advocate private pastoral practice. They began, in other words, to construe pastoral psychotherapy as much more akin to the practice of psychotherapeutic medicine than to the traditional role of the pastor in a local congregation. Seward Hiltner, then a member of the faculty at Princeton Seminary, responded that this movement toward specialization was an effort to turn ministers into crypto-psychologists and psychiatrists, and he defined private pastoral practice as a contradiction in terms. But his protests proved unavailing, as Frederick Kuether of the American Foundation of Religion and Psychiatry in New York, supported by the insurance magnate W. Clement Stone, managed to rally support for an American Association of Pastoral Counselors.[33]

32. Holifield, *History of Pastoral Care in America*, pp. 269–74.
33. Howard Clinebell, "The Challenge of the Specialty of Pastoral Counseling," *Pastoral Psychology* 15/143 (April 1964); 21–22; Seward Hiltner, "The American Association of Pastoral Counselors: A Critique," *Pastoral Psychology* 15/143 (April 1964): 9–14; Wayne Oates, *Protestant Pastoral Counseling* (Philadelphia: The Westminster Press, 1962), pp. 31–32.

The organization flourished, but the debate over it helped to stimulate some rethinking of the meaning of pastoral care. Both Hiltner and Oates warned against the inclination of pastoral writers to seek a borrowed identity from psychotherapy, and by the 1970s other pastoral theologians echoed those warnings. Don Browning of the University of Chicago and Charles Gerkin of Emory University, for example, proposed that pastoral care entailed a concern for questions of ethics and meaning that could not be subsumed under therapeutic categories. And because some of the earlier arguments had sometimes seemed to equate health and salvation, a number of pastoral writers began during the 1970s to accent the differences between them. The Emmanuel Movement envisioned a coming era of pastoral psychotherapy; the most recent publications from the pastoral care movement call for a somewhat different vision.[34]

A similar complexity has marked the relationships between mainstream Protestantism and the harmonial tradition. Neither Worcester nor McComb could have foreseen the extent to which harmonial piety would one day influence attitudes toward health care in America. The language of the harmonial tradition has permeated much of the recent popular discussion of holistic healing, and approving references to holistic health care appear regularly in the statements of the large American denominations. But most churches have remained ambivalent about the harmonial tradition. Recent accounts of harmonial piety have shown it to represent a distinctive religious vision with its own inner logic and symbolic order which resists any easy assimilation into most older Protestant, Catholic, and Jewish traditions. As early as the 1950s, the popularity of Norman Vincent Peale, whose message of positive thinking represented a merging of New Thought with an older Protestant vocabulary, caused some pastoral theologians to draw distinctions more sharply than Worcester and McComb drew them. New Age healing movements, which continue the harmonial tradition, have proliferated, but when they practice the channeling of *prana* (energy) into patients through rituals or touching, or call on the healing power of the "God Within," or employ rock crystals and other healing gems to restore the flow of "odic force" to the body, such practices accentuate the distinctions between these forms of holistic therapy and traditional Protestant, Catholic, and Jewish convictions about God and the world.[35]

American churches have promoted an ideal of holistic medicine even

34. Oates, *Protestant Pastoral Counseling;* Don Browning, *Religious Ethics and Pastoral Care* (Philadelphia: Fortress Press, 1983); Charles Gerkin, *The Living Human Document* (Nashville: Abingdon Press, 1984); James N. Lapsley, *Salvation and Health* (Philadelphia: The Westminster Press, 1972).

35. Wayne Oates, "The Cult of Reassurance," *Religion in Life* 24 (1954–55): 72–82; Seward Hiltner, *Pastoral Counseling* (Nashville: Abingdon Press, 1949), p. 256; Fuller, *Alternative Medicine and American Religious Life*, pp. 91–117.

when they have remained wary of the harmonial tradition, but advocates disagree about precisely what holism entails. For some, it means simply that medical practitioners should attend to persons and not discrete parts of the body; for others, it signifies a far more radical departure from conventional forms of western medicine. The ambiguity has now begun to draw critics who claim that the rhetoric of holistic medicine has outdistanced its achievement and that the religious community should be both more precise and more modest in its language about wholeness.[36]

The third tradition within the Emmanuel synthesis—the helping tradition—has also endured. But the changes in the American hospital system have also rendered more problematic the alliance between the churches and the hospitals that once seemed so promising. American hospitals now administer their work as market institutions; vast economic and corporate forces now govern the operations of most hospitals, which often no longer answer to local authority. Religious denominations that once built scores of hospitals are now beginning to talk of selling them, and a few regional judicatories have already decided that they can no longer bear the financial burdens that hospitals can impose. Catholics in 1986 still operated 10 percent of the hospitals in the United States, but that represented a numerical decline. In 1966 they had operated 943 general and specialty hospitals; in 1986 the number was 737, a decrease of almost 22 percent. And one hears occasional complaints from within the churches that nothing distinguishes denominational hospitals from those operated by other agencies, in any case.[37]

Not that the helping tradition has waned. It has assumed, rather, a variety of forms not foreseen by the earlier proponents of denominational hospitals. A conference in Atlanta on "The Church's Challenge in Health," sponsored by the Carter Presidential Center and the Wheat Ridge Foundation, brought together in October, 1989, representatives from the denominations and from sixty-one church agencies that have developed programs for promoting health. The striking feature of the conference was the sheer variety of health-care activities conducted by church-related organizations. The delegates represented advocacy groups that work to serve the disabled, cut infant mortality, and feed the hungry; community health programs that provide health care for low-income families; and educational agencies that struggle with teen pregnancy, publicize health assessment programs, train health-care professionals, and conduct wellness and fitness programs in local congregations. Most visible were the direct service agencies that care for

---

36. Kristine Beyerman Alster, *The Holistic Health Movement* (Tuscaloosa and London: The University of Alabama Press, 1989; Martin E. Marty, "Theology and Tradition of the Church in Health and Healing," public address at the symposeum on "The Church's Challenge in Health," The Carter Presidential Center, Atlanta, October 26, 1989.

37. Margaret John Kelly, DC, "Toward the Twenty-first Century," in Stepsis and Liptak, eds., *Pioneer Healers*, pp. 179–80.

homeless people who are ill, train parish nurses, serve migrant women, transport people to doctors, offers residential services for disturbed adolescents and alcohol and drug abusers, sponsor mobile dental units, administer Hospitality Houses for the families of hospital patients, provide non-clinical support for the mentally ill, and establish hospices. The sixty-one agencies included six devoted solely to assistance of persons with AIDS; they also included three Church Health Centers that provide medical service for the poor by a full-time staff of physicians and nurses. Many saw themselves as offering ministries of health to persons neglected by the broader American medical system.

One can still find occasional agencies and centers that combine the three traditions—pastoral care, harmonial piety, and religious service and reform—in ways strikingly reminiscent of the Emmanuel Movement. But recent voices have reminded us that the pastoral care tradition is, at the least, more than therapeutic; that the harmonial tradition has its own integrity that resists incorporation into other integral patterns of faith and piety; and that the helping tradition cannot find its primary expression simply through support for hospitals, partly because the financial demands of the hospital systems increasingly outstriping the capacity of the churches to provide meaningful economic help.

As a result of such changes, the relationships among the three sectors have become increasingly complex. Denominational hospitals survive by making profits, attracting governmental grants, and accomodating themselves to federal Medicare and Medicaid programs. Or sometimes now the denominations sell their hospitals to large conglomerates in the health business. Commercial health agencies promote medical techniques that had once been techniques of meditation within traditions of harmonial piety. Chaplains serve in both commercial and state hospitals, often functioning as part of health care teams. And as the conference in Atlanta suggested, the religious communities have also recently developed an array of smaller programs and services in local communities that meet needs ignored by health agencies in the other two sectors. Worcester and McComb would have been unable to imagine the current complexities, and it is not certain that they would have been pleased, but they could not have complained that religious groups had continued to ignore the healing of the body. The three traditions—pastoral care, harmonial piety, and religiously-motivated reform—remain vital, and religious institutions within the independent sector continue to sponsor numerous ministries of health. Without them, the American health system would be decidedly poorer.[38]

38. Denominations have also sponsored recent national and regional consultations on religion and health. The United Methodist Church, for example, sponsored national conferences in Memphis, Tennessee, in 1988 and Des Moines, Iowa, in 1990, along with various regional conferences, exploring issues of religion, health, and healing.

NOTES ON CONTRIBUTORS

DOROTHY C. BASS is associate professor of church history at the Chicago Theological Seminary and visiting professor of theology at Valparaiso University, where she is director of the Lilly project on Theological Education in American Religious Communities. Contributor to *Between the Times,* edited by William R. Hutchison, as well as to a number of other books and journals, she is co-editor of *The United Church of Christ* and *Women in American Religious History.*

CONRAD CHERRY is Distinguished Professor of Religious Studies, adjunct professor of American studies, and director of the Center for the Study of Religion and American Culture, Indiana University, Indianapolis. He is co-editor of the journal *Religion and American Culture,* the editor of several books, including *God's New Israel,* and the author of numerous articles and chapters and books, among which are *The Theology of Jonathan Edwards* and *Nature and Religious Imagination.*

WILLIAM D. DINGES is associate professor of religion and religious education at the Catholic University of America where he specializes in sociological approaches to the study of religion, particularly Catholic traditionalism. The author of a large array of essays on various topics, he also prepared the article on "Catholic Fundamentalism" for the first volume of *Fundamentalism Observed,* edited by Martin Marty and R. Scott Appleby.

J. BRYAN HEHIR, S.J. is Joseph P. Kennedy Professor of Ethics at Georgetown University and Counselor for Social Policy of the U.S. Catholic Conference. Having served as a papal envoy to a United Nations Conference on Arms Control, he writes frequently on public policy questions regarding nuclear issues and international affairs. He is the author of *Religion and Politics in the 1980s and 1990s.*

E. BROOKS HOLIFIELD is Charles Howard Chandler Professor of American Church History at Emory University. Recipient of several significant research fellowships and member of a number of professional and editorial boards, he is a frequent writer for scholarly periodicals and is the author of *The Covenant Sealed, The Gentlemen Theologians, A History of Pastoral Care in America, Health and Medicine in the Methodist Tradition,* and *Era of Persuasion.*

MARY J. OATES is professor of economics at Regis College. Beyond service to a large number of institutes and boards, she has received several important research grants and fellowships. She is the editor of *Higher*

Education for Catholic Women and, along with many articles and chapters, the author of *The Role of the Cotton Textile Industry in the Economic Development of the American Southeast.*

ROWLAND A. SHERRILL is professor and chair of Religious Studies and adjunct professor of American studies at Indiana University, Indianapolis, where he also serves as co-editor of *Religion and American Culture.* He is the editor of *Religion and the Life of the Nation* and the author of *The Prophetic Melville,* as well as a contributor of other journal articles and book chapters.

JAMES F. SMURL is professor of religious studies, adjunct professor of nursing, and adjunct professor of medical genetics at Indiana University, Indianapolis. Winner of several honors and awards and frequently called upon as consultant on issues of medical ethics, he is also the author of many articles and of *Religious Ethics* and *The Burdens of Justice.*

MAX L. STACKHOUSE is Herbert Gezork Professor of Christian Social Ethics and Stewardship Studies at the Andover Newton Theological School. He has filled several named lectureships and overseas professorships, served on numerous boards, and authored a large array of articles and chapters. His books include *The Ethics of Necropolis, Ethics and the Urban Ethos, Creeds, Society and Human Rights, Public Theology and Political Economy,* and *Apologia.*

JOHN WITTE, JR. is associate professor of law and director of the Law and Religion Program at Emory University and, among other significant positions, is a fellow in the Center for Public Justice in Washington, D.C. and chair of the law and religion section of the Association of American Law Schools. Major publications include numerous articles in law school and other professional journals and his co-editorship of *The Weightier Matters of the Law.*

INDEX